Delmy Tania Cruz, Manuel Bayón Jiménez,
and Colectivo Miradas Críticas del Territorio desde el Feminismo
(eds.)

Bodies, Territories, and Feminisms
Latin American Compilation of Political Practices, Theories,
and Methodologies

Delmy Tania Cruz, Manuel Bayón Jiménez,
and Colectivo Miradas Críticas del
Territorio desde el Feminismo (eds.)

BODIES, TERRITORIES, AND FEMINISMS

Latin American Compilation of Political Practices,
Theories, and Methodologies

Bibliografische Information der Deutschen Nationalbibliothek
Die Deutsche Nationalbibliothek verzeichnet diese Publikation in der Deutschen Nationalbibliografie; detaillierte bibliografische Daten sind im Internet über http://dnb.d-nb.de abrufbar.

Bibliographic information published by the Deutsche Nationalbibliothek
Die Deutsche Nationalbibliothek lists this publication in the Deutsche Nationalbibliografie; detailed bibliographic data are available in the Internet at http://dnb.d-nb.de.

Cover picture: © Sonia Madrigal, from the Series *La Muerte sale por el Oriente*. Chimalhuacán (México), 2015

ISBN-13: 978-3-8382-1709-3
© *ibidem*-Verlag, Stuttgart 2022
Alle Rechte vorbehalten

Das Werk einschließlich aller seiner Teile ist urheberrechtlich geschützt. Jede Verwertung außerhalb der engen Grenzen des Urheberrechtsgesetzes ist ohne Zustimmung des Verlages unzulässig und strafbar. Dies gilt insbesondere für Vervielfältigungen, Übersetzungen, Mikroverfilmungen und elektronische Speicherformen sowie die Einspeicherung und Verarbeitung in elektronischen Systemen.

All rights reserved. No part of this publication may be reproduced, stored in or introduced into a retrieval system, or transmitted, in any form, or by any means (electronic, mechanical, photocopying, recording or otherwise) without the prior written permission of the publisher. Any person who does any unauthorized act in relation to this publication may be liable to criminal prosecution and civil claims for damages.

Printed in the EU

Bodies, Territories, and Feminisms.
Latin American Compilation of Political Practices, Theories, and Methodologies

Delmy Tania Cruz, Manuel Bayón Jiménez, and Colectivo Miradas Críticas del Territorio desde el Feminismo.

Publisher: Abya Yala and Instituto de Estudios Ecologistas del Tercer Mundo.

Dedicated to Rosi Govela, part of the passion who has woven this book, who left us when we were best learning to enjoy ourselves.

In memory of Walda, who, from the ethics of mutual care among women, weaved networks of sisterhood, tenderness and respect for life.

Table of Contents

Prologue 9
Introduction 13

PART 1: THEORETICAL-POLITICAL PERSPECTIVES 19
1. Extractivism y (re)patriarchalization of territories 21
2. Women, bodies and territories: between defense and dispossession 39
3. Intersectionalities in the body-territory 53
4. The geopolitics of the womb: towards a decolonial feminist geopolitics in spaces of slow death 69
5. Neodevelopment vignettes in Argentina. Development(s), looting(s) and body/ies between exploitation and struggle . 83
6. Identities, body and territory: 56+1 girls at the "Hogar Seguro, Virgen de la Asunción" fire 99
7. *Kawsak sacha*: women organization and political translation of the Amazonian rainforest in Ecuador 117
8. The Sepur Zarco Grandmothers and their fight for justice. Summary of a conviction 135

PART 2: METHODOLOGICAL APPLICATIONS AND PROPOSALS 151
9. From the body: art, politics and transformation. Sharing *Magdalenas Uruguay-Teatro de las Oprimidas* 153
10. Reaching out, feeling and getting involved: reflections on an investigation into emotions 169
11. Living Mesoamerican methodologies: body, earth and feminisms 181
12. Collective views and walks. Experiences of rural extension and feminist action-research in eastern Uruguay 201

13. The map as a guide: mapping feminicidal violence and feminist progression 217
14. Subverting the geopolitics of sexual violence: a proposal for (counter)mapping our bodies-territory 235

PART 3: DIALOGUES 255
15. On Genders and Territories. Does the land have a gender? 257
16. Women at the forefront of the fight. Conversation with Doña Felisa Muralles, from the Movimiento de Resistencia Pacífica La Puya, Guatemala 267
17. Violence affects the entire community, not just women 285
18. What we talk about when we talk about reproduction. An ecofeminist dialogue between Ivonne Yánez and Cristina Vega 307
19. Mirrors of each other: consciousness-raising in Minervas ... 325

Prologue

There are social times when what Thomas Kuhn called "normal science" breaks down, and those certainties and promises that it offered become weak, or collapse. They are times of crisis which become fertile if they manage to open themselves up to critical renovation of thoughts and practices. *Bodies, Territories and Feminisms: Latin American Compilation of Political Practices, Theories, and Methodologies* is a book which enters various open debates in contemporary social sciences with the aim of presenting in good order ideas and arguments which add to the wide constellation of efforts deployed to break such "normalcy". To challenge the normalcy of what is imposed on us as stifling reality and, at the same time, as a limit to thought and imagination: that is, a willingness to decompose argumental schemata, rigid disciplinary divisions and conceptual keys that hide and bias more than they discover and illuminate.

Thus read, the volume co-ordinated by Delmy Tania Cruz and Manuel Bayón, from the *Colectivo Miradas Críticas del Territorio desde el Feminismo* (Critical Views of Territory from Feminism) is a relevant and accomplished partial synthesis of a set of learning and renewed knowledge which have matured in the last decade. I propose to highlight three key matters. Firstly, throughout the first part of the volume, the authors wonder about a problem that lies at the heart of contemporary struggles in defense of territories attacked by extractivist capitalism and multiform struggles against all the forms of violence which tear at the social body. How and why does the (re)patriarchalization of territories happen, as the devastating extractive and capitalist activities altering the entire continent's geography today extend along those territories? How is the rigid triangle of patriarchy, colonialism and capitalism sustaining the very scaffold of so-called modern life reinforced and expanded?

The five dimensions of what authors call (re)patriarchalization of territories in extractive contexts — political, economic, ecological, cultural, and physical — constitute a fertile analytical tool to connect what appears as fragmentary and scattered when studied from other perspectives. Thus, the complexity of the view put forward by the authors feeds the debate and makes up an argumental framework which can, simultaneously, enlighten problems with renewed strength and connect issues whose separate approach would blunt the sharpest points of criticism. The contributions in the first part of the compilation are grouped around experiences of dispossession, exploitation, expropriation and violence analyzed in Argentina, Mexico, Guatemala and Ecuador, specific and different, which are woven together in a pattern. The pattern of separations and hierarchicalizations condensed in the voracious capitalist-colonial and patriarchal offensive we both inhabit and resist when, alongside many others, we make an effort to subvert it from the constellation of feminisms we forge.

In the second part of the compilation, entitled "Methodological applications and proposals", the authors lead us to a pertinent chain of reflection —situated in Central America, The Andes and the River Plate— on currently legitimate forms of knowledge production, equally multidimensional. As they present their practical experiences of criticism to the modern separation between reason and emotion, subjects of knowledge and objects of study —a central split in academic production established as legitimate—, they document their procedures in different tasks while scrutinizing what was learnt in their own research work. This section leads me to wonder whether it would be fertile to think of research work comprehensively, not just as a meeting and exchange between subjects of knowledge but also, and perhaps firstly, as reciprocal knowledge and potential alliance between subjects of struggle. To think of research work on the most pivotal contemporary issues as a meeting and exchange between subjects of struggle moves us away from the absurd place of neutrality which certain academic knowledge means to hold. However, it also leads us to take charge of the intention animating the research activity explicitly and rigorously. Reflection on this matter, in my view, contributes to co-production of shared horizons of sense which can learn to become common, while still remaining different. And this is a key issue for the connection and interweaving of the wide range of situated efforts carried out by females and males against extractivism, exploitation and violence; this is one of the intentions of the volume which, in its third part, "Dialogues", engages in opening to conversation with those with shared concerns despite differing viewpoints.

Therefore, the book is also a challenge to dominant, eminently patriarchal and colonial views and practices which structure academic knowledge. The authors show their willingness to dialogue, their openness to conversation around current issues. They do not wish to be or position themselves as a "rival theory" against similar voices, or a "competing" perspective before other close views; rather, they make an orderly contribution to the debate, with an effort to nourish and widen what is known.

A third key about the compilation as a whole arises, and I again put it forward as a question. Are the young colleagues whose effort has conceived this volume not promoting a research practice which aims to visibilize, connect and explain problems of great significance and multiple subjects of struggle with a view to overcome them? To provide rigorous and general explanations for the most relevant problems has been a concern for so-called scientific knowledge since it got such name in the 17th century. However, such scientific knowledge was immediately attached to the expansion of colonial capitalism and organized in a ferociously patriarchal way. The canonical Marxist theoretical corpus also went to great lengths to acquire that name, as for more than a century it became a rival theory to the so-called positive science, with which it comfortably shared its old patriarchal features. All that knowledge is in crisis today, and for some decades the collapse of any general explanation of the social phenomenon was dictated. However, is "getting to know the reason of something" not an urgent need now? One of the meanings of the word "explain"? And plenty more, if that "something" condenses the reiterated dynamics which threatens and destroys us as a species. Is it not the most fertile thing we can do to become aware of the capitalist (re)patriarchalization of territories and life as a whole, to build arguments to understand what is happening, and to attempt explanations which can nourish the efforts to subvert and overcome that extreme, if we have the time to research?

Finally, my enthusiasm for the book whose authors have generously invited me to prologue rests on the fresh way in which their work clearly reinstates the discussion on the "being a part" relationship —a part of a tenacious flow of struggle spreading over our territories. To know that we are a part of a life, struggle and reproduction flow with others, as well as to be a part of that flow in the knowing, means to (re)start the walk along an old and contemporary path which feminisms shed light on at present. I am thankful for this effort and I celebrate "being a part" of it: an effort which wishes to become, and is becoming, a torrent.

Raquel Gutiérrez Aguilar

Puebla, September 2018

Introduction

Delmy Tania Cruz Hernández and Manuel Bayón Jiménez

"The world was silent." This is how the prologue to *Half of a Yellow Sun*, one of Nigerian author Chimamanda Adiche Ngozi's books, starts. She writes the contemporary story of a part of Africa: Nigeria. The struggle in this nation to achieve an independent republic, Biafra, towards the end of the 1970s, shapes the civil war and the international ghosts which wandered the NON-separation from Nigeria, due to the interest in its raw materials. Thousands of people lost their lives. The phrase "The world was silent" recalls that, back then, there were no great international echoes claiming "Stop now!" against the cruelty of the massacre in Nigeria. It has been over forty years since then, and in the world we are still silent in the face of injustice. There are many current examples in Latin America and the Caribbean: Nicaragua is one of them. These events remind us of the premise highlighted by the feminist thinker Judith Butler (2010), when she wondered what life is, whether some lives are worth more than others. Butler states that the main problem about how we think of the world and how our epistemologies work has a deficit, since our ontology on what constitutes a life is divided by a moral, rather than an ethical, project. Thus, there are lives that we construct in the collective imaginary which deserved to be cried over, and others that do not. The lives of female and male subjects in Africa, Asia, Latin America and the Caribbean who fight for their territories and are massacred for defending their collective identity appear not to be within our apprehension frameworks of what life is; then, they are simply not important enough and we become deaf to the yell of *¡Ya basta!* ("Stop now!")

This collective project, this book, born of dissident voices from various corners of Latin America, names these female and male subjects invisibilized by History, with a capital letter, the History dictated by the winners, almost all of them men, heterosexual, white, Western and bourgeois. This project in your hands is dissonance in a world of complicit silences, rupture, naming the unsayable, returning protagonism to those who have always fought for life and their territories to build possible, livable worlds for all the beings inhabiting this planet.

For Indigenous peoples, subaltern communities, peoples in resistance and peripheral collectives, the defense of the territory is *a life process in becoming and with an ancestral memory*, which did not start at the beginning of the 21st century. The visibilization that their struggles have nowadays responds to the gory violence they receive from the capitalist, patriarchal and colonial system which, even in self-named "socialist" regimes (Ecuador and Bolivia), combats communities, peoples and collectives and their common goods, criminalizing the fight for the defense of their rivers, mountains, shared lands, farms, parcels, forests; because it hates the defense of their own existence and their dignified rage.

As Zapatists point out, in reference to Mexico —but applicable to all Latin America— the farm administrator is changed, but not the farm system, which runs on the four wheels of the capitalist system: exploitation, dispossession, criminalization and hate; especially towards ways of living that discomfit, disruptive ways of living and being which clash in the concert of established order to say ¡*Ya Basta!* Together with it, as part of that collective clamor, in the margins there is the voice of an echo of unimaginable power incarnated in feminized bodies which say ¡NI UNA MENOS!, not one woman less!

In the last decade, the defense of territory started to figure in the agendas of academy, international co-operation and civil society organizations as an emerging "topic".[1] We posit that it is a long-standing situation, evidenced and incarnated, for over five centuries, in the subjects from organized peoples in the global

---

[1] We enclosed *topic* in inverted commas because we recognize that, for Indigenous peoples, disruptive collectives and subaltern communities, the defence of their existence is a process that has existed over the last five centuries.

South and their struggles, who place their bodies at the center, risking their lives and their chances of existence.

This book is praise for those struggles that preceded ours, a questioning as militants, activists and committed thinkers, a constant open question that demands *what about you?*

We offer this article compilation with a double affiliation to committed academia and margin militancy and activism, as actors, subjects and partners in fights for territory defense, since in our view they mark conditions of possibility and existence in community contexts.

No doubt it was the peoples in resistance who showed us the way, but it was and still is women who evidence the art of organizing hope; still, women of all ages, times and geographies who defend territories are invisibilized, erased and silenced. Even when it is them who reproduce resistance life itself; when their bodies are the first military objectives for dispossession; when they are carers for coming generations; when they must do, in addition to a multiple shift, double militancy (outwards and inside their communities).

The articles in this book take up the call for epistemic justice; we speak on no one's behalf, but with them all, since to us speaking is a mirror to keep rethinking (ourselves) in the struggle for life and dignity in all the Abya Yala territories.

For us, a starting point to try and dialogue with struggles and resistances across our countries is *the body-territory, the body as a territory, the territory as a social body*. We find in feminisms from the South words that orient us and invite us to rename female subjects, whose leaderships are today in the spotlight. Through their voices and looking at the categories [bodies, territories], we want to listen, understand, learn and visibilize resistance practices, movements that carry out new strategies, stopping, and ways of appearing/disappearing in the face of territory dispossession.

Collective creation process in this book

This book in your hands is a compilation with no fixed reading sequence: it can be approached in random order. It is a set of suggestions to place a deep, different look on topics which have experienced a strong surge in interest in the last few years: extractivism, women's struggles, territorial dispossession, resistances, feminicides, territory defense, bodies, feminisms. The diverse bodies who have worked on this book formed the Clacso Workgroup "Cuerpos, Territorios y Feminismos" (Bodies, Territories and Feminisms) and, in it, an excuse to gather together and share knowledge, fight experiences and feelings against patriarchy, and structural racism in the system.

Distances in our continent made us get together by region: Central America, Andes and Southern Cone. Thus, we gathered at conferences, activities, journeys and debates which led us to collective reflections. Many of the articles portray this sharing. Once written, the articles circulated around the regions, adding sides to the formulated reflections, in a collective co-editing process among the entire workgroup. This process finished in October 2018.

Thus, this is a book that aims to leave behind individual standards for knowledge production; while still stating that the article authors are responsible for any imprecisions they might contain. In turn, we acknowledge that these are contributions born from interaction with other collectives, organizations and people who have enriched them.

A first approach to contents

The book is divided into three sections for easier browsing. The first section focuses on the concepts projected on the title: bodies, territories and feminisms, according to different theoretical perspectives which relate them to case studies in the Andes, Central America and the Southern Cone. The eight articles in this section delve into a great variety of topics. First, dispossession that multiplies against women when extractive activities appear, reconfiguration of popular struggles in the last decade, or reasons why women and their bodies are at the center of the fight for the defense of life. A recurring question about transformations and continuities between neoliberal and neo-developmentalist States is identified along all these articles. The second section explains corporal-territorial processes, gathering terrible cases of violence against women, through massacre or slow death processes, and forms of resistance that arise to face them. In this section, there is special interest in relations between different theoretical perspectives: intersectionalities between the categories of body and territory, or proposals such as body geopolitics in the face of coloniality or (re)patriarchalization of territories.

The second section is essential to replicate contents and knowledge for the dispute, since it focuses on work methodologies for the interrelation of bodies, territories and feminisms. Drama, cartography, emotions, participative research-action, popular education or feminist writing lead us to situate ways of approaching work and reflection on resistance processes. These are articles written in the mirror of different regions: methodologies for rural work in Uruguay and Central America, counter-mapping experiences in Ecuador and Mexico, emotions from research in Guatemala or Theater of the Female Oppressed in Uruguay. These are experiences narrated in the first person, a way of doing in the world, which in the interaction produced by the process of elaboration of this book found multiple resonances.

The third section is dialogues around issues still unformulated, which we are still thinking and inquiring, which contain as many questions as statements, and which are produced in the discussion among different bodies that share a questioning of generalized axioms. Thus, we find feminist questionings to Mother Earth naturalization in the Andes, life and organization stories from Guatemala, decolonial dialogues about patriarchal violence, conversations between feminists and ecologists on the concept of reproduction, as well as reflections from consciousness-raising developed in Uruguay. This is a section where writing styles are less attached to essay prose, where choppy dialogues, self-narration and doubts arise, to end the book on paths open to reflection in order to follow the political action of resistance.

The bonuses are the Prologue, by Raquel Gutiérrez, written from the affection of exchange. Our thanks to both of them for sharing so much learning and so many experiences with those who fight to transform bodies and territories from feminisms.

PART 1: THEORETICAL-POLITICAL PERSPECTIVES

1. Extractivism y (re)patriarchalization of territories *

Miriam García-Torres, Eva Vázquez, Delmy Tania Cruz and Manuel Bayón[1]

Where are these reflections born?

After the declaration of oil exploitation of the ITT Block[2] in the Yasuní National Park, Ecuador, in August 2013 by Rafael Correa, who was president at the time, different social movements emerged in the country, taking a stand against this decision. Among these movements, the most important are *Yasunidos* —"Yasunited", an ecologist, mainly urban collective, who put forward a popular consultation to try to stop exploitation in the Yasuní-ITT Block— and, especially relevant, the *Articulación de Mujeres Amazónicas* ("Articulation of Amazonian Women"). The latter, formed by Indigenous women of five nationalities —kichwa, waorani, sapara, shiwiar and shuar— emerged strongly in October 2013, after a demonstration that marched from Puyo (Pastaza) to Quito, in order to reject the oil border extension into their territories.

In this setting, the first reflections of the Colectivo Miradas Críticas del Territorio desde el Feminismo started to take shape

---

* An extract of this chapter was published by *Revista Ecología Política*, no. 54, January 2018.

[1] This article is knowledge by the *Colectivo de Miradas Críticas del Territorio desde el Feminismo* (Critical Views of the Territory from Feminism Collective), in interaction with other organizations and territory struggles. It is the fruit of a joint reflection with the entire collective at different times in the past six years. Those who sign this article have only given concrete words to the collective work and appear in random order.

[2] The 43-ITT Block is formed by the Ishpingo, Tambococha and Tiputini oil fields, located at the very heart of the park.

around what extractive activities imply for the territories, especially for female bodies, and also around the protagonist role of women against extractive activities. These first reflections were summed up in *La vida en el centro y el crudo bajo tierra. El Yasuní en clave feminista* (*Life at the center and oil in the ground. The Yasuní in feminist key*), a book that emerged from exchanges and conversations with Amazonian women who arrived in Quito, and which became our first collective approach to understanding links between territories and feminisms: the defence of the land closely connected to identity and means of life reproduction (water, crops...) in the hands of women in community dynamics, the close links between the material and spiritual dimension of the territory, the resignification of what Amazonian women understand by "poverty", the territory understood as a space of intimacy, protection, where also social and family bonds are reproduced (Colectivo Miradas Críticas del Territorio desde el Feminismo, 2014).

The appearance of women's movements against extractivism across Latin America motivated us to try and give a feminist look to the understanding of territory dynamics: comprehending how and why women are resisting, and looking deeper into the link between the struggles for feminized bodies and dispossessed territories. To this end, the work carried out by community feminists and their conception of body-land territory were a constant source of inspiration and reflection. To think and work on the body-territory allowed us to visibilize how violence on women's bodies is connected to global dispossession processes on territories. The methodologies from the body and senses that we start to gestate and construct, such as the mapping of the body-territory or corporal cartography,[3] became the basis to initiate

---

[3] The mapping of the body-territory or corporal cartography is a methodology that rethinks, recreates, complements and adapts collectively. It consists of using drawings of one's own body to discover how the body lives and feels violences exerted on the territories and where on the body those violences are located. This tool favors consciousness-raising of corporality in the struggle for territories, corporization of aggressions and

multiple dialogues and alliances among diverse women: this allowed us to understand how the territory is (re)patriarchalized with extractive activities, as well as the roots of women's resistances in these struggles (Colectivo Miradas Críticas del Territorio desde el Feminismo, 2017).

In this sense, it is important to highlight that our views and reflections are rooted in the exchange with women from diverse communities and collectives, from Latin America and the Caribbean: feminists from different urban and rural movements, and also from spaces that are shared with organizations and women in the global North, with whom we try to weave links and alliances that allow us to set up joint strategies to stop the multiple violences on our bodies-territories.

With the Red Latinoamericana de Mujeres Defensoras de Derechos Sociales y Ambientales (Latin American Network of Women Defending Social and Environmental Rights), present in ten Latin American countries, we could delve into how the sack of mineral resources for the benefit of mining corporations configures the current system which colonizes peoples, lands, women and nature. Women in mining resistance from the entire Abya Yala allow the construction of an identity that links their territory struggles, documenting, influencing, articulating and shaping actions leading to safeguard female defenders in high risk situations due to their participation in denunciation spaces before mining companies and States. In these dialogues, reflections arising from the (re)patriarchalization of territories by extractive activities and from what this network and its member organizations have been naming as environmental violence against women take place as well.

Our exchanges with Indigenous women from various countries also allowed us to analyze response forms based on gender, class and ethnic group conditions as markers of social

---

resistances against extractive megaprojects, creation of counter-narratives that represent us in other ways, as well as own popular representations of identity and self-representation.

hierarchical organization and of conflict. We can highlight our meetings with Saramanta Warmikuna in Ecuador, an articulation formed by Andean and Amazonian Indigenous women from various peoples and nationalities; the *Federación de Mujeres Campesinas, Artesanas, Indígenas, Nativas y Asalariadas del Perú* (Femucarinap: Federation of Peasant, Artisan, Indigenous, Native and Salaried Women of Peru); Tzk'at-*Red de Sanadoras Ancestrales del Feminismo Comunitario* (Ancestral Healers of Community Feminism Network) in Iximulew, Guatemala; as well as companions from diverse Mexican Indigenous organizations, specifically from Chiapas, through alliances with *Mujeres Transformando Mundos* (Mutram: Women Transforming Worlds). This view was broadened with an approach to sexual diversity collectives such as the lesbofeminist collective La Concha Batukeada, or urban activist collectives such as the Colectivo de Geografía Crítica, the Colectivo de Investigación y Acción Psicosocial o Acción Ecológica in Ecuador, the Centro de Derechos de la Mujer y el Centro de Educación Integral de Base (Ceiba) in Chiapas, or Minervas in Uruguay.

In this reflection, it was also important to hold meeting, reading and discussion spaces with different intellectuals from diverse movements, with whom we had a chance to share time and thoughts. To mention a few, we had meetings with Vandana Shiva from South ecofeminisms, Lorena Cabnal from community feminisms, Ivonne Gebara from theologian feminists, Silvia Federici and Terisa Turner from Marxist feminism, Yayo Herrero from Northern ecofeminisms, Joan Martínez-Alier from political ecology and ecological economy, or David Harvey from Anglo-Saxon Marxism. Academic spaces, such as the first and second *Jornadas de investigación feminista* in Flacso-Ecuador, exchanges with students from Universidad Autónoma de la Ciudad de México or Clacso Workgroup "Cuerpos, Territorios y Feminismos" were discussion, questioning and advancement spaces for this reflection. The conceptualization of territory (re)patriarchalization we propose here is, thus, a result of all this baggage of collective thinking, multiple reflection and diverse criticism.

Women facing extractivism, colonialism, and patriarchy in Latin America

In the last few years, Latin America substituted the Washington Consensus, based on application of structural adjustment and privatization policies, by the Commodities Consensus, based on exportation of raw materials under the mediating role of States, adopted by both neoliberal and so-called progressive governments (Svampa, 2013), who act under the paradigm of systemic competitiveness (Wilson and Bayón, 2017). The growing demand of raw materials by global North countries, as the emergence of Brazil and China as new referents for foreign policy and resource consumers, led the Latin American region to a new oil, mineral and agroexport products boom.

This boom has been accompanied by a spatial explosion of capital megaprojects of all kinds at the territories, at the base of the reprimarization of Latin American economies. The increase of mining and oil concessions under public-private national-transnational models, land ownership concentration and farming model asphyxiation to benefit large agroexport companies is causing land rent to be the base of the economic growth cycle produced in the region (Svampa, 2011).

It is necessary to view this deep capital penetration in territories from the body scale: paraphrasing Rita Segato (2004), territory appropriation also supposes violent possession of women's bodies as part of what can be sacrificed for the sake of territory control. Silvia Federici (2014), in turn, recognizes this link between originary accumulation and patriarchal violence already from the feudalism to capitalism transition period, but her analysis can be perfectly identified with today's extractive contexts.

These processes of dispossession and violence are still configured by race and gender hierarchies in Latin American societies (Hernández Castillo, 2015). As a result of colonial advance of capital penetration processes, Nation-State formation and territory dispossession, Indigenous territories have relocated to increasingly remote spaces. Therefore, territory became a self-government power political category, leading, in some cases, to plurinational States, such as the Ecuadorian or the Bolivian States. However, this political recognition obtained under progressive government administrations has not modified the essence of the extractivist model, still considered the foundation for a development model based on modernity and economic growth. Thus, expansion of extractive megaprojects is a common feature in the whole region, independently from the political sign of each successive administration. The limits to progressive governments show the need to confront not only neo-liberalism, but also capitalism as a colonial system that subordinates peripheries to global accumulation processes (Machado Araoz, 2016).

If, as Machado Araoz (2016) states, extractivism, colonialism and capitalism share historical and geographical links, in this text we will try to also show the connections that those oppression systems keep with the imposition of patriarchy. The role of oil and mining companies, together with the role of a State that mediates and facilitates their activities, found in territory planning, compensatory project offerings and local administration co-optation their main strategies to try to legitimize their activities. These strategies are centered around offering salaries to the male community population; salaries which, though few and short-term, aim at broadening the social base of oil and mining exploitation acceptance. As stated by Terisa Turner (cited in Colectivo de Investigación y Acción Psicosocial, 2017b), the patriarchal alliance is key to implanting extractive projects; as between different ethnic groups and classes, this evidences the patriarchal and capitalist system, favoring a male alliance —under power relations.

As described below, male wage labor provides a tool for integration into national society and hegemonic masculinity canons but, on the other hand, it gives men more power in their families. This increases the gender gap in communities. This is one of the reasons why a majority of women in communities usually oppose extractivism. As they point out, the arrival of megaprojects will only bring more care work, more violence and the loss of their food sovereignty, and thus, more dependence (Colectivo Miradas Críticas del Territorio desde el Feminismo, 2014).

On the other hand, political visibilization of Indigenous women has been growing in the past few decades, and for the past few years they have increasing led struggles for territory defense, becoming a referent against capitalist and patriarchal extractivism. We will study some cases.

In Central America, for example, women movements rose to oppose megainfrastructures associated to Puebla-Panama Plan, highways and hydroelectric projects associated to mine exploitation; they suffer great criminalization and growing violence. In Guatemala, the Xinca women's fight against mining in the Xalapan mountain is emblematic. In Mexico, Chiapas is a resistance territory, and the EZLN (Zapatista Army of National Liberation) shows a growing female political protagonism, with successive women's meetings to defend their territory, starting from their bodies. In the past few years, Ecuador has experienced Amazonia's Indigenous women's demonstrations against oil exploitation: they lead territory defense with interethnic articulations focused on stopping the advance of extractive projects. Women in Cajamarca, Peru, fight together against mining and patriarchy. In Bolivia, the Red Nacional de Mujeres en Defensa de la Madre Tierra have started to raise their voices against mine extractivism, and Mujeres Creando became an icon for the combat against a patriarchal State in connection to capitalist advance and female body criminalization. In Uruguay, women organizations are rising against the soybean model, which leads to land dispossession and impoverishment. In Brazil, the Movimento de Mulheres Camponesas has become a referent for the Vía Campesina, bonding women's role to the fight for the land, globalizing alliances across the region and the world.

Shared experiences by women organized in movements against capitalism and colonialism advance in their territories shows the collusion between economic power and political power, with strong similarities across Latin American countries. There is a generalized response that does violence to bodies, breaks apart life cycles, chains itself to patriarchy with specific violence policies against female bodies: repression, criminalization, reproduction control, political negation, gender violence, etc. Generalized advance of capital megaprojects found in organized women a new resistance front, a social actor whose protagonism has been historically denied.

In urban territories, life reproduction crisis implies survival strategies which place women at the head of daily care responsibilities; they sustain a daily work overload, among the many forms of violence taking place in these agglomeration spaces. In spite of an increase in social policies in the past few years, class, patriarchal and racist power structures have not been altered. Cities are still the prime segregation space, especially large Latin American metropolises. In this sense, it is not possible to observe the dispossession process linked to extractive megaprojects without seeing the other side of urban spaces, increasingly populated, showing a growing life crisis. At the same time, agrarian counter-reforms and the deepening in agrarian liberalization kept increasing impoverished urban population arriving from the country, many of them women also fleeing different forms of patriarchal violence. Migrations not just on a Latin American scale, but moving towards central capitalism spaces, in the United States and Europe, where the care crisis increasingly demands cheap female labor to alleviate it by plundering affection: bodies which will care for the bodies of those who exploit them.

Policies designed to serve the interests of political power have generated dispossession on a wide scope. Extractive megaprojects, segregated urban spaces and forms of violence against women's bodies interweave on several levels: global, national, local, community, domestic, physical. Subsuming territories and bodies to transnational capital met in Latin America an explosive boom of raw materials. Thus, organized women's resistances increasingly join the struggle against capitalist, patriarchal and colonial violence, positioning themselves as new political subjects.

In this context, we propose the concept of *territory (re)patriarchalization* as a way of naming this interweaving of violence forms related to the current capital expansion cycle in the continent, and the response that women give in a joint fight against megaproject territorialization, neo-colonial forms of life space dispossession and patriarchy reconfiguration required by the extractivist model.

The five dimensions of territory (re)patriarchalization

As we have posited, extractive activities configure in territories a new patriarchal order, which converges, takes root, deepens and actualizes the existence of previous sexist relations. We refer to territories not just as biophysical and geographical spaces, but also as social, cultural and corporal life spaces. Studying extractive activities in this perspective makes it possible to understand that logics imposed by large mining and oil projects go hand in hand with a reconfiguration of society-nature relations and a restructuring of gender relations in patriarchal terms. To illustrate this, we will take as the core of our analysis the five dimensions — political, economic, ecological, cultural and corporal— of what we have called *territory (re)patriarchalization* in extractive contexts.

Political dimension: masculinized decision-making

When attempting to identify those who make decisions over extractive project implantation in territories, there is no doubt that they are privileged capitalism subjects, represented by States and national and transnational companies. In other words, it is possible to state that those who make decisions affecting communities' lives and territories are subjects defined by Pérez Orozco (2014) as "*BBVAH*" ("*blanco, burgués, varón, adulto, heterosexual*"): i.e., a white, bourgeois, adult male subject, with normative and heterosexual functionality ("WBAMH").

Besides, when those subjects —companies, or the State— arrive at territories to persuade or impose the extractive option, they often establish individual relationship strategies in order to weaken the communities' collective negotiation capacity. Thus, in many cases companies encourage exclusively male interlocution, whether with sympathetic local leaderships or with male heads of households. This means that women are excluded from decision making over issues that affect their territories and their lives. Therefore, the relationship logic derived from mining and oil activities implies considering women as passive agents without their own voice, who must be under tutelage of male decisions. This happened, for example, in the Mirador mining project in South Amazonia, Ecuador, where women found out about their farms being sold to the company when their husbands had already been persuaded to sign (Colectivo de Investigación y Acción Psicosocial, 2017a).

As a consequence, extractivism favors reconfiguration of interlocution spaces and masculinized decision making, overlapping with previous patriarchal political structures. Thus, one of the factors that motivated women's mobilization and political organization against extractive projects was precisely their historical exclusion from decision spaces and the cooptation of male leaderships by the extractive logic, as in the case of the Amazonian Women articulation in Ecuador against the oil frontier expansion (García-Torres, 2017).

Economic dimension: configuring patriarchal labor structures

Penetration of extractive dynamics in communities leads to a local economy reorganization according to the company's central presence (Fundación Rosa Luxemburg, 2013). In addition to creating a deep reordering of community self-sufficiency economies towards a wage economy, it also generates significant transformations in gender relations: because it is necessary to consider that job expectations brought by extractive industries are strongly associated to male labor and carry new unequal social relations (Himley, 2011; Sharma, 2012; Mukherjee, 2014).

In other words, when extractive industries penetrate and communities are dispossessed of common goods that ensured their autonomous material provision —because they are evicted and displaced, or water, rivers and soil are polluted—, wages obtained from the company become a powerful instrument of dependence and subjection. Men start doing jobs for the companies — temporary, unskilled jobs, often under labor exploitation conditions, as in Kakinte communities at Peruvian Amazonia's hydrocarbon blocks (Campanario Baqué and García Hierro, 2013).

Excluded from labor and natural goods, women lose autonomy and are relegated to a subordinate place in relation to their husbands wages. Consequently, in the new labor structure introduced after extractive industries penetration the figure of the bread-earner male and the woman economically dependent on male wage are reinforced (Himley, 2011; Sharma, 2012; Mukherjee, 2014).

Therefore, expropriation and territory pollution as a consequence of mining and oil activities establishes what Federici (2010) calls "wage patriarchy".[4] Thus, it is possible to state that extractivism, by installing a highly masculinized wage economy, helps widen the structural differences between men and women inside a community.

Ecological dimension: breakdown in life reproduction cycles

Extractive activities imply a break in life reproduction cycles: rivers get polluted, soils stop producing, deforestation drives animals away from forests; as a result, food provision for communities by means of their traditional activities such as hunting, fishing and farming are severely altered. On the one hand, as mentioned above, there is a reorganization of the sexual division of labor by which men, who in ancestral economies made a considerable contribution to reproduction jobs —e.g. hunting, or fishing—, become unskilled workers in the company.

Thus, extractive activities imply an increase of feminization in social reproduction labor. On the other hand, the socioecological impact derived from oil or mining activities deeply affects care work assigned to women. It is them who must face growing difficulties to access clean water sources or guarantee family food provision. Likewise, the rise in diseases and decline in collective health resulting from extractive dynamics causes a growing need for care in the population: a responsibility assigned to women

---

[4] Even though Federici (2010) uses this term in reference to the transition period from feudalism to capitalism, it may well be used to characterize certain extractive contexts in the present.

(Colectivo Miradas Críticas del Territorio desde el Feminismo, 2014).

Therefore, it is possible to state that the introduction of these dynamics results in female care work overload, as well as an increase in stress and anxiety produced by the growing difficulty to solve social reproduction responsibilities that befall them, as in Ecuador's South Amazonia after large-scale mining penetration (Colectivo de Investigación y Acción Psicosocial, 2017a).

In conclusion, in a crisis scenario as the one generated in extractive areas, where reproduction cycles are abruptly broken, the task of trying to rebuild possibility conditions for life falls, invisibilized, on women's backs. It is necessary to manifest, therefore, that extractivist accumulation is structurally dependent on the appropriation of unpaid, hidden and undervalued labor done by women, as much as on the appropriation of nature.

Cultural dimension: deepening sexist representations and stereotypes

The massive arrival of male workers external to the communities in mining and oil areas creates a masculinization of the territory. Often, along with extractivism penetration, there are territory militarization processes by public or private security forces, which deepens space masculinization. For women, this involves new feelings of fear and insecurity, causing what Federici (2010) calls "social isolation", which confines women to the private-domestic space, limiting their mobility in the territory.

On that subject, it is necessary to add that the new dynamics introduced as a consequence of extractive activity penetration generate changes in leisure forms and space occupation, facilitating bar opening and the entry of industrial alcohol. In this scenario, masculinized spaces are formed, in which men monopolize places thus imbued with new power relations, which overlap with previous gender hierarchies (Mukherjee, 2014; Sharma, 2012; Barrientos Delgado et al., 2009) Hence, the implantation of mining and oil activities privileges the conformation of subjects who reinforce hegemonic masculinity stereotypes, where the male pole is linked to domination and control, while the female pole is associated to the idea of a dependent woman, object of control and sexual abuse (Fundación Rosa Luxemburg, 2013).

Thus, for example, women in the mining area of Cajamarca, Peru denounce that they "can no longer go out for coffee because [they] are treated like prostitutes" (Red Latinoamericana de Mujeres Defensoras de Derechos Sociales y Ambientales, 2012, pp. 19-20). In this new masculinized scenario, the imaginary of the "bad woman" is built on those who try to transgress imposed normativity (as in the case of territory and nature defenders), to whom certain behavior models based on the imposition of patriarchal moral attributes are applied (García-Torres, 2017).

Corporal dimension: social control and male violence

Extractive dynamics impose a certain discipline and body control in territories, on sexed and racialized bodies. In other words, violence forms exerted on territories materialize in significantly different ways on sexed and racialized bodies.

In this context of deepening of sexist stereotypes and massive territory masculinization by male workers and public or private security forces, men show a strong sense of appropriation over women and their bodies. Therefore, in mining and oil areas, intimidation, harassment, sexual aggressions and male violence against women increase (Colectivo Miradas Críticas del Territorio desde el Feminismo, 2014; Colectivo de Investigación y Acción Psicosocial, 2017a).

On the other hand, new leisure forms, introduced as a consequence of extractive activities, result in the appearance of brothels in community territories. It is worth mentioning that in many cases these brothels are associated to women trafficking for sexual exploitation purposes (Macassi León, 2015). Thus, there is a strong connection between extractivism and —often forced— sex work, inasmuch as the latter supposes an activity that in extractive contexts is functional to capital accumulation, serving to channel the male workforce's stress (Laite, 2009).

Another form of control over women's bodies happens when they are forced to get employment in vulnerable conditions of domestic exploitation for company workers. In some cases, for example in Chiapas, women are forced to marry "temporarily" in order to serve workers more cheaply (Rojas, 2013, p. 10). Their bodies, wishes, dreams and work are dispossessed in the service of capital.

It is possible to state, therefore, that violence, sexual harassment and social control of women's bodies are part of patriarchal imaginaries powered by mining and oil activity penetration, where both nature and —especially women's bodies— appear as objectified spaces which can be appropriated and sacrificed in the service of capital accumulation.

Xinka women in Guatemala who oppose mining in the Xalapan mountain know this well. Hence they propose the concept of territory-body-land to maintain that the recovery of women's territory-body is a first inseparable part of the territory-land defense. In other words, these community feminists affirm that a territory-land defense is not possible unless accompanied by the emancipatory recovery of —sexed and racialized— bodies who are continually subjected to violence (Cabnal, 2010).

Closing words

These five dimensions of territory (re)patriarchalization allow us to understand that in those Latin America territories where extractive megaprojects arrive, a reconfiguration of patriarchal power relations intersecting with classism and colonialism is generated. Women whose territories and bodies are under dispossession threat linked to oil, mining, agroindustrial or urban projects are gathering to become a river of transcontinental resistance. The concept of territory (re)patriarchalization tries to develop and capture in ideas what for centuries has been ancestral female knowledge: capitalism, colonialism and patriarchy are intimately related. That is why it is necessary to incorporate intersectional feminist perspectives to think of transitions toward post-extractive societies.

Bibliography

Barrientos Delgado, Jaime *et al.* (2009). Minería, género y cultura. Una aproximación etnográfica a espacios de esparcimiento y diversión masculina en el norte de Chile. *Revista de Antropología Iberoamericana* 4 (3): 385-408.

Cabnal, Lorena (2010). Acercamiento a la construcción de la propuesta de pensamiento epistémico de las mujeres indígenas feministas comunitarias de Abya Yala. In *Feminismos diversos: el feminismo comunitario*, ACSUR-Las Segovias: 11-25

Campanario Baqué, Yaizha y Pedro García Hierro (2013). Empresas domiciliadas en países ratificantes del convenio 169-OIT operando en territorios de pueblos indígenas en Perú. El caso de la empresa española Repsol. Coordinación por los Derechos de los Pueblos Indígenas (CODPI). Available at http://bit.ly/2fGPwnU

Colectivo de Investigación y Acción Psicosocial (2017a). La herida abierta del Cóndor: Vulneración de derechos, impactos socioecológicos y afectaciones psicosociales provocados por la empresa minera china EcuaCorriente S.A. y el Estado ecuatoriano en el proyecto Mirador. Quito. Available at https://investigacionpsicosocial.files.wordpress.com/2017/02/herida-abierta-del-cc3b3ndor.pdf

— (2017b). Repatriarcalización de los territorios por actividades extractivas. Salud colectiva, feminismo y ecología política. Paper presented by Eva Vázquez at the II Jornadas de investigaciones feministas y de género sobre la acción política. Flacso-Ecuador. May 2017. Available at https://miradascriticasdelterritoriodesdeelfeminismo.files.wordpress.com/2013/07/ponencia-repatriarcalizacic3b3n-territorios-eva-vc3a1zquez.pdf

Colectivo Miradas Críticas del Territorio desde el Feminismo (2014). *La vida en el centro y el crudo bajo tierra. El Yasuní en clave feminista*. Quito. Available at https://miradascriticasdelterritoriodesdeelfeminismo.files.wordpress.com/2014/05/yasunienclavefeminista.pdf

Federici, Silvia (2014). La revolución inacabada. Mujeres, reproducción social y luchas por lo común. Escuela Calpulli.

— (2010). Calibán y la bruja. Mujeres, cuerpo y acumulación originaria. Buenos Aires: Tinta Limón.

Fundación Rosa Luxemburg (2013). Memoria del Encuentro Regional de Mujeres y Feminismos Populares. June 4-6, 2013. Available at www.rosalux.org.ec

García-Torres, Miriam (2017). Petróleo, ecología política y feminismo. Una lectura sobre la articulación de Mujeres Amazónicas frente al extractivismo petrolero en la provincia de Pastaza, Ecuador. Master's Thesis. Quito: FLACSO: Ecuador.

Hernández Castillo, Rosa Aída (2014). Cuerpos femeninos, violencia y acumulación por desposesión. In Belausteguigoitia Ruis y María Josefina Saldaña-Portillo (Coords.), *Des/POSESIÓN: Género, Territorio y luchas por la autodeterminación*. México: UNAM-Programa Universitario de Estudios de Género (PUEG), pp. 79-100.

Himley, Matthew (2011). El género y la edad frente a las reconfiguraciones en los medios de subsistencia originadas por la minería en el Perú. *Apuntes XXXVIII* (68): pp. 7-35.

Laite, Julia Ann (2009). Historical perspectives on industrial development, mining, and prostitution. *The Historical Journal 52* (3): pp. 739-761.

Macassi León, Ivonne (Coord.) (2015). *Diagnóstico sobre trata de mujeres, niños y niñas en ocho ciudades del Perú*. Lima: Centro de la Mujer Peruana Flora Tristán. Available at http://bit.ly/1CIXPRG

Machado Araoz, Horacio (2016). El debate sobre el "extractivismo" en tiempos de resaca. *Rebelión*. Available at http://www.rebelion.org/noticia.php?id=211020

Mukherjee, Sonali (2014). Mining and Women: The Case of the Maria of Chhattisgarh. *Social Change 44* (2): pp. 229-247.

Olivera Bustamante, Mercedes (2014). *Subordinaciones estructurales de género. Las mujeres marginales de Chiapas frente a la crisis*. San Cristóbal de las Casas: Universidad de Ciencias y Artes de Chiapas/Centro de Derechos de la Mujer.

Pérez Orozco, Amaia (2014). Subversión feminista de la economía. Aportes para un debate sobre el conflicto capital-vida. Madrid: Traficantes de Sueños.

Porto-Gonçalves, Carlos Walter (2009). De Saberes y de Territorios: diversidad y emancipación a partir de la experiencia latinoamericana. *Revista Polis*. Venezuela: Universidad Bolivariana.

Red Latinoamericana de Mujeres Defensoras de Derechos Sociales y Ambientales (2012). Memorias. Encuentro Latinoamericano de ecofeminismo y protección. Cajamarca, Perú. September 1-4, 2012.

Rojas Rosa, Alma Rosa (2013). La trata de las personas en San Cristóbal. *Colectivo de Educación para la paz y los derechos humanos*. Available at http://www.cepazdh.org/wp/wp-content/uploads/trata-sancristobal2013.pdf

Segato, Rita (2004). La escritura en el cuerpo de las mujeres asesinadas en Ciudad Juárez. Buenos Aires: Tinta Limón.

Sharma, Sanjay (2012). The impact of mining on women: lessons from the coal mining Bowen Basin of Queensland, Australia. *Impact Assessment and Project Appraisal, 28* (3): 201-215. Available at http://dx.doi.org/10.3152/146155110X12772982841041

Svampa, Maristella (2013). *"Consenso de los Commodities" y lenguajes de valoración en América Latina*. Available at http://nuso.org/articulo/consenso-de-los-commodities-y-lenguajes-de-valoracion-en-america-latina/

— (2011). *Pensar el desarrollo desde América Latina*. Available at http://www.maristellasvampa.net/archivos/ensayo56.pdf

Wilson, Japhy y Manuel Bayón (2017). *La selva de los elefantes blancos*. Quito: Abya Yala/IEETM.

2. Women, bodies and territories: between defense and dispossession[1]

Delmy Tania Cruz Hernández[2]

Vicenta tells that, ever since the Acteal tragedy, her body became empty; in her body-territory map she only placed a cross in the heart, the rest of her figure was uninhabited. She mentioned in Tsotsil[3] that, for as long as there was no justice in her territory, she would not be able to feel anything else in her body.[4]

---

[1] Even though I author the text, the arguments that build it could not have been constructed without work and reflection by the collectives I am a part of: *Miradas Críticas del Territorio desde el Feminismo, Mujeres Transformando Mundos* and the *Centro de Educación Integral de Base*. In addition, the premises I show are part of my doctoral thesis and the fieldwork I did between January and September 2017 at the Comiteca Plateau in Chiapas, Mexico and the Southeast of Ecuadorian Amazonia.

[2] Delmy Tania Cruz Hernández is a feminist, anti-racist, popular educator, southern ecologist, animalist, companion to women who defend their territories, and feminist militant from below and to the left. Doctoral student in Social Anthropology CIESAS-Mexico. Coordinator of the Subject Pedagogy program in Cesder-Puebla and member of *Mujeres Transformando Mundos* A.C. in Chiapas. Co-coordinator of the GT "Cuerpos, Territorios y Feminismos" (Bodies, Territories and Feminisms) Member of the *Colectivo Miradas Críticas del Territorio desde el Feminismo* (Critical Views of the Territory from Feminism Collective).

[3] Tsotsil is one of the nine Indigenous languages spoken in Chiapas, with the greatest number of speakers.

[4] Workshop organized by Miradas Críticas del Territorio desde el Feminismo, Mujeres Transformando Mundos and the Centro

As Vicenta tells her experience, in Rosa's face there is a tear. She speaks after Vicenta, and the first thing she says is: "I feel our companion's pain right here in my heart", as she touches her stomach.

Rosa grabs her map and starts, loudly:

> I drew my house, I placed some mountains where some trees are left. In the part of the chest I put the *milpa* because that's our living, corn is sown to eat in the family, and in my belly, the trees, because this is part of our lives and I like the flowers and animals. I put a hill where they are digging and there is a machine to draw sand out and down to the feet there is the black water river, which is the only thing left to us... (Rosa, Barrio la Concepción Jocnajab, Comitan, Chiapas).

Both Rosa and Vicenta are enunciating their lives in their territories through their own bodies: in one of them there is nothing more than a search for justice, in the other there are milpas, trees, damaged hills, and an excess of black water, dust and sadness due to the pollution in the river.

Both women invite us with their narrations to think the body as a central place to inhabit, hear, feel, perceive the territory.

Women's bodies, as some feminists suggest, is the first site of struggle; however, questions arise when territories are forced by paramilitarism, or when there are threats that extractive companies will arrive in their spaces. What happens to women's bodies? Do feminized bodies in community contexts claim the same autonomy as in urban environments, where the individual paradigm is a premise?

The article presented here articulates feminized bodies and dispossession in Indigenous territories, and captures the meaning of territory defense in women's hands, lives, voices and bodies. It places special emphasis on daily life as a defense strategy.

---

de Educación Integral de Base in October 2015 in Comitán, Chiapas.

Colonized territories and criminalization of defense

One of the twentieth century Latin America scenarios is the increase in territory disputes, especially those inhabited by ancestral peoples. The structural violence we are in has increased due to State policies closely linked to neoliberal plans which affect mostly Indigenous territories. Starting from the political economy analysis of late capitalism currently developed by Harvey (2003), after Luxemburg (1978)'s ideas, we see that originary accumulation never finished. Previously, colonial powers employed natural resource dispossession, as well as colonized peoples' alternative production and consumption forms. Currently, these forms of dispossession still happen, but with different, bloodier faces, generating new territory configurations: because unexpected actors appear, such as organized crime and its alliances (Segato, 2017). Paraphrasing Eduardo Galeano, Latin America and the Caribbean's veins still bleed.

Mining, hydrocarbon and agroindustry extractive projects find more and more geographies to settle in all Latin America. Business is always accompanied by large transnational companies and, in the past few years, we can identify the addition of some State companies. As Gartor (2014) suggests, "if neoliberal and progressive governments coincide on anything, it is on consolidating a neo-developmentalist model with an extractivist basis."

We know that dispossession was never a peaceful act. Historically, violence has been a constant capital accumulation method, not just in its genesis but until today (Luxemburg, 1978). However, Indigenous peoples from various Latin American latitudes sought ways to defend their territories. As pointed out by Zapatists, peoples' resistances, from the Colony to nowadays, are an affront to a power trying by all means to impose its hegemony.

Violence is legitimated from the top when those defending their territory are Indigenous peoples (Gilly, 2006, p. 53). One of States' repression strategies to confront dissident voices is removing them from the "legal" framework, in order to charge them as criminals. In addition, those females and males considered leaders face police harassment and threats to their families (Hernández Castillo, 2015, pp. 80-81); in this sense, situations of political violence cause significant damage to health, or even death.

Criminalization of women has specific features, since the focus of violence is on their bodies and the intimidation of their being "women" in communities, where moral behavior is brought into question.

> At one point I stopped asking the men's organization for things; I didn't even want to participate, because every time I asked, they laughed at me. Once I asked for money to make the women's house, for us to talk, have workshops, get together there, and they started saying in the assembly that I wanted it to get money in the bar that, according to them, I have in Puyo [a city close to Amazonia]; my little daughter was there, she heard everything (Female leader, Lorocachi, Pastaza, 17 July 2017).

When organized women raise their voices to defend their territory, they face a hydra with many heads: being Indigenous, they transgress the racial space constructed by Westernized government and party politics, which consider that racialized women have no place in that space. As if having attention and hearing for their Indigenous demands implied having to separate from their body and their language. "Their Indigenous bodies had to split from their tongues, which spoke a broken Spanish" (Belausteguigoitia, 2006). An example of this racism is the attitude taken by Ecuadorian government, led at the time by Rafael Correa, when in October 2013 he did not receive the Amazonia women's march to the city of Quito; they repudiated the oil frontier expansion (XI Ronda) and the public bid for blocks in their territory, in order to avoid soil, river and forest pollution, as well as other social and cultural forms of impact. Besides, being women they violate and transgress the patriarchal space carefully constructed for centuries in their own communities, and reinforced by State policies; Segato (2011) proposes the notion of "State-colonial pact" to account for this.

"The Indigenous women's transgression is punished by discrediting them", states Belausteguigoitia, showing how women suffer two-fold criticism when they resist invasion to their lands or bodies, since they are considered traitors to both their community and the nation.

active Indigenous women, who push away military forces and yell, demanding official orders that justify and legalize advancement and invasion, owners —even for the briefest time— of their lands, defenders of their space, are transgressors not just in the eyes of the State and the army, but also of their own socio-cultural traditions and practices (Belausteguigoitia, 2006, p. 242).

Women facing the extractive fight

In the last few decades, the number of studies that address the experience of territory defense in several Latin American countries has increased. However, little has been said about what women's organization in territory defense is like, and almost nothing is known about what women defend.

The voice and the fight of women organized in the defense of their territories took visibility in the past decade, even though women have defended their territory ever since Spaniards arrived (Hernández Castillo, 2015). Mechanisms adopted by dispossession of territories and natural, social and cultural resources in them framed different scenarios which made women evince their previously-hidden struggles. In the past decade, they had to face the re-emergence of extractive industries supported by Latin American governments pushing for the sale of their territories. In addition, exacerbated wealth accumulation and concentration in the hands of a minority of businessmen and financers (Olivera *et. al.*, 2014), what Segato (2017)[5] called "*dueñidad*" ("lordship", power in the hands of a few owners), caused the creation of a "global borderless geopolitics with new domination forms between imperialist and dependent countries" by means of the free market (Segato, 2017). This affects peripheral countries, especially rural areas and peasantry, excluded from the neoliberal accumulation

---

[5] Since 2016, Segato has worked on the concept of "dueñidad" in several interviews. In her keynote address at the 50-year celebration of Clacso-Central America, in the city of Guatemala, 24-26 October 2017, she explained this concept, assigning the "dueñidad" specific features that, according to the author, can be found all across Latin America.

equation, even though their work as laborers, their consumption and their care work support the capitalist system. Not finding relief in the system-imposed market, many men decide to migrate to "rich" countries or take up arms and join drug trafficking, while women opt to join informal labor, not leaving aside reproduction work in their communities nor territory defense.

Current scenarios dictated by the capitalist system to all the people in the world-system affect Indigenous peoples especially, with peculiar features in the case of their women, and even more so when in their territories there are valuable raw materials whose extraction adds to accumulation.

Previously considered life spaces, territories become hostile places to inhabit when patriarchal alliances between capital and community sexist relations leave women alone in the territory defense.

Argumentation in the present text starts from regarding women as political subjects who face the great capital and expounds how they, in their daily practices, construct their political reflection to defend territories, how that territory defense organization is experienced and how they involve their bodies in the fight in spite of the systemic violence they live every day.

Territory defense in women's voice and body

If we argue that women have been referents in territory defense, how can we explain their invisibility in struggle processes? There is no conclusive answer to this question; I do not know whether that is intended. Undoubtedly, I believe that it is a series of strategies that nowadays have led women to become a "new" Indigenous political subject to be considered in territory defense analysis.

Surely the women voices we hear today are driven by the kind of alliances configured in the territory within certain circumstances. In order to start telling the story, we could discuss the active female presence in events and processes alongside liberation theology in all Latin America. They promoted organizational processes that led to an organized base demanding, in places like Mexico, fair land distribution and abolition of diverse oppressions to which the

Indigenous population, in slavery conditions, were subjected. Many of the women who got organized in Latin America after the calling of liberation theology gained organizational experience, in spite of not achieving land ownership or visibility (Olivera, 2005).

In Latin America, a significant watershed which gave women notoriety was the Ley Revolucionaria de las Mujeres (Women's Revolutionary Law), driven and enacted by militiawomen in the Ejército Zapatista de Liberación Nacional (EZLN, Zapatista Army of National Liberation) in 1994. This law made women's voices resonate and showed their ever present participation in broad social movements (Olivera, 2005).

In spite of the racism, male chauvinism and classism faced by organized Indigenous women nowadays when they raise their voices and use their bodies to defend their territories, they are referents in the struggle.

What do organized women defend in their territories? That will be the focal point of our analysis. First, we will focus on the body scale, since that is where capital is reproduced (Federici, 2004) and where territory conquest spaces have been recreated (Hernández Castillo, 1998; Freyermunth, 1998; Olivera, 1988, 1995, 1998, 2001, 2014).

Feminized bodies are a target for territory control (Segato, 2008). In fact, as expounded by Federici (2004), the capitalist system was developed by the dispossession of knowledge from women's bodies and their exploitation. Currently, the dispossession process of feminized bodies continues, according to the author, who names it "permanent originary accumulation" (2014).

A crucial side to study territory defense by women is looking at daily life, as it is in that space-time that organized women construct their strategies-reflections for the defense of their body-land, body-territory. However, in order to make reflection more complex, looking at daily life as a category of analysis implies framing it in the current context of violence, as mentioned above.

Violence and daily life in territory defense

Violence in Latin America, especially in Indigenous peoples' territories, is a defining element for territory defense by women; it disrupts their daily life and removes the significance of placing their bodies in that resistance.

Violence against women is not an isolated fact, nor is it exclusive between women and men, nor does it happen in "private" spaces; rather, it is a historical continuum which nowadays adopts diverse faces and attacks women's lives and bodies (Segato, 2017). This violence, undoubtedly, articulates with territory dispossession. Even though it is true that women's relationship with the land has always been conflictive and mediated by exclusion, territory is the representation of their care, being and existing; it is, in part, the definition of their material existence forms, thus its dispossession affects their daily lives and their bodies directly.

In order to approach violence in women's daily lives, Nancy Scheper Hughes, Philiphe Bourgois, Venna Das, Pierre Bourdieu, Eduardo Gudynas, Silvia Federici and Rita Segato's perspectives help us understand how violence interacts in social structures but also in our everyday lives. Specifically, Bourgois (2001, 2010), Hughes (1987, 1996, 2004) and Bourdieu (2002, 1999) articulate three violence manifestations which are invisible: structural, symbolic and normalized. The continuum they are in is impregnated with power, which makes them permeate hierarchically one over the other as they simultaneously overlap horizontally, reproducing themselves as well as the inequality political structures that drive and promote them. I believe that articulating these three sides of violence which are not immediately visible allows us to demonstrate the links between manifestations and specific violence forms that are virtually infinite and found in daily life along history. With Segato (2003, 2007, 2016) and Venna Das (1997, 2008) it can be seen how women and their bodies get a special treatment in the violence phenomenon, because its epiphenomenon is women's bodies; dialogues for the male world are inscribed in them.

Segato (2016) posits that twentieth-century war has a new tone; new configurations and their faces are more subtle, since there is an attempt to hide existing schemes among state policies, extractive transnational companies and drug trafficking. In her opinion, violence against women has worsened and its multiple heads[6] have changed; nowadays there is a new form of appropriation of women's bodies originated from non-formal wars, the territorial paradigm and the change in political culture. Thus, as stated by Segato (2004, 2007) and Aida Hernández (2016), when the territory is seen as a body, the body becomes a space in dispute.

In the study of violence on women's bodies, there is an emphasis on how the phenomenon is systemically materialized on the sexual sphere. Although it is true that the exercise of sexuality is a fundamental part of the violent reconfiguration of bodies in territories, the intention of body dispossession is linked to it enclosing wisdom, knowledge, networks and life reproduction (Federici, 2014); that is, from *daily reproduction, new forms of community life are constructed, and the ways to do politics and the political are transformed.*

But how does daily life happen? What do we do in it and what do we reproduce? Questionings are a key to think that daily life is a place that articulates existence, that it is mediation, prefiguration and a space of invention; it is a place of repetition, seriality, naturalization; thus, it is a social practice (Giddens, 1988), the time and place where we are, where we happen. It cannot be conceived of apart from the structure that produces and legitimates it. It is the place where life reproduction happens, materially and symbolically. For Heller (1998), daily life is reproduction of the particular, where the particular is the human being; in it, humanity reproduces. All humanity has a daily life, even if each of those lives has peculiarities. Daily life is the perfect space to understand *habitus* reproduction (Bourdieu, 1999), where women organized as political subjects reproduce social and material life, where they

---

[6] Paraphrasing the Zapatist movement and their analogy of capitalism as a many-headed hydra.

experience several forms of violence and create strategies for territory defense. Even though structure determines social subjects, they also break with determinations and often create ruptures in the system. Organized territory women shake their territory when they pronounce for life and defense of the spaces they inhabit, even if they are not legally their owners.

The women organized at the Meseta Comiteca, in Chiapas, show clear examples of resistance and territory defense in daily life.

A strategy that women find fundamental to make their voices resonate is reappraising their and their daughters and sons' reproductive work, even when such activities trouble other people in the community, because they break with marked gender stereotypes in their communities.

> [...] women work the most in the community, some men don't want to see this... (Sara, another organized woman, laughs), some others do. Me, for example. I teach my son to make *tortillas*, *tortear*, although when they go by and they see him doing it, or washing dishes, or gathering wood, or feeding the animals, they tell him he'll become a woman, they shout things at him... Well, for me, it's important that in the community they see how our work is valuable. How will they value us, otherwise? This way, we can talk and make our words valuable. [...] (Tere, San Nicolás, Trinitaria, interview extract, 12 August 2017).

Reappraising and evidencing reproductive work, women do politics for territory defense and visibilize their everyday production; they show how, through their work, territory becomes the place of resistance and reconstruction of values and, at the same time, community senses.

Likewise, women organized in the collective El Colibrí, living in the Chiapas borderland, *promote the non-capitalist "use" of natural resources: land, water, mountains; and they have opposed nature commercialization.*

> In our community, there's the San Vicente river; here it flows very wide, and it goes into the canals to water the cane. All the agrochemicals in the avocado processing plant go in the river. It gets polluted and disappears, the cane landowners have appropriated it. What do we do? We used to do nothing... now we talk about it, we must get together with the other communities that are affected, and reproduce the information we hear. We must say in the

assembly that the river is for everyone (Zenaida, First "toxitour", Tzimol, Chiapas, 6 November 2017).

Women say that before they were organized, they could see the changes in their communities: river pollution and water hoarding by the cane landowners. But they did not feel capable of speaking about it, or much less confront it. Once they started their reflection process with women from other territories and their own community, they saw the importance of raising their voices, but most of all, as Zenaida says:

> [...] We've plucked up courage and lost our embarrassment, we've learned to stop speaking in darkness. Besides, that river problem affects us more... If water is dirty, it's more work for women. And if the river is dirty, well, we look for other rivers, and we go to other places further away, like our *compañeras* [companions] in San Nicolás. (Reflection workshop "What is organization and how is it useful to us women?", Comitán, Chiapas, 15 May 2017).

Rosa and Zenaida share the same worry. At the beginning, we showed how Rosa, though her body cartography, narrated the sadness she felt on seeing the polluted river. That's why she filled in her feet with smelly black waters, going up to part of her thigh and into her vagina. When her companion Zenaida asked her the reason for that water "up inside", she replied that "when the water is dirty, it kills inside, too, in the soul." Zenaida has Tojolabal Indigenous roots; she is from Meseta Comiteca, at the border between Mexico and Guatemala. The idea of territory that she shares with her friend Rosa is that their territories are bodies and bodies are territories. That is, the body is not only natural: it is also constructed socially and politically (Esteban, 2004; Bordo, 2001). According to statements and examples from organized women at territories in resistance, we could assert that, in addition, it is built territorially, especially in community contexts. Thus, body-territory becomes an indispensable conjunction to live and understand the place to inhabit from a different cosmogony. Therefore, polluted water invades inside or, in the lack of justice, the body only has a cross over the heart, as Vicenta told.

The territory as a body is a space of daily, historical-material and symbolic interaction in dispute. A fundamental stronghold for their defense are the voice, resistance practices and individual-community strategies that organized women bring into play when they feel their lives, jobs, knowledge and spaces are threatened. Nevertheless, organized women at the Comitán borderland developed a diagnostic and discussion process on issues that directly affect them, their families and their communities; organized, they generate new ways of understanding the territory, their being women, their bodies, their lives, putting their voices forth onto the debate — saying how they want to live, and how they will confront the dispossession they experience daily.

Bibliography

Belausteguigoitia, Marisa (2006). Descarados y deslenguados el cuerpo y la lengua india en los umbrales de la nación. In M. Belausteguigoitia and M. Leñero, *Fronteras y Cruces: cartografías de escenarios culturales latinoamericanos*. México: PUEG-UNAM, pp. 63-84.

Bordo, Susan (2001). El feminismo, la cultura occidental y el cuerpo. *Revista de estudios de género la Ventana*, 14. Guadalajara: Universidad de Guadalajara.

Bourdieu, P. (2000). *La dominación masculina*. Madrid: Anagrama.

— (1999). *Meditaciones pascalianas*. Madrid: Anagrama.

— [1997] (1999). *Razones prácticas*. Madrid: Anagrama.

Bourgois, Philippe (2003). *En busca de respeto. Vendiendo crack en Harlem*. Mexico: Siglo XXI.

— (1996). In Search of Masculinity: Violence, Respect and Sexuality among Puerto Rican Crack Dealers in East Harlem. *British Journal of Criminology 36* (3).

— (1989). Ethnicity At Work: Divided Labor on a Central American Banana Plantation. Baltimore: Johns Hopkins University Press.

Das, Venna (2008). Violence, gender and subjectivity. *Annual Review of Anthropology* 37: pp. 283-299.

— (1997). Language and Body. Transactions in the construction the pain. In Arthur Kelimman, Venna Das and Margaret Lock. *Social Suffering*. Santa Cruz: University California Press.

Esteban, Mari Luz (June 2004). Antropología encarnada. Antropología desde una misma. *Papeles del CEIC* 12. Basque Country.

Federici, Silvia (2014). La revolución inacabada. Mujeres, reproducción social y luchas por lo común. Oaxaca: Escuela Calpulli.

— (2004). La acumulación de trabajo y la degradación de las mujeres. La construcción de la "diferencia" en la "transición al capitalismo". In *Calibán y la bruja. Mujeres, cuerpo y acumulación originaria.* Madrid: Traficantes de Sueños.

Freyermunth, Enciso Graciela (1998). Antecedentes de Acteal: muerte materna y control natal, ¿genocidio silencioso? In Rosalva Aída Hernández Castillo (ed.). *La otra palabra: mujeres y violencia en Chiapas antes y después de Acteal.* México: Centro de Investigaciones y Estudios Superiores de Antropología Social (CIESAS), pp. 63-82.

García, T. Miriam (2014). El feminismo reactiva la lucha contra extractivista en América Latina. *Periódico la marea.* Available at https://www.lamarea.com/2014/02/17/ecuador-extractivismo-mujeres/

Giddens, Anthony (1997). Modernidad e Identidad del yo. El yo y la sociedad en la época contemporánea, Barcelona: Península/Ideas.

Giddens, Anthony [1988] (2006). La constitución de la sociedad. Bases para la teoría de la estructuración. Buenos Aires: Amorrortu.

Gilly, Adolfo (2006). Historia a contrapelo una constelación. México: Era.

Gudynas, Eduardo (2016). Summary of key ideas presented in the course "Los derechos de la naturaleza y los extractivismos", presented with Alberto Acosta, in Flacso, Quito, July 11-12. Hosted by Flacso y CLAES, supported by Rosa Luxemburg Foundation. Available at http://ecologiasocial.com/wp-content/uploads/2016/09/GudynasDerNaturalezaExtractivismosEc16P.pdf (7 November 2017).

Heller, Agnes (1998). *Sociología de la vida cotidiana.* Barcelona: Península.

Hernández Castillo, Rosalva Aída. (2014). Cuerpos femeninos, violencia y acumulación por desposesión. In Marisa Belausteguigoitia Ruis and María Josefina Saldaña-Portillo (Eds.). *Des/POSESIÓN: Género, Territorio y luchas por la autodterminación* (pp. 79-100). Mexico: UNAM-PUEG.

Luxemburgo, Rosa (1978). La lucha contra la economía natural. In *La acumulación del capital.* Barcelona: Grijalbo.

Olivera Bustamante, Mercedes (2014). *Subordinaciones estructurales de Género. Las mujeres marginales de Chiapas frente a la crisis.* San Cristóbal de las Casas: Universidad de Ciencias y Artes de Chiapas/Centro de Derechos de la Mujer.

— (2001). Igualdad de género y etnia: desafío para las mujeres indígenas chiapanecas. In Olivia Gall (ed.), *Chiapas: sociedad, economía, interculturalidad y política* Mexico: CEIICH-UNAM.

— (1998). Acteal: Los efectos de la guerra de baja intensidad. In Rosalva Aída Hernández Castillo (ed.). *La otra palabra: mujeres y violencia en Chiapas antes y después de Acteal* (pp. 114-124). Centro de Investigaciones y Estudios Superiores de Antropología Social (CIESAS).

— (1995). Práctica feminista en el Movimiento Zapatista de Liberación Nacional. In Rosa Rojas [Comp. and Ed.], *Chiapas ¿y las mujeres qué?* 2nd ed., tome II. México: Ediciones del Taller Editorial La Correa Feminista.

— (1988). Nicaragua: el poder de las mujeres. Nicaragua: Cenzontle. (Colección Realidades.)

Scheper-Hughes, Nancy (1996). Small Wars and Invisible Genocides. *Social Science & Medicine*, pp. 5-43.

— (1987). The Mindful Body: A Prolegomenon to Work in Medical Anthropology. *Medical Anthropology Quarterly 1*, 1, pp. 6-41.

— and Philippe Bourgois (2004). Introduction: Making Sense of Violence. In Nancy Scheper-Hughes and Philippe Bourgois (ed.). *Violence in War and Peace: An Anthology*. Oxford: Blackwell Publishing.

Segato, Rita (2016). *La guerra contra las mujeres*. Madrid/Buenos Aires: Traficantes de sueños/Tinta Limón.

— (2004). La escritura en el cuerpo de las mujeres asesinadas en Ciudad Juárez. Buenos Aires: Tinta Limón.

— (2003). Las estructuras elementales de la violencia: ensayos sobre género entre la antropología, el psicoanálisis y los derechos humanos. Buenos Aires: Prometeo 3010.

3. Intersectionalities in the body-territory

*Alicia Migliaro González, Dina Mazariegos García,
Lorena Rodríguez Lezica, Juliana Díaz Lozano*

Presentation. Many bodies and other territories

Many bodies walk across our America. Diverse tones, a *mestizo* palette concentrating and diluting pigments. Various forms, stretching or thickening in different latitudes. Bodies as meeting points for the memory inside our veins, the territories we inhabit, and all those females who inhabited it before us. Bodies and territories. Sexualized, racialized geographies. Flesh and bone oppressed in their places of origin or thrown into the diaspora of a continent overflowing its borders.

In these lines, we propose to collectively think, discuss, debate the contributions that the concept of intersectionality can make to the body-territory construct. We will start by positing a conceptual definition of intersectionality, highlighting its roots on non-hegemonic feminist movements, later to develop a brief genealogy of the concept, historical contexts and fights that originated it. Then, using the concept of intersectionality as an analytical tool, we will discuss crossings in the body-territory construct in some Latin American feminist movements. Last, we will share some reflections on the challenges of intersectionality in and from the body-territory construct to contemplate some of the challenges in current Latin American reality.

Intersecting. What do we talk about when we talk about intersectionality?

> "There's the catch, when under the excuse of not getting lost nor wandering off along the way, feminism only attends to gender oppression. Because, who are the women who are only affected by gender oppression? Those who are white, heterosexual, bourgeois, member of a non-colonized people, diagnosed as women at birth and whose functional abilities abide by the norm. They really are a minority, a socially privileged minority."
> Itziar Ziga, Malditas. Una estirpe transfeminista.

ALICIA MIGLIARO GONZÁLEZ, DINA MAZARIEGOS GARCÍA,
LORENA RODRÍGUEZ LEZICA, JULIANA DÍAZ LOZANO

Intersectionality as a concept is a proposal by feminist theory from the late twentieth century (mainly dissident US American black feminism), which attempts to account for successive domination and oppression forms that befall some women. It refers to the articulation of socio-cultural features that define subjects and can be regarded as categories of social stratification and, thus, of political domination. Hence, adscription to class-race-gender configures possibility conditions for the different exploitation forms experienced by subjects, upon which society is organized. It takes a denunciation stand, pointing at the impossibility of analyzing inequality dimensions in isolation, or as the sum of different inequalities. On the contrary, it posits that inequalities interweave in subjects' and collectives' lives in complex ways, and that we need to place ourselves in that complexity to approach them.

The concept arose in academia in an effort to resist the homogenization of feminism, broadening and sophisticating the approach to domination modes. Thinking in terms of intersectionality implies two epistemic warnings. First, the acknowledgement of multiple domination systems which, far from acting as separate channels, interconnect and propel each other. As stated by Valdes (2005), the domination system is multiple, but structured as one; therefore, even if it is possible to read the traces of structural inequalities, it is necessary to refine the tools used to understand them. Second, the need to heterogenize the subjects of knowledge, which will no longer be an ideal type (mirroring the white, bourgeois, heterosexual male), but rather the protagonists of singular and collective stories actualizing inequalities.

Understanding social inequalities and their multiple articulation has been a concern for social sciences. Accounting for how these inequalities are produced, multiplied and articulated is no easy task. In this sense, the concept of intersectionality offers an explanatory potential that allows to transcend the arithmetic metaphor (multiple domination as a sum of inequalities) into a geometric metaphor (multiple domination as the intersection of diverse inequalities embodied in the subjects). Even though certain critical voices posit that intersectionality does not solve the problem, insofar as it still presupposes differentiated and pre-existent oppression roots, there is agreement that, at least, it offers new readings on a complex problem (Dorlin, 2009).

Based on these epistemic turns, intersectionality becomes an analytical tool, as it allows us to understand how different oppression dimensions act simultaneously and actualize in flesh and blood subjects' vital trajectories (Platero, 2012). Following these feminist traditions, it became a privileged tool to enunciate the multiple and interdependent inequalities in the world we live in (Brah and Phoenix, 2004). As stated by Viveros Vigoya (2014), in addition to a paradigm, intersectionality is a social analysis tool; it makes it possible to understand and interpret the complexity of the social issue. Moreover, it evidences and elaborates on the crossing and combination of gender, class, race, age identities and others, translated into the domination and oppression actions experienced especially by women and feminized bodies. On the other hand, it also visibilizes power relations and their impact on individual or collective persons, sophisticating the study of inequality production.

We believe, as put forth by María Lugones (2007), that the intersectional perspective is not the only one; there are other possible categories and frameworks to discuss relations between power orders and inequality. For example, while studying gender, class and ethnic categories, Lugones names them as "warp" and "weft", since in her view they express the integrity observable in a fabric; the individuality of weaves becomes diffuse in drawing or fabric (Lugones, 2000). However, due to intersectionality's use and spread, it must be acknowledged as having created conceptual spaces that facilitate comprehension of "historical disputes over control of sex, collective authority and intersubjetivity" (Lugones, 2000: 79). The point is accounting for these differences in interconnection, since these elements constitute the capitalist, Eurocentric and globalizing model established by the power relations pattern. In order to situate intersectionality's political action, it is necessary to remember that this feminist perspective questions those subordinations and dominations which have their historical bases on privileged social constructions and normatives, for the male, white, heterosexual and land-owning male. This subject belongs to the dominant epistemic logic and culture, and from there the exclusion or privilege are established, constructing systemic stereotypes such as racism, classism, and unequal power relations.

Likewise, Patricia Hill Collins (2000) affirms that intersectionality is a specific way to understand how the interweaving of different oppression systems is installed and mutually strengthened. She refers specifically to the domination matrix in the power organization in a society. In any matrix there are two features: (i) it has oppression systems that intersect historically and socially, (ii) oppression's intersection systems are specifically organized by means of interrelated domination systems: structural, disciplinary, hegemonic and interpersonal (Collins, 2000, p. 8).

In short, the concept of intersectionality, rather than explaining, offers a metaphor, a radical image of new thinking to understand women's oppressions (in the plural: not just white, bourgeois, heterosexual) and feminized bodies.

Memories. A brief genealogy of the concept

The intersectionality concept is not well dated, nor does it have a single origin. Moreover, several feminist authors (Brah and Phoenix, 2004; Ziga, 2014; Viveros Vigoya, 2016) coincide when they state that the notion of intersectionality is previous to its denomination, and it clearly evidences how feminist thought has produced an epistemic rupture inside social sciences (Dorlin, 2009). As López affirms, the notion emanates from prior developments from certain feminist traditions and their thoughts on inequality: "Emma Goldman had already narrated in her memories how the need for revolution for workers' emancipation was closely linked to women's emancipation, as the experience of working women and class society-forming structures could not be regarded as independent from each other" (López, 2013, p. 239).

However, the 1970s and US American black feminism are considered founding milestones in the conceptualization of intersectionality. Female Afro-Americans criticized white feminism, considering that it only responded to certain women's needs, disregarding other realities and cultures different from the Western ones. At the same time, socialist feminists (mainly the Italian ones) visibilized connections among racism, sexism and class privilege in their studies on "women and labor", where they adequately used Marxism's theoretical tools to fight racism and colonialism.

The intersectionality concept was enunciated as such in 1989 by the Afro-US American lawyer Kimberlé Crenshaw, in the context of a legal dispute in defense of black female workers at General Motors (Viveros Vigoya, 2016). It was proposed as an empirical reference strongly supported by the black feminism tradition (clearly linked to the 1977 Combahee River Collective black feminist manifesto[1]). She put forth the proposition during the defense of a paradigmatic working women's case in Missouri, where the court responsible for hearing the complaint made by a group of female workers, who had been dismissed by the General Motors Assembly Division (1976), refused to grant them compensation. Then, the jury refused to acknowledge sex and race discrimination simultaneously, arguing that, according to applicable United States law, discrimination complaints could be presented for sex or race, but not as a combination of both (Rey, 2008, p. 259).

In that sense, Crenshaw empirically evidences that the women she defended were at a crossroads, and this is the image she uses to put forward the concept of intersectionality. In her defense, she establishes that there are inequalities that cannot be identified as a simple sum: rather, they intersect consubstantially at the personal-

---

[1] Combahee River Collective, a feminist collective of black and lesbian women in the city of Boston, active between 1974 and 1980. Its name comes from the guerrilla action led by Harriet Tubman on 2 June 1863, at the Port Royal region of South Carolina state. This action freed more than 750 slaves and is the only military campaign in US American history that was planned and led by a woman (Davis, 2004, p. 50).

social level, evidencing power relations in society. She posits that gender, class, race and other categories are not natural: instead, they are socially constructed and are interrelated to include or exclude individually or collectively. Years later, Crenshaw herself, surprised at the concept's repercussion, devoted herself to theorizing it. In her text *Mapping the margins* (Crenshaw, 1991), she sets out a systematic analysis of intersectionality in two keys: structural intersectionality (race, gender and class are interrelated power structures determining subjects' lives) and political intersectionality (addressing the conflict that interweaving these dimensions implies for State and social movements' political agendas). Intersectionality emerges to nominate what is evident and also to evidence the constriction of social and political traditions from which domination is signified.

However, as mentioned above, intersectionality has no precise birth date or parentage. Furthermore, mentioning one would silence those voices which in diverse times and geographies have risen to name dominations. Likewise, Viveros Vigoya (2016) affirms that this perspective finds its historical precedents over two centuries ago, and mentions several personalities; among them, Olympia de Gouges, who establishes a comparison between colonial and patriarchal domination. On the other hand, drawing analogies between women and slaves, she mentions Sojourner Truth and her paradigmatic 1851 speech "Ain't I a woman?" As to including the intersectionality concept in Latin American feminism, she highlights some critical voices, such as Martha Zapata Galindo or María Lugones, who state that the concept contributes little to our continent's realities. Unlike these views, Viveros Vigoya posits that, around the 1980s, Latin America starts to promote debate from the so-called dissident feminism (black, Indigenous, lesbian, trans women), who started to criticize feminism on its disregard for non-hegemonic femininities. She especially mentions the case of Peruvian Clorinda Matto de Turner, who in her book *Aves sin nido* (Birds Without a Nest) points out the ethnic-racial and gender vulnerability to which Indigenous women of the colonial era were subjected (Viveros Vigoya, 2016, p. 4). The political and epistemological relevance of the intersectionality concept arises from linking it to the decolonial perspective, in which the social subject needs to be addressed in their heterogeneity.

In a more recent analysis on intersectional theory, Elsa Dorlin (2009) states that the concept was useful to put forth two approaches to domination. On the one hand, an analytical approach, by which all domination in itself expresses intersectionality insofar as it is not possible to isolate the class, race and gender dimensions — a position that often makes the notion redundant. On the other hand, a phenomenological approach, by which what is intersectional is subjects' experience as their embodiment of class, race and gender categories, but not social categories themselves.

Even though the notion of intersectionality does not solve all issues,[2] it has been greatly useful to supersede the abstract hegemonic women model by liberal feminism and understand all women's experiences, meanings and issues.

Intersectionality in Our America's body-territory

Now, if we are to look closely at our latitudes: how is intersectionality intervowen with Latin American feminism?

Aura Cumes (2009), a Maya-Kaqchikel researcher, writes about the complexity of Indigenous women's struggles in Guatemala. Considering the US American feminist bell hooks,[3] she focuses on how the overlapping of different oppressions, as well as the Indigenous and the feminist movements' exigency of a certain position to be taken. Thus, she criticizes reductionism in the analytical-political viewpoints by different movements, as they focus on a single axis, whether gender, ethnic group-race or social

---

[2] For instance, the concept does not solve the articulation of the domination dimensions.

[3] bell hooks (in lowercase) is a pen-name for Gloria Jean Watkin, US American black academic and feminist. Her intellectual production, in close dialogue with her political practice, focuses on the articulation of class-gender-race domination systems.

class; instead, she takes up the proposal to analyze racism, patriarchy, classism as domination systems which do not work separately but in interrelation, as well as operating differently on women and men. In a double stand aimed at questioning the Indigenous movement and the feminist movement, she posits that, as we must question apparently gender-neutral ethnic revendications, as supported by power relations, we must also regard women's voices plurally, in their diversity. Thus, she opens debate on rejection of "essentialist" revendications of Indigenous women posed by ethnocentric hegemonic feminism, considering it entirely mistaken. She invites ethnocentric hegemonic feminism to question the image of Indigenous women passive to Indigenous men, as an exercise that has no intention of "hiding the existence of power relations and domination relations, but visibilizing and valuing the creative struggles of those Indigenous women" (Cumes, 2009, p. 13). On the other hand, she debates with the Guatemalan Indigenous movement, criticizing an Indigenous essentialism that seeks to justify male chauvinism and sexism as Colony-exclusive products. She also states that, even though essentialism as a fighting strategy has been crucial in a deeply racist society, "culture cannot continue being more important than women themselves, as long as the way she lives and the power conditions she undergoes are not revealed" (Cumes, 2009, p. 47). The author recovers the principles of complementarity and duality, difference and identity, present in Guatemalan Indigenous movements and the Mayan cosmovision, resignifying them. She tries to distance herself from discourses which refute the existence of domination relations between women and men, and states the need to vindicate the concepts of complementarity, duality "by understanding how they work, in a dialogue with reality and political propositions which do not forget questioning existent oppression relations" (Cumes, 2009, p. 37). Her proposal intends to resignify difference, in dialogue with "other" (non-hegemonic) feminisms; it begins by acknowledging some Indigenous women's difficult relation with feminism, and clarifies that the difference that is revendicated

> is not that which justifies unequal treatment, but that which procures liberating processes; which is not built on hierarchy, but in horizontality; which is not imposed, but revendicated from the female subjects in a complex, critical framework. [...] in domination situations, difference has been constructed as a mechanism of excluding, discriminating practices; but in struggles for justice, difference is constructed as an affirmation of diversity (Cumes, 2009, p. 44).

Cumes finds a bridge to feminism in the difference from which diversity is approached, and with decolonial feminism, inasmuch as it denounces the foundation of colonial societies on the unequal treatment between Indigenous and not Indigenous, but also between women and men. It deepens the view of Indigenous women's fight to the extent that they are questioned both from the Indigenous movement and multiculturalism and from the women's feminist movement itself. When they fight as women, they are delegitimized by the Indigenous movement, accused of being divisive, traitors who endanger the community social fabric, who can damage organizations' autonomy or Westernize them, especially if they adopt feminist discourse. In contrast, from a different front they are questioned for adopting ethnic revendications, and singled out for indecision and lack of women's fight prioritization. Thus, she denounces the reproduction of racist practices by some feminists, who use their privileges and see multiculturalism as a distractor for women's universal fight, echoing the way in which the left accused the Indigenous and the women's fights of dividing the movement. Last, she criticizes the image of women trapped in ethnic struggles, incapable of questioning male power in their communities, when domination power is not made explicit among women themselves, denouncing that

> white and mestiza women's racism carries as much weight as white, mestizo and Indigenous men's patriarchy [...] In Latin America, white women have largely had a relationship of mistress-servant, proprietress-slave or matron-girl with Indigenous and Afro-descendent women. History has made us unequal, and it would be very unfortunate to hide those asymmetries under the fallacious argument of universality in a way to be women, raising a single liberation flag (Cumes, 2009, p. 34).

ALICIA MIGLIARO GONZÁLEZ, DINA MAZARIEGOS GARCÍA,
LORENA RODRÍGUEZ LEZICA, JULIANA DÍAZ LOZANO

It is visible in the black women's movement how, from the articulation of race, class and gender variables (fighting flags historically raised by black and female movements in Brazil), feminist revendications are *blackened*, as black movement's proposals and revendications are *feminized*. One of the voices in the black women's movement, Afro-Brazilian feminist Suelí Carneiro (2001), echoes the Indigenous women's claim, questioning Brazilian hegemonic feminism for its Eurocentric bias which may have omitted race centrality in gender hierarchies, black women's differentiated historical experience of the effects of an oppression qualitatively different to the one suffered by white women, as well as the history of resistances and struggles which they have led. The harsh historical conditions which objectified black persons in general, and black women in particular, are part of a Latin American history marked by sexual appropriation of black and Indigenous women's bodies by white masters, colonial sexual violence constituting the base of the race and gender hierarchical system current in today's society. Thus, Carneiro questions the institutionalized feminist movement, stressing the difference in patriarchal oppression experienced by racialized women's bodies. She takes her stance from the specific condition of being black and a woman, questioning the female fragility myth on which hegemonic feminism claims men's oppression over women takes root:

> [...] Which women are they talking about? We —we black women— are part of a contingent of women, probably a majority, who never recognized this myth in themselves, because they were never treated as fragile. We are part of a contingent of women who for centuries labored as slaves, working the land, or in the streets, as sellers or prostitutes. Women who did not understand when feminists said that women had to take to the streets and work! We are part of a contingent of women with an object's identity. Yesterday, at the service of fragile young ladies and stupid noble men. Today, domestic help for liberated women. When we talk about breaking with the household queen myth, the muse idolized by poets, which women are we thinking of? Black women are part of a contingent of women who are queens of nothing, who are portrayed as the anti-muses of Brazilian society because the aesthetic female model is the white woman. We are part of a contingent of women who are the target of hiring advertisements with the phrase "Good presence required", whose subtext is *black women need not apply* (Carneiro, 2001, p. 22).

Although not on the ethnic-racial but the class dimension, something similar happened with the rich anarchist movement tradition in the River Plate at the end of the nineteenth and start of the twentieth century. Laura Fernández Cordero (2017) addresses crossings between libertarian thinking and criticism to gender inequalities. River Plate *anarquismo obrerista* ("worker anarchism") was a *mestiza* movement which fed from the libertarian ideal brought by European immigrant workers, reconfigured within the limits and possibilities in the Latin American scene. Even though revolutionary figures such as Virginia Bolten, Juana Rouco or María Collazo questioned class oppression and patriarchal oppression equally from popular publications, feminism was not discussed. The feminism field was hegemonized by bourgeois liberal feminism, which expressed complete disdain and incomprehension for the issues experienced by women from the popular classes. It was years before any encounters between feminism and popular movements enough to alter the strategic and organizational perspective of left organizations took place. In connection with this encounter, it is worth highlighting the studies on feminism in the Argentine *piquetero* (picketing) movement from the late nineties and early 2000s, where the multiplicity of inequalities became a necessary condition to consider the emergence of *piqueteras* (picketing women) as political subjects (Andujar, 2014). In this respect, Andujar emphasizes that popular women did not appear in the political scene only then; rather, hegemonic social sciences, blind to intersectionality, erased differences and invisibilized women.

Thus, from north to south and east to west of our continent intersectionality questions and appeals to us. As women who are migrant, Indigenous, black, *mestiza*, from the countryside or the metropolis' precarious outskirts. Women who set the world rolling with our own hands, and who raise our voices to be acknowledged from all the borders limiting the bodies we incarnate.

ALICIA MIGLIARO GONZÁLEZ, DINA MAZARIEGOS GARCÍA,
LORENA RODRÍGUEZ LEZICA, JULIANA DÍAZ LOZANO

Final reflections: dialogues in, from and through intersectionality

As mentioned above, the concept of intersectionality allows us to focus on how domination forms interweave and knot as threads in a loom, and operate both structurally and historically in a given space and time. Still, for an intersectional approach not to imply a vision "from the top" and "from outside" of social relations, as if a scenario could be created by crossing inequalities outside the subjects who live them, we propose to regard intersections from their experiences. That means to configure a viewpoint which recognizes and unravels oppressive relations, but also visibilizes in the same fabric the dispute strategies and resignifications carried out individually and collectively.

In fact, in gender and feminist studies there is a debate that significantly contributes to developments around the category of experience. Authors such as Mary Nash have pointed out the category's usefulness to draw links between personal experiences and historical processes and women's paths as a dynamic social collective. This author refers to women's historical learning processes in their fight experience and gender power relations (Elizalde, 1998). In the same vein, feminist theory points out personal life as a political, public site, a place of transformation and (re)production of existing relations (Vargas, 2008), as well as stating that "change in gender relations is closely linked to questioning the existence of both spheres and places of belonging assigned to women and men in them" (Andújar, 2005). In turn, decolonizing perspectives regard experience as a key category to recover those narratives which have been ignored in imperial patriarchal and androcentric narration. Diverse Latin American feminists have highlighted experiences by women subalternized by their social class, ethnic group, gender, nationality, as elaborations that can express hegemony-resisting forms. However, it is necessary to say that there is not always a direct connection between the subaltern place occupied by these women and the generation of hegemonic system questioning or transformation experiences. Still, this experience is not transparent to research in itself but, as complex material, it enables reading layers or levels where continuity, but also impugnation of dominant logic forms, can be interpreted. We believe that, from an experience-based approach, it can help us understand the dimension of intersectionality.

To sum up, analyzing the world in an intersectional key is an attempt to rescue what in different women's vital experience remains hidden: it is a call to suspicion. In Joan Scott's words:

> The only alternative, it seems to me, is to refuse to oppose equality to difference and insist continually on differences — differences as the condition of individual and collective identities, differences as the constant challenge to the fixing of those identities, history as the repeated illustration of the play of differences, differences as the very meaning of equality itself (Scott, 1988, pp. 174-175).

This warning sets us on the right path to understand the intersection of inequalities in connection to subjects' vital experience. That is, categories presented to us as natural and transparent are far from being so. On the contrary, they are socio-historical constructions, models to approach comprehension of this dynamics; therefore, they are abstractions that hardly manifest in their pure form. In this sense, we conceive of intersectionality as a category of analysis that is interwoven in vital trajectories. We share the disruptive character assigned by Scott to gender as a category, mainly since it allows to make apparently simple questions complex: *what is it to be a woman? What is it to be a non-hegemonic male? What is it to be trans, transvestite, queer, dissident? What is it to work (inside and outside the household)? What is it to care for children and elders? What is it to get organized and participate in politics? What is it to defend a territory or denounce environmental damage?* Assuming that it is not to be just one thing or a sum of things, but rather it is to be a woman in a historical and social time and in material relationships of existence, perhaps questions should also focus on *how*. Regarding intersectionality as a category of analysis offers new ways into the issue, focusing on these women's experiences. On how they live these or other roles, spaces and identities that are indivisibly embodied in their own life stories. We contemplate making the questions more complex: *what is it and what is it like to be a woman? How do these women fight and what do they fight for? Do* they see themselves as ecologists, union members, feminists? All of them, some, none? How do they understand and signify their life stories?

We women emerge as social subjects to evidence the limits of hegemonic constructions. But resistance comes from several fronts, and we also emerge in history to question the totalizing notions of Woman which exist, as stated by Basque feminist Itziar Ziga (2014) in her criticism of liberal feminism, only in the likeness of the white, bourgeois, heterosexual woman. To be able to visualize and support an approach that shows the multiplicity of dominations looming over subjects is nowadays an urgency. Intersectionality allows us to view critically what science has said, and most especially what it has not said. It also enables us to free the category "woman" out of the liberal corset that recognizes only some women, all of those who are not those others who can eventually cause uneasiness. Thinking, reading, researching, intervening, writing from intersectionality and feminist epistemology sharpens the ear, touch and sight to understand life experiences and significances.

Bibliographical references

Various Authors (1977). Manifiesto colectivo del río Combahee: Una declaración negra feminista. Available at http://www.herramienta.com.ar/manifiesto-colectiva-del-rio-combahee (2 November 2017).

Andújar, Andrea (2014). Rutas argentinas hasta el fin: mujeres, política y piquetes 1996-2001. Buenos Aires: Fundación Rosa Luxemburgo.

— (2005). De la ruta no nos vamos: las mujeres piqueteras (1996-2001). Paper presented at the X Jornadas Interescuelas. Departamentos de Historia, Rosario, 20-23 September.

AWID (2004). Interseccionalidad: una herramienta para la justicia de género y la justicia económica. *Derechos de las mujeres y cambio económico* 9. Available at https://www.awid.org/es/publicaciones/interseccionalidad-una-herramienta-para-la-justicia-de-genero-y-la-justicia-economica

Brah, Avatar and Ann Phoenix (2004). Ain't I a Woman? Revisiting intersectionality. *Journal of International Women's Studies* 5(3): 75-86.

Carneiro, Sueli (2001). Ennegrecer al feminismo. La situación de la mujer negra en América Latina desde una perspectiva de género. Feminismos disidentes en América Latina y el Caribe. *Nouvelles Questions Féministes* 24 (2): pp. 21-26.

Cumes, Aura (2009). Multiculturalismo, género y feminismos: mujeres diversas, luchas complejas. In Andrea Pequeño (ed.). *Participación y políticas de mujeres indígenas en América Latina*. Quito: Flacso-Ecuador/Ministerio de Cultura del Ecuador.

Davis, Angela (2004). *Mujer, raza y clase*. Madrid: Akal.

De Veaux, Alexis (2004). Warriors Poet: A Biography of Audre Lorde. USA.

Dorlin, Elsa (2009). Sexo, género y sexualidades. Introducción a la teoría feminista. Buenos Aires: Nueva Visión.

Elizalde, Silvia (2008). Debates sobre la experiencia. Un recorrido por la teoría y la praxis feminista. *Revista Oficios Terrestres* 23, año XIV. La Plata: Facultad de Periodismo y Comunicación Social-UNLP, pp. 18-30.

Expósito, María Carmen (2012). ¿Qué es eso de la interseccionalidad? Aproximación al tratamiento de la diversidad desde la Perspectiva de género en España. Available at https://revistas.ucm.es/index.php/INFE/article/viewFile/41146/39358 (8 June 2017).

Fernández Cordero, Laura (2017). Amor y anarquismo. Experiencias pioneras que pensaron y ejercieron la libertad sexual. Buenos Aires: Siglo XXI.

Gómez, Fany (2003). La interseccionalidad en la discriminación. Actividades relacionadas: Conferencia Mundial de Naciones Unidas Contra el Racismo, la Discriminación Racial, la Xenofobia y Otras Formas de Intolerancia. Available at http://www.inmujeres.gub.uy/innovaportal/file/21589/1/15_la_i nterseccionalidad_en_la_discriminacion.pdf (11 November 2017).

Hill Collins, Patricia (2015). *Intersecting Oppressions*. Available at http://www.heroinas.net/2015/01/combahee-river-collective.html (6 June 2017).

Krenshaw, Kimberlé (1989). Demarginalizing the Intersection of Race and Sex: A Black Feminist Critique of antidiscrimination Doctrine, Feminist Theory and Antiracist Politics, University of Chicago Forum.

La Barbera, Mª Caterina (2015). Interseccionalidad un "concepto viajero": orígenes, desarrollo e implementaciones en la Unión Europea. *Interdisciplina* 4(8). México: UNAM.

Lugones, María (2008). *Colonialidad y género*. Vestal: Binghamton University.

López, S. (2013). Intersecciones: cuerpos y sexualidades en la encrucijada. *Revista Española de Ciencia Política* 32 (pp. 239-242).

Platero, Raquel (Lucas) (2012). *Intersecciones: cuerpos y sexualidades en la encrucijada*. Barcelona: Bellaterra.

Rey, Mª Fernando (2008). La discriminación múltiple. Una realidad antigua, un concepto nuevo. *Revista Española de Derecho Constitucional* 84, septiembre-diciembre, pp. 251-283.

Scott, Joan ([1988] 2008). *Gender and the Politics of History*. New York: Columbia University Press. Translated to Spanish by Consol Vilà I. Boadas: *Género e historia*. México: FCE.

Valdés Gutiérrez, Gilberto (2005). Diversidad y articulación en América Latina de los desafíos de los movimientos sociales ante la civilización excluyente, patriarcal y depredadora del capital, *Revista Dialéctica* 37, year 29 (pp. 37-64).

Vargas, Virginia (2008). Nuevas formas de participación política y de luchas feministas en lo local y en lo global en el nuevo milenio, Rosario, paper presented at the IV Congreso Iberoamericano de Estudios de Género.

Viveros Vigoya, Mara (2016). La interseccionalidad: una aproximación situada a la dominación. *Debate Feminista* 52. UNAM-PUEG, pp. 1-17. Available at http://www.sciencedirect.com/science/article/pii/S0188947816300603 (12 May 2017).

Yuval-Davis, Nira (2006). Intersectionality and Feminist Politics. *European Journal of Women's Studies* 13(3): 193-209.

4. The geopolitics of the womb: towards a decolonial feminist geopolitics in spaces of slow death

Sofia Zaragocin[1]

Parts of the body create particular territorialities. In this chapter, I suggest that in spaces determined by *settler colonialism*, where slow violence (Nixon, 2013) and preventable death (Povinelli, 2011; Berlant, 2007; Povinelli, 2002) are naturalized, the womb creates its own territoriality. I take as an example the embodied resistance by Épera (Eperara Siapidaara) women from the north of Esmeraldas, in Ecuador,[2] who, in order to prevent extinction, propose the womb as a place from which to confront collective death. Épera women counteract multiple forms of spatial violence, creating territories from their reproductive roles and corporalities, resulting in *womb geopolitics*. My contribution is situated at the intersections of Anglocentric feminist geopolitics and Latin American decolonial feminism, in a *settler colonial* context intimately related to the slow death of spaces and bodies. I start by situating *settler colonialism* as an analytical framework for Latin American borderlands, followed by a literature review on the body in Anglocentric feminist geopolitics and Indigenous feministance perspectives. Based on this theoretical framework I situate a form of decolonial feminist geopolitics that I call *geopolitics of the womb*.

---

[1] Decolonial feminist geographer. Member of the Colectivo de Geografía Crítica del Ecuador (Ecuador Critical Geography Collective), Visiting Professor and Associate Researcher at the Sociology and Gender Studies Department, Flacso-Ecuador.

[2] The ethnographic work in this doctoral research can be found in other articles under review. In this article, I am interested in highlighting theoretical aspects of the body-territory-death relationship.

Settler Colonialism as a colonial territorial analytic

This article makes the case for *settler colonialism* along Latin American borderlands.[3] Settler colonialism is the systematic elimination of Indigenous peoples not as an event or a series of isolated events, but rather as a structure of invasion (Wolfe, 1999). In contrast with genocide or ethnocide, structural settler invasion, in addition to eliminating Indigenous populations, attempts to appropriate their territories (Wolfe, 1999; Veracini, 2011; Veracini, 2014). This is an analytical proposal of colonialism based on dispossession and territory appropriation, which explains contemporary forms of Indigenous peoples and nationalities' elimination, characterized mainly as a territorial project. Territorial appropriation based on Indigenous peoples' elimination or death is possible for settlers under contemporary forms of biopower (Morgensen, 2011). It is in these contemporary processes of continual colonialism that racialized geographies relate to white supremacy (Bonds & Woods, 2016), and white hetero-settler masculinity (Gahman, 2016) is intensified. Settler colonialism, as analyzed below, is therefore a highly racialized and sexualized territorial project.

Feminist Indigenous intellectuals writing on the spatial-corporal injustice in the context of settler colonialism in countries such as United States, Canada and Australia identify from their own notions of decolonial feminism determined by their spaces of enunciation. In tune with Latin American decolonial feminism, in this text I will develop a dialogue between feminist Indigenous intellectuals in the north with peripheral feminisms from racialized and colonized women's experience in Latin America (Zaragocin, 2017). Thus, I suggest that the intersecting analyses between settler

---

[3] This colonial framework has been applied in geographical contexts such as the United States, Canada, Australia, and other countries regarded as part of the metaphorical "Global North". The use of this theoretical framework for the Latin American context is very recent.

colonialism and Indigenous feminist critiques are pertinent to study racialized and gendered processes of slow death in Ecuador. From these theoretical intersections, elimination of Indigenous peoples and nations answers the question of the how and when of death.[4] Under Patrick Wolfe's "elimination logic", death is both cultural and physical. The collective death of racialized peoples under settler colonialism is slow and preventable (Povinelli, 2011; Berlant, 2007). An example is collective death caused by pollution resulting from environmental racism or racialized capitalism. The Épera die for lack of drinking water and pollution in the Cayapas river, their main subsistence source. In this water space (Oslender, 2002), they eat, drink and bathe; and it is also a recreation place for children. However, due to pollution caused by African palm production, wood industry, mining and State negligence of basic service provisions, people die of preventable and curable diseases such as diarrhea. The fact that Indigenous peoples and nationalities die in everyday spaces normalizes children and youths' deaths, justified by health services that claim that young people die of natural causes. Thus, preventable deaths are naturalized and normalized to the extreme. Cultural assimilation is another kind of slow death explained by settler colonialism (Wolfe, 1999), which supposes cultural assimilation of peoples and nationalities, as another way of eliminating racialized populations. Racialized peoples die collectively, either physically or culturally, in everyday space-times that normalize their gradual disappearance.

---

[4] This question is highly problematic due to body-space essentialisms: thus this article will refer to settler colonialism in relation to Indigenous peoples and nationalities, specifically Indigenous women. Other writings refer to the elimination of non-Indigenous populations facing settler colonialism (Pulido, 2017).

Death-body-territory from settler colonialism

Territorial struggles by racialized women relate body and land in an intimate manner. This text will address the death-body-territory relationship, where the death of a place[5] converges with the death of bodies. Fierce contamination resulting from environmental racism and racial capitalism intoxicates bodies. As posited by some authors, bodies and territories are ontologically a whole (Cruz Hernández, 2016; Cabnal, 2010). Simultaneous violence exerted on body and space has been theorized in different forms, emphasizing the spatial determiner of experience and its conceptualization. From a Latin American perspective, different visions on feminist spatialities[6] stress the intrinsic relation between gender violence and specific spatial dynamics. For instance, there is a direct relation between the increase of gender based violence in areas of extractivist activity (particularly mining) (Ulloa, 2016; Colectivo Miradas Críticas del Territorio desde el Feminismo, 2014), territorialized violence of femini(geno)cide (Segato, 2012, 2013), and feminicide geographies (Zaragocin, Silveira and Arazola, in press).

Communitarian feminisms (Cabnal, 2010), in turn, put forward the existence of an ontological and epistemological relation between the body-territory, where, for instance, it is possible to understand that if the body is sick so is the space: therefore, healing of the body-territory is mutually dependent.[7] In turn, decolonial

---

[5] In this text, I use several spatial identities, in addition to territory. This is due to my feminist geography formation, where gender relations create different kinds of spatialities besides territory. In this text, I propose the use of the term *feminist spatialities* precisely in order to span these other spatial identities that are being promoted from feminist perspectives.

[6] I draw a difference between this viewpoint and Astrid Ulloa's, who mentions territorial feminisms.

[7] During Lorena Cabnal's visit to Ecuador, the Acción Ecológica organization set up a *toxitour* to the Sucumbíos province (in

feminisms (Paredes, 2008) relate sexual violence against the Indigenous female body with colonial penetration in ancestral lands. Ulloa groups some of the issues mentioned as territorial feminisms, defining them as "territorial-environmental struggles led by Indigenous, Afro-descendent and peasant women, focusing on the defense of territory, body and nature, along with a critique of development and extractivism processes [...] based on a vision of the continuity of life articulated in their territories" (Ulloa, 2016, p. 136). For this author, extractivist activity relate women's body-territories with appropriation and processes of dispossession (2016). Absent from these reflections are the processes of individual and collective deaths of racialized peoples and their spatialities.[8] In order to contribute to discussions on territorial feminisms (Ulloa, 2016) and feminist spatialities in Latin America, I will mention key reflections made by intellectual Indigenous women who put forth their views from the spatial effects of settler colonialism, which they define as a structure dependent on unfair geographies and spatial injustices (Goeman, 2017).

Settler colonialism as a racialized and sexualized project

Settler colonialism makes place-dependent ethnic elimination explicit, often solidifying heterosexual patriarchy, so that everyday space becomes a place of control and colonial vigilance (Denetdale, 2017), as well as a centrally racialized and sexualized project (Baker, 2017; Goeman, 2013; Goeman, 2017). The elimination of an ethnic group unavoidably affects racialized women's bodies, due to their reproductive abilities and their role in the continuation of life (Smith, 2005). The connection between racialized women and

---

Ecuadorian Amazonia), to witness oil spills. In these spaces, Lorena healed the land as a way to heal our bodies.

[8] I use the term *spatialities* from feminist geography, where the chance to discuss other space dimensions besides territory is encouraged.

reproduction in contexts of ethnic elimination is necessarily related to the role women play in continuing life.⁹ As a result, women's bodies are intrinsically implied in death-body-land processes. The ethnic elimination logic affects Indigenous women's bodies, precisely because it is from their reproductive functions that the colonial structure aimed at their collective death can be confronted (Smith, 2015).

Indigenous feminist theories mentioned here have focused on counteracting dominant spatialities on bodies and daily life, resulting in racialized and sexualized territorial configurations (Baker, 2017). The Indigenous intellectual Mishuana Goeman (2013), from the ancestral territory Seneca, contends that the spatial ideology of Nation-states is based on colonial heteropatriarchal spaces where a patriarchal heterosexuality order was imposed on space and bodies, and especially on Indigenous women. In this context, she affirms that achieving spatial decolonialism is a form of spatial justice, made possible by geographies embodied by Indigenous women who create other social relations leading us in directions that transcend the settler heteropatriarchal mapping of space (Goeman, 2013). For this author, creating other spatialities from Indigenous women's embodiment is a way to counteract settler colonialism's heteropatriarchal space, and consequently, the elimination of Indigenous peoples and nations. These reflections are helpful to understand strategies put forth by Indigenous women facing their ethnic group's elimination (Zaragocin, in press) from their corporealities and a specific part of their bodies.

The meeting point between proposals by Indigenous feminisms in settler colonialism contexts and Latin American feminist territorial[10] movements mentioned above is that both

---

[9] Indigenous women's cultural and physical reproduction has been put forth at debates on women's rights and Indigenous rights. See Speed, 2008; Picq, 2012; Cumes, 2012.

[10] In her visit to Ecuador, Lorena Cabnal mentioned that the community feminism she proposed was not necessarily decolonial.

concur that the coloniality of gender defines gender relations in a place *(Espinosa-Miñosa et al.*, 2014; Zaragocin, in press). In turn, the body-land relation is highlighted, where Indigenous women's bodies become a possible target for violence exerted by colonial structures (Goeman, 2017). Patriarchal heteronormativity, materialized in spatial injustices (Goeman, 2017), is linked to racialized women's biological and social reproduction in Latin America. Control for a people's elimination, as well as resistance against ethnocide, cause the womb to be regarded as a geopolitical entity by decolonial feminist geopolitics (Zaragocin, in press), as I discuss below.

Towards a decolonial feminist geopolitics

Bodies exist in places and, at the same time, are places (McDowell, 1999). For the past two decades, Anglocentric feminist geography[11] has favored the scale of the body (Longhurst and Johnston, 2014), using the term *embodiment* (Johnson, 2008). In this intellectual tradition, the body was theorized around maternity and, on a wider scope, as a geopolitical entity (Longhurst and Jonhston, 2014). Feminist geopolitics, a sub-discipline of feminist geography, shows force relations operating through and on bodies, causing certain subjectivities and corporealities to be exploited and violated in connection with security, population, territory and nationalism (Dixon and Marston, 2011, p. 455). The feminist geopolitical imaginary (Hyndman, 2001) incorporates bodies, subjectivities and corporealities, theorizing on them from the everyday *scale* and turning them into *sites* where, by means of socio-spatial practices, geopolitical tensions are displayed. The relation between power scales through the body and situated experience is a foundation of Anglocentric feminist geopolitics. It is in this logic that emphasis was placed on the intimate scale and the everyday space-time, in order to understand power relations in spaces where State power

---

[11] By Anglocentric I mean the theoretical corpus —mainly in English— produced in knowledge power centers in the metaphorical "Global North".

has barely been analyzed. Thus, there has been an exploration of how the geographies of emotions are used geopolitically. For example, the connection between fear experienced by women at home as a consequence of gender violence, and that which is caused by the State with its omissions in the face of feminicide (Pain and Smith, 2008; Zaragocin, Silveira and Arazola, in press). Sara Smith's work (2012) is especially pertinent, since it posits an intimate geopolitics where territorial struggles take into account love, bodily reproduction and children, where, in turn, bodies are not only territories, but territories immerse in geopolitical projects (Smith, 2012). Thus, feminist geopolitics opens a conceptual space to understand different interpretations of death-territory-body in a plurality of geographies where women face collective death of their peoples, by means of specific approaches which, in turn, create their own spatialities. This makes it necessary to include an added conceptual reflection directed towards a decolonial feminist geopolitics, which allows for the conception of the geopolitics of the womb.

For some time, hegemonic Anglocentric production[12] in feminist geography has been analyzed due to its determining role in international academic debate (Garcia Ramon, Simonsen and Vaiou, 2006). Compared to other critical geography schools, feminist geography has included feminist geography voices from outside the Anglocentric world, in journals such as *Gender, Place & Culture* (Garcia Ramon, Simonsen and Vaiou, 2006). However, while some geographers from particular countries see as epistemic inclusion, feminist geographers in Latin American contend that there has been limited conceptual interaction. Following the intellectual tradition of feminist geography, feminist geopolitics was based on Western and universals ontologies and epistemologies (Naylor, 2017). As in the rest of the critical geography field, post-colonial schools of thought were put forth; however, efforts to decolonize the discipline are still recent

---

[12] Understood as feminist geography produced in academic or research centers in the United States, England and Canada.

(Sundberg, 2014; Radcliffe, 2017; Naylor, Daigle, Zaragocin, Ramirez and Gilmartin, 2017).

In order to posit the womb as a geopolitical entity I propose to start from decolonial feminist geopolitics, where spatial analysis of gender colonialism is seen from a plurality of geographical viewpoints (Zaragocin, in press). Specifically, I define decolonial feminist geopolitics as a feminist geopolitics which "considers the coloniality of gender and sexuality of imperialist-colonialist state-formations while acknowledging gendered and racialized spatial resistances related to auto-determination or competing notions of sovereignty (Indigenous and others). It opens a conversation between critical geopolitics and the plurality of decolonized feminist proposals that are introducing alternative body-land based epistemologies, ontologies and geopolitics." (Zaragocin, in press). The use of the womb by Épera women from Santa Rosa de los Épera is an example of decolonial feminist geopolitics. It is an example of spatial-corporal resistance arising from physical and cultural reproduction. In Colombia, the Eperara Siapidaara (Épera) are one of the Indigenous groups risking extinction, and in Ecuador this nationality has around 400 persons. According to the *Organización Mujeres Épera del Ecuador* (Épera Women Organization from Ecuador), in order to face the ethnic group's possible collective death, Éperas reproduction is proposed, so as to ensure the continuity of Indigenous life. Corporal regulation put forth by Épera women is a problematic proposal: and I do not intend to simplify the complexity of pure culture reproduction at the moment.[13] I do wish to highlight the spatial-corporal resistance implied by their using their womb as a geopolitical entity.

Womb geopolitics

When Épera women vindicate their wombs in the face of their people's elimination, they assign power against territorial

---

[13] I study this in other articles for *Antipode* and the *Journal of Settler Colonial Studies*, currently in revision.

dispossession and slow death from a specific part of their bodies. It is from this part of the body that resistance is made, not from the whole body. This becomes even more important in a context of dominant narratives on racialized bodies. They are depicted as oppressed, sexualized, weak, and led towards a future collective death (Tallbear, 2016). On the road to this place-dependent expected death, bodies can transcend and confront the same global and hegemonic powers that cause their slow demise. In this sense, it is suggested that there are some parts of the body that can resist differently: using certain body parts strategically to create their own territoriality. This reflection is different from Maria Rodó-de-Zárate's analysis on geographies of intersectionality, in which she shows how certain variables of embodied difference (sexual orientation, age, gender) are place-dependent (2014). In contrast with Rodó-de-Zárate (2014), who focuses on spatial configuration from identity and variables of embodied difference, I suggest that there are parts of the body that feel more in some spaces than others. Consequently, there are parts of the body that have more political potential in particular space-times than others. In contexts of slow death and violence causing ethnic elimination of entire peoples, the womb becomes a geopolitical entity, because it is from this embodied place that the structures of the logic of elimination are confronted. The geopolitics of the womb does not reinforce the idea of compulsory maternity; on the contrary, it seeks to show that in contexts of the elimination of racialized peoples' this part of the body can confront the logic of elimination.

As several authors have pointed out, the body creates territoriality. But there are parts of the body that create different territorialities. The womb-territory connection takes on diverse and interrelated forms, depending on the place. Territoriality created by the womb has already been put forth by several feminist movements, including debates on abortion, sexual rights and empowerment. I do not relate the womb directly to women or motherhood. This is part of understanding the womb as a geopolitical entity. Decolonial feminist geopolitics allows us to affirm that Épera women are acting geopolitically from a part of their bodies, as they confront the effects of settler colonialism. As such, they are creating other spatial identities including territorialities from a part of their bodies.

Conclusions

The death of territory and its intimate connection to the body is part of continuum of colonialism found in settler colonialism. In this scenario, there are a variety of body-space resistances, including space of self-determination, from which spatial injustices are disputed. The womb, as a geopolitical entity, and from a decolonial feminist geopolitics, shows several possibilities. In this text, I have only discussed one of them: the womb as a geopolitical entity against the death of spaces and bodies, where women vindicate this body part to create territories of resistance. In existing literature on the relation between spaces and bodies affected by the logics of slow death and violence, it is necessary to give attention to what happens to the body under these dynamics. This opens conceptual possibilities around the body-land, body-territory or territory-body-land relationship. Additionally, it encourages other notions of corporality (including other parts of the body), according to a variety of spatial identities in specific contexts where death of a place co-exists with death of the bodies.

Bibliography

Baker, J. (2017). *Critically Sovereign: Indigenous, Gender, Sexuality and Feminist Studies*. Durham: Duke University Press.

Berlant, L. (2007). Slow Death (Sovereignty, Obesity, Lateral Agency). *Critical Inquiry* 33(4): 754-780, Summer.

Bonds, Anne and Joshua Inwoods (2016). Beyond white privilege: Geographies of white supremacy and settler colonialism. *Progress in Human Geography 40*, 715-733.

Cabnal, L. (2010). Acercamiento a la construcción de la propuesta de pensamiento epistémico de las mujeres indígenas feministas comunitarias de Abya Yala. In ACSUR (Ed.). *Feminismos diversos: el feminismo comunitario* (pp. 10-25). Las Segovias: ACSUR.

Colectivo Miradas Críticas del Territorio desde el Feminismo (2017). *Mapeando el cuerpo-territorio. Guía metodológica para mujeres que defienden sus territorios*. Quito: Instituto de Estudios Ecologistas del Tercer Mundo.

— (2014). *La vida en el centro y el crudo bajo: el Yasuní en clave feminista*. Quito: Colectivo Miradas Críticas del Territorio desde el Feminismo.

Cruz Hernández, D. (2016). Una mirada muy otra: los territorios-cuerpos femeninos. *Solar: Revista de Filosofía Iberoamericana* 12(1), year 12: 35-46.

Cumes, A. (2012). Mujeres indígenas, patriarcado y colonialismo: un desafío a la segregación comprensiva de las formas de dominio. *Hojas de Warmi* 17: 1-16.

Denetdale, J. (2017). *Return to "The uprising at Beautiful Mountain in 1913"*. Durham y Londres: Duke University Press.

Dixon, D., and S. Marston (2011). Introduction: feminist engagements with geopolitics. *A Journal of Feminist Geography* 18(4): pp. 445-453.

Espinosa-Miñoso, Yuderkis et al. (2014). *Tejiendo de otro modo: Feminismo, epistemología y apuestas descoloniales en Abya Yala*. Popayán: Universidad del Cauca.

García Ramón, M., K. Simonsen and D. Vaiou (2006). Does Anglophone hegemony permeate Gender, Place and Culture? *Gender, Place and Culture. A Journal of Feminist Geography* 13(1): 1-5.

Gahman, L. (2016). White Settler Society as Monster: Rural Southeast Kansas, Ancestral Osage (Wah-Zha-Zhi) Territories, and the Violence of Forgetting. *Antipode*, pp. 314-335.

Hyndman, J. (2001). Towards a feminist geopolitics. *Canadian Geographer*, 2, 210-222.

Goeman, M. (2017). Ongoing Storms and Struggles. Gendered Violence and Resource Exploitation. In Joanne Barker (Ed.). *Critically Sovereign: Indigenous Gender, Sexuality, and Feminist Studies*. Durham: Duke University Press.

— (2013). *Mark my Words: Native Women Mapping our Nations*. Minneapolis: University of Minnesota Press.Longhurst, R., and L. Johnston (2014). Bodies, gender, place and culture: 21 years on. *Gender, Place and Culture. Journal of Feminist Geography* 21(3): pp. 267-278.

McDowell, L. (1999). *Género, identidad y lugar. Un estudio de las geografías feministas*. Madrid: Cátedra.

Morgensen, S. (2011). The biopolitics of settler colonialism: Right Here, Right Now. *Settler Colonial Studies* 1(1): pp. 52-76.

Naylor, L. (2017). Reframing autonomy in political geography: A feminist geopolitics of autonomous resistance. *Political Geography 58:* pp. 24-35.

Naylor, L., M. Daigle, S. Zaragocin, M. Ramírez and M. Gilmartin (2017). Interventions: Bringing the decolonial to political geography. *Political Geography XXX:* pp. 1-11.

Nixon, R. (2014). *Slow Violence and the Environmentalism of the Poor.* Cambridge/London: Harvard University Press.

Oslender, U. (2002). The Logic of the River: A spatial approach to ethnic-territorial mobilization in the Colombian Pacific Region. *The Journal of Latin American and Caribbean Anthropology* 7(2): pp. 86-117.

Pain, R., and S. Smith (2008). *Fear: Critical geopolitics and Everyday Life.* In Rachel Pain and Susan Smith (Eds.). Burlington: Ashgate Publishing.

Paredes, Julieta (2008). *Hilando fino: desde el Feminismo Comunitario.* La Paz: Comunidad Mujeres Creando.

Picq, M. (2012). Between the Dock and a Hard Place: Hazards and Opportunities of Legal Pluralism for Indigenous women in Ecuador. *Latin American Politics and Society* 54(2): pp. 1-33.

Povinelli, E. (2011). *Economies of Abandonment: Social Belonging and Endurance in Late Liberalism.* Durham: Duke University Press.

— (2003). The Cunning of Recognition: Indigenous Alterities and the Making of Australian Multiculturalism. *Gender, Place and Culture. Journal of Anthropological Research* 59(3): pp. 385-387.

Radcliffe, S. (July 2017). Decolonizing geographical knowledges. *Transactions of the Institute of British Geographers.*

Rodó-de-Zárate, M. (2014). Developing geographies of intersectionality with Relief Maps: reflections from youth research in Manresa, Catalonia. *Gender, Place and Culture. A Journal of Feminist Geography* 21(8): pp. 925-944.

Segato, R. (2013). *La escritura en el cuerpo de las mujeres asesinadas en Ciudad Juárez. Territorio, soberanía y crímenes de segundo estado.* Buenos Aires: Tinta Limón.

Segato, R. (2012). Femigenocidio y feminicidio: una propuesta de tipificación. *Herramienta* 49.

Smith, A. (2015). *Conquest: Sexual Violence and American Indian Genocide.* Durham: Duke University Press.

Smith, S. (2012). Intimate Geopolitics: Religion, Marriage and Reproductive Bodies in Leh, Ladakh. *Annals of the Association of American Geographers* 102(6): pp. 1511-1528.

Speed, S. (2008). *Rights in rebellion: Indigenous struggle and human rights in Chiapas.* Palo Alto: Stanford University Press.

Sundberg, J. (2014). Decolonizing posthumanist geographies. *Cultural Geographies*, 21(1): pp. 33-47.

TallBear, K. (2016). Genomic articulations of Indigeneity. *Social Studies of Science* 43(4): pp. 509-533.

Ulloa, A. (2016). Feminismos territoriales en América Latina: defensas de la vida frente a los extractivismos. *Nómadas* 45: pp. 123-139.

Veracini, L. (2014). Understanding Colonialism and Settler Colonialism as Distinct Formations. *International Journal of Postcolonial Studies 16(5)*, pp. 615-633.

— (2011). Introducing Settler Colonial Studies. *Settler Colonial Studies* 1: pp. 1-12.

Wolfe, P. (1999). Settler Colonialism and the Transformation of Anthropology. The Politics and Poetics of an ethnographic event. London: Cassell.

Wolfe, P. (2006). Settler Colonialism and the Elimination of the Native. *Journal of Genocide Research*, pp. 387-409.

Zaragocin, S. (2017). Feminismo Decolonial y Buen Vivir. In S. Varea and S. Zaragocin (Eds.), *Feminismo y Buen Vivir: utopías decoloniales*. Cuenca: Pydlos/Universidad de Cuenca, pp. 17-25.

Zaragocin, S. (in press). Decolonized feminist geopolitics: coloniality of gender and sexuality at the centre of critical geopolitics. *Journal of Political Geography*.

Zaragocin, S., M. Silveira and I. Arazola (in press). Hacia una geografía del femicidio en Ecuador. In *Género y producción del espacio de la exclusión a la reivindicación del derecho a la ciudad*.

5. Neodevelopment vignettes in Argentina. Development(s), looting(s) and body/ies between exploitation and struggle

Mariano Féliz

From development to neodevelopment through (neoliberal) crisis

The idea and strategy of development historically became the way to channel class contradictions in the framework of capitalist social formations (Negri, 2002; Dalla Costa, 2009). In Argentina, after the fall of neoliberalism towards the end of 1990s, development discourse regained vitality. While in the neoliberal era development appeared in the guise of adjustment and restructuring by a State which had to retire but never did, from 2000 onwards the return to development discourse takes back to historical developmentalism forms from mid-twentieth century, only with a different class content.

"Development" as an idea does not consolidate in South American periphery until shortly after the Second World War, in mid-twentieth century. In the thirty years after early Forties to late Sixties, developmentalism consolidated as big national capital's strategy to integrate into the simultaneous irruption of a massified labor class, along the growing advance of foreign capital. From Getulio Vargas in Brazil and Perón in Argentina, between the Thirties and Forties, to military governments starting in 1964 and 1966 in the same territories, among others, developmentalism became a dominant social reproduction pattern, as a hegemonic project's axis willing to contain and channel demands put forth by worker masses and, as mentioned, to attempt a conflictive integration of the cycle of local capital to imperialist capital internalization process.

In the twentieth century, neodevelopment is similarly constituted to contain the irruption of popular classes' new political composition. Today, as yesterday, it also expresses transformation in the social and technical composition of capital as a whole, whose new dominant fraction is the great capital with a transnational tendency.

In Argentina, in particular, in the same way as historical developmentalism arose as an effect of transformations in class compositions in the first half of the twentieth century (end-of-century agro-exporting Argentina crisis), neodevelopmentalism appeared as a mediated response by the dominant classes to emerging contradictions in the neoliberal era. If development arose to contain the irruption of the new (internal) industrial/male/migrant working class, which consolidated through the first years of Peronism, neodevelopment was proposed as a solution to the irruption of (international) picketing/female/migrant precariat in the (late) neoliberal political scene.

The developmentalist crisis in the late Sixties started a path to a rearticulation in the development strategy. It would be a global crisis, produced by the fight by the weakest links in the imperialist chain and, simultaneously, by diverse fractions of the working people at the center of capitalism as well as in dependent peripheries. This crisis was expressed as a circulation of struggles: from the Afro-descendants' battles for their basic civil rights in USA in the Sixties, to the fights in the 1969 French May; from the Argentine *Cordobazo* barricades, to Iceland's 1975 Wages for Housework Campaign and Women's Strike; from the 1959 Cuban Revolution (and its 1961 Socialist radicalization), to Italy's 1969 Hot Autumn.

Neoliberalism would act as a long transition to overcome that crisis, with structural adjustment and enlarged-scale violence as the new face of development. These violence forms (indeed adjustment is, above all, violence) act with global reach, widely ranging their modes of attack to the forms of popular resistance to the capital's project. Most evident were external debt violence and military-civic dictatorships in dependent countries, accompanied by a Statist authoritarianism radicalization in the center (Negri, 2003). Later, the neoliberal crisis itself would pave the way to the construction of a new neodevelopment strategy as a means to contain the renewed fight cycle born from adjustment.

Thus, development and structural adjustment, Keynesianism and neoliberalism are faces of the same process of capital's expanded reproduction. Likewise, in each historic era there are different facets, more or less popular, conservative or liberal, still all framed in the need to channel social, political and economic contradictions in the capital valorization process.

The development that neoliberalism left us

The transition to neodevelopmentalism in Argentina takes up the conclusions of neoliberalism. It proposes its dialectical overcoming, negating it in order to express a new qualitative phase of its class content (Féliz and Pinassi, 2017).

First, neodevelopment expresses the need to consolidate a new social and technical composition of capital. The great transnational capital emerges as a dominant power within the whole of capital, after three decades of fierce struggle.

On a global scale, capital becomes more flexible, expanding and self-financializing (Marini, 2007; Ceceña, 2000; Harvey, 2004, 2005). In Argentina, this capital penetrates most aspects in the economy, concentrating especially in those moments of the cycle of capital with the capacity to produce and appropriate extraordinary rent: mining and hydrocarbons, agribusiness, logistical and financial branches (Azpiazu and Schorr, 2010). This new composition is a consequence of the world's neoliberal transformation, it constitutes a new colonial-imperialist matrix, and it configures a new form of production, appropriation and surplus value use in Argentina. A more extractivist production, a more transnational, more financialized appropriation, with a more sumptuary use of created value. Kalecki explained that the mass of surplus value is constituted macroeconomically from capital's expenditure decisions (Kalecki, 1977). Capital internationalization and its concentration in the local-international chain of owners/appropriators (Veblen's "leisure class") leads to its extroverted, extractivist, sumptuary constitution.

Second, neoliberalism leaves neodevelopmentalism to come with a new working class composition, with those-who-live-from-their-labor (paraphrasing Antunes, 2000). Within this composition, extended forms of overexploitation and precariousness are on the rise. Labor force use forms which flexibilize its management multiply, while invisibilizing real domination and exploitation relations behind "autonomous" forms of employment (self-employment, false co-operatives, service agreements, etc.). In this new social and technical composition, many layers of workers are on the periphery of the social factory, in conditions of super-exploitation. Around each transnational there is a myriad of nuclei contributing to it immense value quota (i.e., of alienated, abstract life-labor time), and compensating in it the large volumes of constant capital invested (means of production and material inputs which do not produce value or surplus value). Modern great capital cannot exist, or be valorized, without that mass of super-exploited labor on the edges of the social factory.

Third, as mentioned above, transnational-based extractivism becomes the dynamic core of valorization. This process has an increasingly imperialist foundation; every second of value and ounce of use value (gold, soybeans, timber, water and land, etc.) is intended to satisfy demands by the circulating fraction of constant capital (raw materials, non-human energy and inputs) of imperialist capital.

Real subordination of nature to capital (Sabattella, 2009) reaches new heights. The use of nature reaches super-exploitation levels as productive practices develop scales and modes that destruct nature's universal metabolism (Bellamy Foster, 2013). This destructive power imitates the social practices of patriarchy, which places women's bodies-territories as exploitable material (Segato, 2013; Palermo, 2017). Territories, the capitalism battle front in its neo-extractivist aspect, become primary nodes in human trafficking networks and unlimited exploitation of women's bodies. Women's bodies are bodies-territories that capital development intends to expropriate and exploit, but they resist (Segato, 2013).

Extraordinary rent appropriation and natural resource plundering for export is the axis of capitalist value production in dependent economies. That extraordinary rent is permanently disputed by different capital fractions and by working class fractions. Within the former, there is a tendency to consolidate a new socio-political formation linking the material interests of imperialist/extractivist great capital with non-working middle class fractions who live from income appropriation (directly from the land and/or derived forms such as real estate or financial rent) or from share appropriation in great capital's surplus value (transnationalized hierarchical management).

This process is sustained by high capitalization levels (capital centralization and concentration): that is, with high organic composition levels in the extractivist-rentier branches. This implies that, although these branches employ relatively little direct labor, they appropriate plenty of surplus labor (surplus value) in the form of extraordinary profits. The other side of this profitability concentration in great capital is, as already noted, the strengthening of labor force super-exploitation forms and the employment precarization in the rest of the branches and in smaller capitals, which must give up through unequal exchange part of the labor they exploit.

Finally, the triangle closes in a growing pressure on life reproduction labor, in the sphere of care, carried out mainly by women (Féliz and Díaz Lozano, 2018). Precarization of paid labor forms, especially in the working class periphery, increases pressure on them to be the last (and first) adjustment variable. On the one hand, daily precarization of neighborhood and community life forces a need for women to sharpen their imagination to solve more with less. In addition to this growing mental and time burden, there is the need to complement or complete insufficient household income with a search for paid labor. Pressing needs and the precariousness of care networks (including the State's increasingly limited task), force women to accept jobs with poor incomes and working conditions. In particular, these are often care jobs in family homes of the dominant fractions or the best paid workers; likewise, these gender-class relations are racialized, since a significant part of care workers are migrants from neighboring countries (or from poor provinces of the 'interior' of the country), which makes them even more vulnerable.

The core of the working class, concentrated around the branches and companies that organize the valorization process, compensates conditions of growing precariousness in the work with organizational capacity that allows them to compensate it (even partially) by means of hours worked and salary. The formal, male, institutionalized working class core acts as a containment dam; great capital overflows its desire for exploitation in an exacerbated surplus labor extraction in the valorization spaces that concentrate the most precarized, feminized, unpaid or badly-paid labor force. Labor super-exploitation has a woman's face.

Thus, neodevelopment is constituted on the basis of the historical fire triangle of capitalism, but in new conditions. Historical super-exploitation of labor in dependent capitalism (Marini, 1973) is deepened by pressure from imperialist extractivism forms over nature in the capital transnationalization era. Articulation between both processes structurally amplifies the super-exploitation of women's bodies in production and reproduction areas.

State configurations in neodevelopment

The neodevelopment strategy is a result of the explosion of contradictions that express its conditions of possibility. The new political composition of the working people allows for the configuration of a new form of State and political system. The new composition of capital as a whole marks the limits of that State reconfiguration.

The new formal labor force composition forces dominant sectors, and especially their hegemonic factions, to call for institutional channeling of demands. In the neoliberal crisis, companies faced demands that were expressed in the streets, decentralized, dispersed, outside the institutional framework, therefore outside the control of state forms. From mid 2002, in combination with the prevailing union form as an organizational strategy for formalized work, existing demands were contained by revitalizing pre-existing institutional forms; in particular, collective labor conventions (*convenciones colectivas de trabajo, CCT*) by activity branch and minimum wage policy recovered their dynamism.

These institutions enable containment of the labor conflict created around workers' grassroots organization, particularly in the area of large companies where that organization is more stable and articulated. Conflict institutionalization allows for neutralization of the most radical facets, but at the cost of redistributing a fraction of extraordinary profit among the best-integrated workers.

In parallel, demands from precarized fractions —in the periphery of the social fabric— are progressively integrated into new state configurations (basic universalist social policies). From the beginning, the Argentine *piquetero* movement (articulated around unemployed women and men on the outskirts of large urban centers) raised demands for work, dignity and social change (Dinerstein, Contartese and Deledicque, 2010). This was done in theoretical-political and practical terms, by means of self-organization, self-managed productive practices, co-operatives, and forms of territorial organization with a prefigurative projection (leadership without chiefs, grassroots democracy, political autonomy).

These recently organized fractions of fighting people (*piqueterxs*) initially reject institutionalization practices, which are social control and systemic integration forms. However, a combination of policies conflictively and progressively normalizes these demands, without allowing for their autonomization (Dinerstein, Contartese and Deledicque, 2010).

In contrast to the integration strategies of the formalized and unionized workers' movement, state strategy when faced with the *piquetero* movement operated on the basis of recognizing the demand for income, while dismissing the demand for dignified work. Throughout the neodevelopmental decade, social policies were consolidated as money transfers in exchange for care tasks performance: the unemployed heads of household program (*Programa Jefes y Jefas de Hogar*), family plan (*Plan Familias*), universal allowance for children (*Asignación Universal por Hijx, AUH*). At the same time, a certain amount of formalization for "domestic service" employment is promoted, with salaries close to minimum wage, at the cost of losing the right to AUH. In fact, these policies are based on the sexual division of labor imposed by patriarchal capitalism, and reinforce it (Féliz and Díaz Lozano, 2018). On the one hand, they express a recognition for women's social weight among the fighting people and society in general; however, they attempt to limit their role to that of "caregivers".

The neodevelopmentalist state supports social control based on the reproduction of the patriarchal-capitalist matrix of labor division. Formalized men consolidate historical institutionality (by means of the union form), strengthening their relative well-being within the labor force. Women, on the other hand, are conflictively normalized within historical productive and reproductive work fragmentation patterns. CCTs and minimum wage policy protect unionized men, while women receive income transfers conditioned to their care work, and some formalization of commoditized reproductive work (basically, paid home domestic service) but with incomes sustainedly below the averages for men and below the poverty line.

Non-paradoxically (although contradictorily), in neodevelopment the State reconstructs policies for political containment of social conflict that express the social fragmentation in the class-that-lives-from-their-labor. Intersectional fragmentation between men and women, between formal and informal, between employees of large capitals and precarized workers, productive and reproductive, remunerated and unremunerated, exploited and super-exploited, is consolidated in State practice in the era of neodevelopment.

Neodevelopmental hegemony and popular resistances

The neoliberal crisis opened a necessary space for the reconfiguration of capital hegemony forms. The fracture of neoliberal common sense — through the organic crisis — created a hiatus that had to be closed by means of a relegitimization process. Reconstruction of a development strategy to recreate the myth of a possible capitalism in a dependent territory was the main task for political forces who intended to lead the State apparatus (Féliz, 2016).

Once the crisis was over, once the limits of the Convertibility Plan (1991-2001) as a government technique (and not just as an "economic program") were exceeded, the macroeconomic and socio-political conditions were ready to start on the path of hegemonic reconstruction. In this sense, two issues are worth noting. On the one hand, hegemony as a category refers to the ability of certain fractions of the dominant social forces to impose their world view as common sense and strategy. That ability is supported by a social materiality, a historically and socially determined capacity to create reality from dominant positions in society. Capital domination is expressed in the State as a social form (as a real abstraction: Salama, 1979) and it is through that social form that the hegemonic fractions within capital work to constitute social hegemony.

Additionally, political forces seek to present themselves as articulators in the political system sphere as expressions of the social forces in dispute at the material level. They do not construct social hegemony by themselves: rather, they contribute to strengthening the social hegemony of dominant fractions (such as the "order parties") or, eventually and against socially dominant tendencies, to the transformation of (objective, subjective, symbolic) material conditions that allow for a change in the correlation of social forces in favor of non-dominant classes. Thus, political forces in the State occupy it as a form of political regime, as an expression of social forces in struggle (à la Poulantzas) and not as a direct expression of certain social fractions (à la Miliband).

Neodevelopmentalism is constituted on the basis of a new State form that materially expresses the social domination of a particular fraction of capital as a whole, as mentioned above. That form does not operate linearly, but rather expresses in politics the contradictions of concrete social forces in struggle and (emphasis on "and") the strategy of the political force in State power. Social forces in struggle impose their social power on the State; and the State (and its political forces) respond in terms of these forces and their strategic orientation. During neodevelopmentalism in its constitutive phase (2002-2008), Kirchnerism oriented its strategic action to configuring a form of "serious capitalism" around the formula "growth with social inclusion" (Féliz, 2017).

The macroeconomics of neodevelopment, or capitalist development as a strategy

The neodevelopment strategy managed to consolidate a capital accumulation pattern in the periphery, sustained in a new social and technical capital composition, and in a new political composition of the popular classes.

From the point of view of expanded capital reproduction, the strategy sought to support a macroeconomic policy that would build an extroverted demand pattern and allow accumulation to multiply on the basis of extraordinary rent appropriation and labor super-exploitation. Economic policy had to value the materiality of the new composition of capital, taking the most advantage of its potential for surplus value production.

The expensive dollar policy (devaluation of currency and the national labor force) was the chosen tactic, and it made it possible to take advantage of the favorable international situation (expanding imperialist economies and high prices for export commodities until 2008) in order to keep a five-year cycle of variable capital (employment) accumulation in super-exploited labor and nature conditions. In that period, several million jobs were created, and the limits of mining, soybean and oil exploitation were extended.

This only operates as a feasible policy in an expansive context, which provides a margin for the partial redistribution of extraordinary rent and with a margin to partially absorb popular demands (especially those that operate within marginal income redistribution). When that space narrows, adjustment inevitably begins and neodevelopment loses its progressive luster and garb, starting to show its (exploitative and destructive) capitalist essence. This policy of competitiveness via national currency devaluation is only operative if it succeeds in devaluing the labor force, reducing the relative real wage (Shaikh, 1991) and/or if it increases the intensity of reproductive labor. Without material changes in production or social reproduction organization (that is, without higher productivity levels), greater competitiveness only expresses higher absolute exploitation levels (more extensive and intensive super-exploited labor).

During the 2000s, Argentina's dependent economy was able to sustain the myth of growth with inclusion as long as the international appropriation of domestic value (unequal "outwards" exchange) was compensated with labor, nature and women's bodies super-exploitation forms (unequal "inwards" exchange). Greater competitiveness through greater absolute exploitation (and social resistance to it) is the limit faced by dependent economy.

The world market expansive cycle exhaustion starting from 2007-2008 marked the limits of the strategy. From then on, pressure to compensate for dependency conditions became unsustainable. This is expressed both in tensions in the direct capital production/appropriation space and in the specific State mediation.

Growing inflation began to operate as a means to wage devaluation (Féliz, 2015). The dispute for income appropriation (and surplus labor reduction) in the productive capital space and in the social reproduction space begins to show openly as inflationary tensions. The business demand for wage restraint increases; however, the loss of competitiveness cannot be avoided. A growing contradiction operates, since real wages stop recovering, but State policies do not manage to overcome inflationary tension; a pattern of inflation and stagnation is configured (Féliz, 2015).

In the social reproduction sphere, the redistributive policies reach their limits in the neodevelopmentalist framework, with basic universalism expansion in the form of *AUH*. From the 2002 *Jefes y Jefas* plan to the *AUH*, a redistribution pattern that only manages to avoid socio-political explosion in dependent capitalism social frontier spaces is consolidated. Even so, facing the impossibility of sustaining marginal income redistribution, the transitional neodevelopment crisis opens the way for certain forms of symbolic recognition (of rights), which aim to mediate and fragment rising social conflict (Féliz and Díaz Lozano, 2018). Thus, political forces in the State seek to compensate for the "growth with social inclusion" myth losing reality with operating modalities that, from the construction of (limited) citizenship rights, would allow the hegemonic alliance's solidity to be maintained.

Supported by a new configuration of productive-reproductive labor and women's bodies' super-exploitation, the hegemonic project is blocked because it cannot guarantee the continued reproduction of its legitimization forms. Working people's political composition has undergone a new mutation throughout the decade, now within the socio-political space of neodevelopmentalist social formation (Féliz, 2015). Indeed, political forces who promote neodevelopmentalist articulation at the Kirchnerist stage cannot understand this mutation: they are witnessing the dissolution of the materiality of those political relations that placed them at the top of the power-bloc. Income redistribution sought to articulate an appropriation matrix dominated by men in formal employment, while women were institutionalized as a reproductive labor force, by means of specific labor legislation that still speaks of "housewives", or social policies of conditional income transfer (such as *AUH*).

As far as the precarious redistributive matrix loses its material foundations, political forces in the State lose their capacity for hegemonic articulation. However, as long as the people's political composition is not recomposed in terms of struggle and hope but in terms of resignation and opportunism, the bases of neodevelopmentalist materiality are perpetuated and intensified through their own crises (Féliz, 2017).

The fire triangle of dependent capitalism and its limits

The capitalism-patriarchy-extractivism triangle runs across the dynamics of production and social reproduction in our territories. Especially in Argentina, throughout the era of neodevelopment in its Kirchnerist stage, those general patterns of expanded reproduction of violence forms towards female and feminized bodies morphed into subtler and sometimes more sinister forms.

Extroverted patterns of accumulation based on natural wealth plundering and super-exploitation deepened. The transnational financialization of capital subjects the advance of spoliation to speculation ups and downs. Recently, the renewed attack on Mapuche communities, and the repression, criminalization and murder of militant defenders of lands and communities, all clearly express the beachhead of this battle for control of the bodies. Simultaneously, the violence of plundering affects all territories. Subsumed in it is violence against women, who appear at the borders of capital as the last line of resistance to the advance of dead work over life itself. At the same time, women are the main focus for the attacks of patriarchal capitalism, which responds with violence to women's rebellion. On the one hand, neodevelopment and its crisis intensify the circuit of human-trafficking networks, especially those directly articulated with oil and mining extractivism, of high impact and territorial concentration. On the other hand, women embody resistance leadership. Their struggles gestate radical oppositions: to megamining (e.g., the assembly against Famatina mountain's exploitation), to soybean extractivism (e.g., the Ituzaingó mothers' assembly in Córdoba against Monsanto's glyphosate fumigations), to urban extractive activities (e.g., the thousands of organized *piquetero* women in slums) and, of course, to feminicide and violence against women (e.g., the International Women's Strike and the *Ni Una Menos* movement).

Life reproduction and its defense express the absolute limit to the advance of the fracture of its metabolism, caused by patriarchal capitalism. Forms of generalized super-exploitation of bodies are articulated, shamelessly penetrating different fractions of the working people's daily lives. The neodevelopment State tries to consolidate a new stable social and political hegemony, capable of productively containing for capital all social forces emanating from the experience of common life.

The paradox lies in the collective resistance to societal metabolism's extended and growing fracture not yet having an expression in forms of political recomposition of the people which are capable of containing the destructive tendencies. For the time being, popular movements have not been able to block this dialectical process of historical overcoming within capitalism. However, the battles against extractivism and plundering, the Indigenous, native and peasant communities' struggles, and feminist women's fight are reconfiguring the parameters of these resistances, nowadays and for some time already (Féliz, 2017b). They appear as the mobilizing core in new forms of political composition of the people. They are the key to future fights, an example of organization modalities and practical-critical horizon for the prefiguration of social change. They hold within them the new flames, those new fires which will light the way to freedom.

Bibliographical references

Antunes, Ricardo (2000). La centralidad del trabajo hoy. *Papeles de Población* 6(25). Toluca: Universidad Autónoma del Estado de México.

Azpiazu, Daniel and Martín Schorr (2010). *Hecho en Argentina*. Buenos Aires: Siglo XXI.

Bellamy Foster, John (2013). Marx y la fractura en el metabolismo universal de la naturaleza. *Revista Herramienta Web*, 15. Buenos Aires.

Ceceña, A. E. (2000). Tecnología y organización capitalista al final del siglo XX. In R. M. Marini and M. Millán (eds.). *La teoría social latinoamericana. Cuestiones contemporáneas* (pp. 95-104), t. IV, 2nd ed. (1996). México: UNAM/El Caballito.

Dalla Costa, Mariarosa (2009). *Dinero, perlas y flores en la reproducción feminista*. Madrid: Akal (Cuestiones de Antagonismo, 58).

Dinerstein, Ana, Daniel Contartese and Melina Deledicque (2010). *La ruta de los piqueteros*. Buenos Aires: Capital Intelectual.

Féliz, Mariano (2015). Limits and barriers of neodevelopmentalism: Lessons from Argentina's experience, 2003-2011. *Review of Radical Political Economics 47*(1): 70-89. URPE.

Féliz, Mariano (2016). Till death do as apart? Kirchnerism, neodevelopmentalism and the struggle for hegemony in Argentina, 2003-2015. In Ingo Schmitt (ed.), *The Three Worlds of Social Democracy: A Global View from the Heartlands to the Periphery* (pp. 91-106). London: Pluto Press.

Féliz, Mariano (2017). Argentina, de la crisis neoliberal a la crisis del neodesarrollo de Kirchner a Macri. Hipótesis sobre el tiempo que nos toca. In Mariano Féliz and María Orlanda Pinassi (Eds.), *La farsa neodesarrollista y las alternativas populares en América Latina y el Caribe* (pp. 47-68). Buenos Aires: Herramienta.

Féliz, Mariano (2017b). Marxian Dependency Theory in Latin America After the Pink Tide. Lessons Learned from Popular Movements and its Struggles. Ponencia presentada en *14th Annual Conference of Historical Materialism*, 9 al 12 de noviembre de 2017, SOAS. London: University of London.

Féliz, Mariano and Juliana Agustina Díaz Lozano (2018). Trabajo, territorio y cuerpos en clave neodesarrollista. Argentina, 2002-2016. *Revista Perfiles Latinoamericanos*, 52, July-December. México: Flacso-México. (In press.)

Féliz, Mariano and María Orlanda Pinassi (eds.) (2017). *La farsa neodesarrollista y las alternativas populares en América Latina y el Caribe*, Buenos Aires: Herramienta.

Harvey, David (2005). El "nuevo" imperialismo. Sobre reajustes espacio-temporales y acumulación mediante desposesión (parte II). *Revista Herramienta*, 29, June. Buenos Aires.

— (2004). El "nuevo" imperialismo. Sobre reajustes espacio-temporales y acumulación mediante desposesión. *Revista Herramienta*, 27, October. Buenos Aires.

Kalecki, Michal (1977). Los determinantes de las ganancias [(1933)1954]. In *Ensayos escogidos sobre dinámica de la economía capitalista (1933-1970)*. México: FCE.

Marini, Ruy Mauro (1973). *Dialéctica de la dependencia*. México: Era.

Marini, Ruy Mauro (2007). Proceso y tendencias de la globalización capitalista. In *América Latina, dependencia y globalización*. Buenos Aires: Clacso/Prometeo.

Negri, Antonio (2002). Keynes y la teoría capitalista del Estado después de 1929. In *Crisis de la política. Escritos sobre Marx, Keynes, las crisis capitalistas y las nuevas subjetividades* (pp. 11-36). Buenos Aires: El Cielo por Asalto.

Negri, Antonio (2003). *La forma-Estado*. Madrid: Akal.

Palermo, Hernán (2017). La producción de la masculinidad en el trabajo petrolero. Buenos Aires: Biblos.

Sabattella, Ignacio (2009). Crisis ecológica y subsunción real de la naturaleza al capital. *Íconos*, 36: 69-80. Quito: Flacso-Ecuador.

Salama, Pierre (1979). État et capital. L'État capitaliste comme abstraction réelle. *Critiques de l'économie politique (nouvelle série)* (pp. 7-8). Paris: Maspero.

Segato, Rita Laura (2013). La escritura en el cuerpo de las mujeres asesinadas en Ciudad Juárez. Buenos Aires: Tinta Limón.

Shaikh, Anwar (1991). Competition and Exchange Rates: Theory and Empirical Evidence. *Working Paper*. New York: New School for Social Research.

6. Identities, body and territory: 56+1 girls at the "Hogar Seguro, Virgen de la Asunción" fire

Walda Barrios-Klee(†)[1] and Dina Mazariegos[2]

Dedicated to Walda Barrios-Klee, who left us too soon, we celebrate your life and your legacy.
The impossibility of governing young people's bodies incites the application of an iron-fist policy manifested in the confinement and extermination of these bodies as an eugenics or "social cleansing" factor, added to discourses on surveillance and panoptic control of youth practices, discourses that no longer show young people as "rebels" and label them as "dangerous": it will be necessary to control their bodies as proof of the impossibility of dominating their thinking (Heffes, 2013, p. 3).

Introduction

Guatemalan society cannot be understood without recalling that this is a post-conflict country, where wounds caused by the falsely-called 'internal armed conflict'[3] still have not healed completely; as a result, we face an ailing democracy. Although the Peace Accords, signed in 1996, were a watershed that allowed for recomposition of

---

[1] Walda, academic, activist and friend, you transcended to a new dimension, while the book in its English version was in the process of publication. Walda you remain in our memory, you are one more link in our lineage and feminist ancestors, whom we must thank, honour and celebrate their legacy.

[2] Coordinator for the Flacso *Programa de Estudios de Género y Feminismos* ("Gender and Feminisms Studies Program"), academic seat: Guatemala. Researcher for Iumusac and doctoral student in Social Sciences, Universidad de San Carlos, Guatemala.

[3] It was not armed conflict: the term implies parity between combatants. In Guatemala, the State apparatus repressed unarmed civil population and applied a scorched earth policy.

the social movement and emergence of new social protagonists who were previously totally excluded, such as Indigenous peoples and women, political will was insufficient to carry out public policies aimed at strengthening institutions created as a result of the Accords (see Méndez and Barrios-Klee, 2010).

Guatemala experiences a continuous state of emergency, where one crisis follows another, and the State has been looted by the same oligarchy who appropriated the country more than five centuries ago, alongside army fractions who were entrusted with repression during the counter-insurgency period.

Juvenicide and feminicide fuse extreme violence against young women, which has increased in recent decades in different countries throughout the region. Guatemala is regarded as the country with the third highest incidence of extreme violence against young women. From this perspective, we search for the origin and the organizational structure that allowed for and generated those violent actions: that is to say, we are looking for the root causes of the dispossession, exclusion and death of countless young Guatemalan women at certain political moments, and at their recomposition in the current society.

Being a child or adolescent: a condition for exclusion in Guatemala

This article is a denunciation and reflection on the dreadful situation that girls and adolescents in Guatemala experience nowadays, as a consequence of the institutional weakening of the State. The Peace Accords signing in 1996 brought great hope and optimism for changes in the country, but the authoritarian and hardly inclusive character of the successive governments after the Accords hindered the country's transition towards a participatory democracy, as well as the possibility for human development.

One of the Accords' achievements was the visibility of women and Indigenous peoples as subjects of rights. However, there was a lack of public policy and the corresponding budgetary allocations to effectively fulfill these rights.

In this context, on 8 March 2017 there was a tragic incident of a fire at the "Hogar Seguro Virgen de la Asunción" ("Virgen de la Asunción" Safe House), in which 41 girls between the ages of 13 and 17 died. This was not an isolated event: it was a "chronicle of a death foretold", because the system's shortcomings had been reported several times before.

The statistics on children and adolescents' situation are horrifying: one in every two children under 5 years old suffers from chronic malnutrition; in 2015, 83483 girls and adolescents between 10 and 17 years old became pregnant (OSAR), most of them as a result of rape. In 2016 there were 7338 criminal complaints of sexual violence against minors, and 14698 of physical abuse (MP); in the same period, there were 809 violent deaths of children and adolescents, 90% of them caused by firearms.

In 2012, the United Nations Development Programme (UNDP) issued the country report "Guatemala, a country of opportunities for youth?", which identified four basic rights that children, adolescents and youth require to achieve human development: the right to live, which implies health, healthy and responsible sexual life initiation, and security; the right to know, which involves schooling, but also access to cultural goods, and interests to preserve their cultural heritage; the right to participate progressively in social life in the political, economic, social, and cultural spheres; and the right to enjoy leisure time. "Joy as a right, also pointed out in the research we carried out in Flacso/UNFPA, regarding the dramatic situation of girls who become mothers (2015)."

The Minister of Education (interview PL/15-10-16) recognized that 800,000 adolescents between 13 and 18 years old are not in the educational system, in addition to 800,000 or 900,000 others older than 18 who should also have gone through school, but did not. Therefore, there are 1,600,000 adolescents outside the educational system. These figures demonstrate that formal education coverage does not reach a large part of the population.

Guatemala is wasting its demographic dividend by having a young population without opportunities for development; for a rural Indigenous girl, the situation is even more concerning and excluding.

Girls and adolescents, negotiable territories in Guatemala and elsewhere

For as long as can be remembered, women's bodies have been considered disputed territories and spoils of war. In Guatemala, repression in rural areas by means of a scorched earth policy has resulted in the rape and killing of women as a way of humiliating communities. In ancient Greece and Rome, women's bodies were considered to be appropriable and, therefore, spoils of war.

In 1884's *The Origin of the Family, Private Property and the State*, Friedrich Engels noted that private property was guaranteed through the expropriation of women's bodies. Men needed to ensure their paternity of sons and daughters for the sake of property transmission.

Women's bodies have always been linked to patriarchal power's mandates; thus, they are intended to "have as many children as God commands," unable to make decisions about their fertility regulation and intergenerational intervals. In addition, their bodies are subject to legislation; for example, through the criminalization of abortion. Maternal death is an indicator of inequality and lack of care for women's health and bodies. It is inconceivable that, in the 21st century, women in Guatemalan rural areas still die in childbirth.

In Guatemala, we are faced with the constant violation of sexual and reproductive rights directly linked to adolescents' and women's bodies. No right can be lived outside the body. The body, then, becomes a territory where the cultural meanings of sexual differences and patriarchal mandates take place. Consequently, the female body will always be the space that suffers attempts to control it. This is why the French feminist Monique Wittig wrote "woman, vile and precious commodity". In Guatemala, there are many examples of girls and young women being given to older men in exchange for livestock or money (see Barrios-Klee, 2015).

The research cited (Barrios-Klee *et al.*, 2010, p. 51) used the concept of hegemonic masculinities posited by Connell to explain the body expropriation of which girls and adolescents are victims. This masculinity shows the following features: 1) naturalization of violence and discrimination against girls and adolescents; 2) regard for women's, girls' and adolescents' bodies and lives as property and possession: bodies as territories for others to appropriate; and 3) control of women's, girls' and adolescents' sexuality, in an attempt to limit behaviors that go beyond the norm and favor autonomy.

The second wave of the feminist movement claimed contraception as the way to allow women to exercise control over their own bodies, to regulate their own fertility as a right. This led to the transition "from family planning to reproductive health" (Barrios-Klee and Pons, 1995) and, later, to sexual and reproductive rights.

Based on findings from research conducted by Flacso/UNFPA, *¡Me cambió la vida! Uniones, embarazos y vulneración de derechos en adolescentes* ("My life was changed! Unions, Pregnancies and Rights Violations in Adolescents", 2015), these results are shown: early marriage influences early childbearing; adolescents are unaware of contraceptive methods and their own bodies' functions, making it almost impossible to regulate fertility. Adolescent girls and women have a low schooling rate, which prevents them from knowing their rights and exercising them. These conditions contribute to the expropriation of bodies and the exercise of submission becoming an imperative of patriarchal power over women's bodies.

Burnt Bodies: Victims or result from witnessing institutional violence against girls and adolescents in Guatemala

The 56+1 girls and adolescents who were immolated on March 8, 2017 at the Hogar Seguro Virgen de la Asunción had been temporarily confined in that state institution which, according to its creation agreement, was paradoxically instituted to give protection to children and adolescents whose rights had been violated.

After contextualizing the situation, condition and position of children and adolescents in Guatemala, it is necessary to profile the Guatemalan institution responsible for the integral care of children and adolescents whose rights had been ignored and abused. This institution has obviously not been efficient, responsible and committed in its endeavors, especially the restitution of violated or denied rights. The result was a devastating effect on this population group, specifically in the case of the 56+1 girls burned to death that fateful day.

According to Castoriadis (2005), each society builds its institutions and meanings; furthermore, it elaborates tools, procedures and methods to help face everyday problems. In Guatemala there is a legal framework that promotes the creation of institutions for the integral protection of children and adolescents.

Moreover, since 26 January 1990 the Guatemalan State has been a signatory of the *Convention on the Rights of the Child*, the United Nations General Assembly international treaty that recognizes the basic human rights of children and adolescents.

In this sense, responsible commissions have been created to achieve the objectives set by the *Ley de protección integral de la niñez y adolescencia* ("Law for the Integral Protection of Children and Adolescents"): first, the *Comisión Nacional para la Niñez y Adolescencia* ("National Commission for Children and Adolescents"), responsible for the creation of public policies for integral protection that guarantee children and adolescents the full enjoyment of their rights and freedoms, composed of those State and civil society organs that are focused on their development.

Second, the *Comisiones Municipales para la Niñez y Adolescencia* ("Municipal Commissions for Children and Adolescents"), with participation from municipal corporations, government institutions and social organizations that work in the town and are responsible for formulating policies for the comprehensive protection of children and adolescents at the municipal level.

At the time of the tragedy, the Presidential *Secretaría de Bienestar Social* ("Social Welfare Secretariat"), one of the public institutions 'specialized' in the formulation of public policies for the implementation of comprehensive protection for children and adolescents, was led by the Head of the Hogar Seguro Virgen de la Asunción. This secretariat was created on April 29, 1963 and its Organic Regulations were passed in 2006.

It is the 'competent and responsible' authority for carrying out actions regarding compliance with sanctions imposed to adolescents in conflict with criminal law, as well as protection measures for children and adolescents whose rights have been violated, through programs and services devoted to prevention, integral protection, integral reinsertion and resocialization at a national level with equity and equality.

For a clearer view of the causes that led to these 56+1 children and adolescents' immolation, a critical approach to the complex problem of minors' institutionalization in Guatemala is necessary. According to experts, this type of institutionalization has two modalities: minors institutionalized for having been in trouble with the law, and those confined in institutions as a protective measure due to their condition of vulnerability.

Children and adolescents who are victims of physical, psychological and sexual violence in their family spaces, and daily contexts are considered vulnerable. Also, as established by the Statute of the Social Welfare Secretariat, minors with some disability, in situations of abandonment, homelessness, irregular adoptions, addiction, and/or victimization of commercial, labor and economic sexual exploitation and trafficking, are placed at risk daily, and are considered vulnerable as well.

Guatemala is regarded as one of the countries in Latin America with the largest number of institutions to house children and adolescents. However, these lack the quality standards established for institutions of this type; standards such as "temporality of the child's stay, fulfillment of an adequate infrastructure, access to education and psychological attention, and others". Furthermore, in August 2010, the *Consejo Nacional de Adopciones* ("National Adoptions Council") authorities pointed out that only seven institutions out of one hundred and ten registered private entities had the official authorization to operate (RLAF, 2011, p. 12).

These homes are meant to be temporary and, in principle, should offer professional care and security, taking into account that institutionalized minors are in State custody because their families are in crisis. In this sense, the State is responsible for their health, education, nourishment, security, as well as the basic elements for their comprehensive development.

According to Valeria Brahim (2016), a Brazilian specialist on children's rights, institutionalization should be the last resort for children and adolescents living in vulnerable conditions, "since removing the child from the family is more violent than violence itself." Moreover, the *World Report on Violence against Children* establishes that institutional violence is six times greater than in alternative family programs.

As for the Hogar Seguro Virgen de la Asunción, journalists Enrique Naveda and Carlos Arrazola state in their *New York Times* article of 10 May 2017 that it was founded in 2010, later becoming the main minors' shelter run by the Secretaría de Bienestar Social. The Secretaría should have provided the Hogar Seguro from the beginning with protocols for "differentiated attention", since from the beginning it sheltered children and adolescents with different issues, such as family abandonment and/or domestic violence, trafficking victims, young people in trouble with the law and disabled minors.

Clearly, in Guatemala, the institutionalization of minors is punitive in nature, so that its only effects have nothing to do with prevention, protection, recovery, reintegration, or behavior resocialization. The methodologies employed in the Hogar Seguro Virgen de la Asunción so far described by surviving minors point to repression, which considers punishment as a social function: a tool used in power procedures by which the body is subjected to force by a social body. The institutional administrative apparatus in which minors are confined turns punishment into torture and, as Mably (1789) states, this affects the soul more than the body itself. In turn, Foucault identifies torture as part of the punishment ritual, where the person who suffers it must be pointed out [... T]orture itself, although its function is to 'purge' the crime, does not reconcile; it traces around, or rather, on the very body of the condemned person certain signs that must not be erased; [...] And by the justice that imposes it, torture must be resounding, and be verified by all, somehow as its triumph (Foucault, 2002, p. 33).

In general, it can be said that, from its colonial, patriarchal, racist, and classist roots, Guatemalan society is discriminatory, exclusionary, punitive, and violent, and uses corporal and psychological punishment as a form of control. This is how the horror of daily punishment is built, then experienced daily, by a majority of children and adolescents. "Young people have been turned into dangerous enemies of society. Youth and danger, or youth and crime, have become synonyms, interchangeable words whose effect is to naturalize the institutionalized violence exercised against young people" (Reguillo, 2003, p. 11).

For the most part, the victims at the Hogar Seguro Virgen de la Asunción were children and adolescents who came from places where punishment was also a constant. Therefore, their first experience of torment was not at the Hogar Seguro: unjustly, and in full violation of their elementary rights, they had already experienced physical, psychological, and even sexual violence in the spaces they occupied every day. However, the torture experienced at the Hogar Seguro led them to an agonizing death they had never imagined, which shattered their dreams and devastated their families' lives and Guatemalan society as a whole.

As mentioned earlier, the Hogar Seguro Virgen de la Asunción was part of a so-called national protection system for children and adolescents: that is, an institution meant to provide security. However, according to different reports from the investigation carried out by prosecutors from the Public Ministry (information which was published in various media), it was established that, since its opening, the Hogar Seguro Virgen de la Asunción had been the scene of countless abuse and violence situations: beatings, trafficking, rapes, and even a murder. Among specialists in minors' care, the notion that the protection center had become a place of abuse and torture spread.

Apparently, through its officials, this institution employed a system of control and discipline aimed at modifying thoughts and appropriating the adolescents' bodies-territories, turning them into subjects of punishment, appropriating them and subjecting them to torments of extreme violence by means of the "lordship" of these girls and adolescents. The "lordship" (*dueñidad*) category is delineated by the feminist anthropologist Rita Segato in her book *La guerra contra las mujeres* ("The War against Women") to identify the different facts attempting against the body-territory and sovereignty of women; "lordship" appropriates not only these subjects' physical body, but also their life and death. "Since 2013, dozens of complaints have been filed with the public prosecutor's office and the *Procuraduría de los Derechos Humanos* ("Human Rights Ombudsman's Office") for sexual abuse and humiliation committed against children in the safe house where the tragedy occurred" (Naveda and Arrazola, 2017).

What does all this torture mean? The abuse of power and control relationships that girls and adolescents lived daily in front of the dehumanized, patriarchal and adult-centered system enforced at the Hogar Seguro through its officials, which evidences that behind minors and adolescents' institutionalization there are real systems of torture and abuse.

This punishment system is a tool used by the staff to subdue not only the adolescents' bodies but also their very beings. According to the testimony of several survivors, and of many others who have now been silenced forever, their bodies-territories were used for sexual trade in exchange for security or fewer punishments. On the topic of women's bodies' subjugation, the sociologists María Luisa Femenías and Paula Sosarossi emphasize that

> Its effectiveness lies precisely in the fact that actions are public and their consequences are displayed to the public in "exemplary bodies"; that is, disciplined, terrified, submissive, passive, dead bodies. The message is clear. By action or omission, they write a coded public message to society in blood [...] The range is broad: it goes from insulting or disaffirming a woman (or women in general) to the most extreme cruelty: "We will be in charge again, even if this means increasing cruelty by appropriating women's bodies and

inscribing in them our power and domination message" (Femenías and Sosarossi, 2009, p. 64).

Institutionalization denies the right to be children or adolescents to those who, for whatever reason, are detained in these institutions; places where, although they function within a legal framework, they do not fulfill their responsibilities or the public policies from which they emanate. They do not respond to the reality of most of the youth in Guatemalan population.

Juvenicide and feminicide: the last link in systemic, systematic, stigmatizing and widespread violence against young women in Guatemala

Undoubtedly, many countries in the world live in patriarchal and adult-centered regimes, not caring to implement projects aimed at youth; as a consequence, young people's deaths become irrelevant. Just as women's bodies are considered disposable, so are young people's bodies.

Juvenicide is a social science category which makes it possible to analyze the persistent condition of generalized violence on adolescents and young people. The origin of this concept is attributed to the Mexican activist and academic Víctor Quintana, from the Universidad Autónoma de Ciudad Juárez, who since 2010 has studied juvenile murders perpetrated in Ciudad Juarez during the last decades.

> Juvenicide allows us to understand why some young men are turned into killable subjects, disposable subjects that anyone can kill, as their death, according to Giorgio Agamben, has no legal consequences because they are not even mentioned as homicides. They are called executions. This is the importance of calling them juvenicides (Valenzuela, 2012, p. 2).

In turn, Juan Antonio Vega Báez and Rosalba Elizabeth Rivera Zúñiga, in their article "Juvenicide in Mexico and Central America in contexts of generalized violence: before and after Ayotzinapa," focus this social phenomenon on the tragedy of collective, selective, systematic and persistent disappearances of adolescents and young people which recurs both in Mexico and in Central American countries. In this region, an impressive number of young people and adolescents have disappeared in the last decade; according to the study conducted by Vega and Rivera, this already exceeds the death statistics in countries experiencing traditional armed conflict such as Sudan, the Republic of Congo, and Afghanistan (Vega and Rivera, 2010, p. 4).

In this regard, it is necessary to mention that according to the United Nations Children's Fund (UNICEF) report, *Ocultos a plena luz* ("Hidden in the Light", 2016), Guatemala is one of the three highest countries in the world where children and adolescents die violently.

As a starting point, to classify the massacre of 56+1 girls and adolescents in the Hogar Seguro on 8 March 2017 as juvenicide, we considered the three central aspects established by Vega and Rivera to characterize juvenicide. First, "the non-combatant character of the victims": all the girls and adolescents who suffered torment that day were victims of an indolent, corrupt and violent system.

Second, "the possibility of the existence of State violence, by direct or indirect action or by responsible omission". Indeed, it was and continues to be a violent action committed by the State through its officials; and third, "the structural context of impunity, both *de jure* and *de facto*." Clearly, this criminal act that locked up the girls in an overcrowded space and allowed them to burn without giving them any help exemplifies the rampant impunity enjoyed by State institutions. Furthermore, it particularly describes "the use of violence by system actors against populations regarded as vulnerable" (Vega and Rivera, 2010, pp. 2-4).

This violent act was also a feminicide; Marcela Lagarde, who established this category, states that there is feminicide "when the State does not give guarantees to women and does not create conditions of safety for their lives in the community, at home, or in their workplace, the street or leisure spaces."

To understand this concept, we must first understand how power relations between men and women are established in our societies. Men not only appropriate women's bodies, but also, in a subjective sense, apply social control, and when that control is lost, social sanction comes. Because, in fact, feminicide is not the murder of women executed by a man, but by society as a whole, which constructs masculinity and educates men to appropriate women's bodies, subjectivity, and lives. For all these reasons, the extreme violence with which these 56+1 girls and adolescents were treated can clearly be identified as a feminicide.

The *Informe de Violencia Homicida en Guatemala* ("Report on Homicidal Violence in Guatemala") presented by the *Grupo de Apoyo Mutuo* ("Mutual Support Group", GAM) and the *Instituto Nacional de Ciencias Forenses* ("National Institute of Forensic Sciences", Inacif) showed an increase in crimes committed against women. Women's murders increased by 40.07% compared to the same period in 2016 (January-September). According to the report, the greatest number of victims range from 18 to 39 years old and their deaths can be classified as hate crimes, given their characteristics (Gándara, 2017, p. 8).

The confinement in subhuman conditions to which the 56+1 girls were subjected the night before and the morning of that fateful day at the Hogar Seguro, when they were denied any possibility of safeguarding their fragile lives by preventing them from leaving that burning prison, is a flagrant attitude of hate and contempt that exposes the inhumane, adult-centered, patriarchal and racist system that prevails in institutions that control and dominate institutionalized children.

This feminicide and juvenicide reflects how Guatemalan society condones the extreme violence experienced by young women in Guatemala, and demonstrates how this violence is a founding and sustaining part of the male or patriarchal domination system focused on sexual desire that promotes control of women's bodies and their freedom.

> Women's bodies have always carried an additional symbolic value as a guarantee for closing conflicts or as a power exercise place to humiliate, dishonor, deny, or send coded messages to other men. [...] Only feminist exegesis has managed to begin to reveal how this logic of domination operates (Femenías and Sosarossi, 2009, p. 13).

Therefore, this article employs the category of juvenicide, making an intersectional connection with that of feminicide to highlight how little importance and attention young people receive in exclusionary societies. In other words, without leaving aside symbolic, occupational and psychological violence, we can focus our attention on brutal physical violence, whose extreme expression is the violation of women's bodies, their mutilation and murder (Femenías, 2008).

Who were the adolescent girls burned in the Hogar Seguro?

The girls in the Hogar Seguro were adolescents who lived in poverty, discrimination and exclusion conditions. They came from dysfunctional families, who had to face conditions of violence in their homes and closest communities. These circumstances placed them in a situation of complete vulnerability, preventing them from developing life projects, with violence as their only way to regard themselves and survive.

Theirs are 56 life stories, 41 of which were truncated as a result of the fire; 15 are survivors who were scarred physically, emotionally and spiritually after the tragedy; one of them, with an eight-month pregnancy during her stay in the Hogar Seguro. They saw their lives and dreams linked to the punishment and submission to which they were subjected by the Guatemalan State child protection system through Guatemala's Secretaría de Bienestar Social, specifically in the Hogar Seguro Virgen de la Asunción. These adolescents were between 13 and 17 years old: "they were not delinquents: at least they were not sent there to serve a corrective sentence. The State became the girls' legal guardian; in some cases they did not have a relative to take responsibility for them, or they had been victims of abuse and violence by relatives" (Rojas, 2017, p. 1).

> For some of the girls, residing in marginal areas where criminal groups seek to recruit minors to commit illicit acts became the reason to live in a State shelter, a place where they would supposedly be safe. Others were marked by an environment of deprivation, with limited or no access to education, basic services and limited recreation, compounded by family dysfunctions. Sexual abuse is another recurrent scourge, which led several of them to show

rebellious behavior, and even end up in the safe house as a "protection" measure (Muñoz, 2017, p. 1).

Despite articles 116 and 182 of the *Ley de Protección Integral de la Niñez y Adolescencia* ("Law for the Integral Protection of Children and Adolescents") establishing that the institutionalization of children and adolescents in vulnerable situations should be avoided as far as possible, in the case of these 56+1 girls institutionalization was considered their only option for survival — ignoring that, in fact, it would be an option for death.

After characterizing the situation, condition and position of the group of adolescents immolated that fateful day, the intersectionality of identities can be delineated: they were young, female and did not have the minimum conditions for human development. The neoliberal-patriarchal and racist context in the Guatemalan State led to this State crime with specific names: simultaneously juvenicide and feminicide.

These 56+1 life stories are unforgettable: trapped in a punishment and submission system that through a social body took over their physical bodies and their integral beings, that fateful 8 March 2017. It is impossible not to recall the 123 workers immolated at the Triangle Shirtwaist factory in New York in 1911, and the 43 students disappeared from Ayotzinapa, Mexico in 2014. They all died after they had denounced the injustices they experienced while they were alive and fought for their rights and their freedom.

Final considerations

In order to try to measure the massacre of the 56+1 girls and adolescents of the Hogar Seguro Virgen de la Asunción, which took place on 8 March 2017 in Guatemala City, we must deepen our knowledge of the contexts and scenarios that led to this feminicide and juvenicide. This implies identifying the State's responsibility by direct or indirect action or by omission of responsibilities. This is a consequence of the degradation of those institutions whose responsibility is the integral care of children and adolescents who have been "threatened in their rights".

These elements truncate children and adolescents' dreams and mark their families' lives and the country's history, forcing us to face the violence and terror they experience daily. In turn, they show how women's bodies are used symbolically and concretely as a place to exercise male power logic in all its expressions, normalizing extreme violence and regarding young women's bodies as disposable.

For this type of violence not to be repeated, it is necessary to investigate with greater depth the structural problems that young people experience in their daily lives; in addition, the State must assume its responsibility and strengthen institutions in order to guarantee the defense of Guatemalan children and adolescents' human rights, attending to them with equity and cultural relevance.

Bibliography

Barrios-Klee, Walda and Leticia Pons Bonals (1995). *Sexualidad y religión en los Altos de Chiapas*. Tuxtla Gutiérrez: Universidad Autónoma de Chiapas.

Barrios-Klee, Walda (ed.) (2015). ¡Me cambió la vida! Uniones, embarazos y vulneración de derechos en adolescentes. Guatemala: Flacso/UNFPA.

De Mably, G. (1789). Que el Castigo, si se me permite hablar así, caiga sobre el alma más que sobre el cuerpo. De la legislation, *Oeuvres completes*, t IX, p. 326.

Femenias, María Luisa and Paula Sosarassi (2009). *Poder y violencia sobre el cuerpo de las mujeres*, Porto Alegre: Sociologías.

Foucault, Michel (2002). *Vigilar y Castigar: nacimiento de la prisión*. Buenos Aires: Siglo XXI.

Gándara, Natalia (2017). Asesinatos de mujeres van en aumento. *Prensa Libre*, Guatemala, 22 October, p. 8.

Heffes, Alejandra (2013). *El cuerpo y la memoria como emblemas de participación juvenil*. Buenos Aires: IEHS-UNICEN/Tandil.

Méndez, Luz and Walda Barrios-Klee (2010). *Caminos recorridos: luchas y situación de las mujeres a trece años de los Acuerdos de Paz*. Guatemala: Unión Nacional de Mujeres Guatemaltecas (UNAMG)/Editorial de Ciencias Sociales.

Muñoz Palala, Geldi (2017). 41 vidas truncadas por la negligencia. *Prensa Libre*. Guatemala, April.

Naveda, Enrique and Carlos Arrazola (2017). La tragedia de "un sistema de protección fallido". *New York Times*, 10 March.

Reguillo, Rossana (2003). Ciudadanías Juveniles en América Latina. *Última década* 11(19): 11-30, November.

Rojas, Alex (2017). ¿Qué menores habitan el Hogar Virgen de la Asunción? *Prensa Libre*, Guatemala, 8 March.

Segato, Rita (2016). *Contra-pedagogías de la crueldad*. Facultad Libre y Virtual. Available at https://www.youtube.com/watch?v=f92n-GSJDso

Vega Báez, Juan Antonio and Rosalba Elizabeth Rivera Zúñiga (2015). *Juvenicidio en México y Centroamérica en contextos de violencia generalizada: antes y después de Ayotzinapa*. Mexico: UNAM-Estudios Latinoamericanos/CIESAS-DF Antropología.

Valenzuela Arce, José Manuel (2012). *Sed de mal. Feminicidio, jóvenes y exclusión social*. Mexico: El Colegio de la Frontera Norte/ UANL. Available at http://www.lecturalacaniana.com.ar/que-es-el-feminicidio.

7. *Kawsak sacha*: women organization and political translation of the Amazonian rainforest in Ecuador

*Lisset Coba and Manuel Bayón**

In a context of capitalism global restructuring, in 2013, close to 200 Indigenous women marched from the Ecuadorian Amazonian rainforests to the country's capital, Quito, carrying an economic-political-cosmological proposal: the *Kawsak Sacha* or "living forest".

This is the alternative by the Pastaza Amazonian peoples to stop the oil frontier expansion in their territories. In their journey, the walkers were accompanied by other organizations: ecologists, Indigenous people, women, and trade unionists. The political work of Indigenous Amazonian women has gone alongside internal struggles in their grassroots organizations. In this article, we will study the ways of their politics, their capacity for self-organization, their place in Indigenous protests, and in turn understand their role as interpreters of forest politics.

Rainforest translators

> And finally, as Indigenous peoples grounded on our cosmovision, on our rights, we propose that we begin to generate a proposal at a global level, at a country level, not only based on rights, but also on the sacredness that the Amazonian cosmovision is for us, our territorial space, and that this model be declared a living forest, that it not be declared an area of national interest, but rather declared a life zone, excluding all oil exploitation.
> Patricia Gualinga, Amazonian leader
> Before the Asamblea Nacional ("National Assembly"). Quito, 22 October 2013.

On 12 October 2013, in an act of symbolic inversion to commemorate the "discovery of America," a group of female leaders from south-central Ecuadorian Amazonia began a march to

---

* With contributions by Miriam García Torres.

Quito. Some weeks before, they had sailed, stopping in villages to establish alliances and gather forces. Full of courage and with few economic resources, Kichwas, Saparas, Waoranis, Shiwiars, who would later be joined by Shuar and Achuar women, had undertaken the march to the capital on a 250-kilometer route. As they passed through towns and cities, sympathetic supporters of other Indigenous organizations, women, students, workers and ecologists gave them shelter, food and company. The protest was led by women who, indignant, denounced the expansion of oil frontiers[1], the threat to their way of life.

In a context following the 2013 elections, in which President Correa was re-elected for the third time,[2] oil exploitation was declared in the Parque Nacional Yasuní ("Yasuní National Park") ITT (Ishpingo-Tambococha-Tiputini) Block, and the 11th Bid Round for wells in the Pastaza Province was announced. Thus, the old political triangle was revived on an Amazonian scale: Indigenous movements, the State, and local and transnational extractive agents. Oil is a strategic resource proclaimed of "national interest" in the Constitution; it generates foreign currency-income for the State to provide health, education, sanitation, and housing services to the most impoverished populations, including those in Amazonia. However, it also implies high contamination and violence. Days before, the announcement of oil exploitation in the Parque Nacional Yasuní —repealing the *Iniciativa Yasuní ITT* ("Yasuní ITT Initiative") that proposed to leave the oil underground

---

[1] The 11th Oil Bid Round carried out by the Ecuadorian government in order to obtain international investment for the sector —whose impact would fall mainly on central-southern Amazonia— is the State's legitimisation of native peoples' territorial rights' transfer to transnational oil companies.

[2] The third regime administration was inaugurated with a deepening of its inclination towards a rentier economy based on the exploitation of raw materials as a transition towards Good Living, stipulated as Plan Nacional del Desarrollo del País ("National Plan for the Development of the Country"; Senplades, 2013).

in exchange for international compensation — undoubtedly blurred the chance for an environmental justice horizon, causing rejection to the development model in place.[3]

Pastaza is a province where different Amazonian political-organizational traditions converge. In 1992 its inhabitants achieved the collective titling of 1.5 million hectares of ancestral territories, after a march where women played a crucial role — though invisibilized in the narratives. That year, the 500 years of "resistance" against the Colony were remembered and vindicated. Central-southern Amazonia was historically composed of Indigenous peoples who had fled several expulsion processes. Since the 16th century, different waves of Catholic missions catechized the territory; in the mid-19th century, rubber tree exploitation in northern Amazonia impacted the region. The war with Peru at the end of the 1940's, the arrival of evangelical missions and the installation of multinational oil companies during the 1950's caused the reorganization of ancestral territories.

In late 20th century, many protests and Indigenous uprisings took place; the Amazonian Indigenous organizational process was consolidated at the national and international levels, and it peaked with the marches of the 1990s. However, gradually the State administration and the oil companies intervened, weakening an Indigenous movement whose leaders were seduced by the benefits of oil exploitation — although it promoted high conflict scenarios. Nevertheless, violence continues and so does the capacity to carry out national political proposals with international impact. The *Sumak Kawsay* or "Good Living" stipulated in the Ecuadorian Constitution of 2008 has been promoted by Indigenous organizations such as OPIP (1980-2000) and Confenaie (2000), and

---

[3] Multiple protests, organizations and Amazonia-supporting NGOs collected signatures to call for a national referendum on the issue. The women's movement united against the regime's patriarchal and colonizing authority, equating extractivism with male chauvinism.

their insistence has stimulated the creation of Indigenous and nature rights.

National plans for Development and Good Living redefined in the last decade the rentier character of the State, based on territorial expansion for the extraction of minerals, including oil. Thus, the Indigenous approach was blurred. In response to this threat, various Indigenous organizations have stated that Good Living is not possible without the Living Forest or *Kawsak Sacha*, the place where the protective beings that make forest regeneration possible inhabit (conversation with Juan Gualinga, September 2017). Respect for the *Kawsak Sacha* is fundamental to the existence of the *Sumak Kawsay*.

Many women are experts in plants and the secrets of forest cultivation. Being responsible for daily food provision, they know the effects of oil exploitation. In October 2013, female leaders of various Indigenous organizations decided to march and deliver the *Kawsak Sacha* or Living Forest Mandate to the President of the Republic. They took up authority because many men, they say, negotiate the lives of the *ayllus* and give in easily.

Understanding the intelligence and political outrage that led them to take over march organization is our main aim. Spatial reflection considers the multidimensionality of social struggles, providing us with a non-linear understanding of space-shaping movement, as well as border porosity (Oslender, 2002). Defense of the place grows in complex scenarios, in scales crossed by different power coordinates, in unexpected assemblages between life perspectives. This puts forth the importance of recognizing geopolitical hierarchies and capitalist globalization territoriality (Gibson and Graham, 2002). Indigenous fights as emergencies in post-colonial times are the field from which we start to reflect on women's political space.

Reviewing the *Kawsak Sacha* as a document that claims recognition of the forest as a "living place", of subjects full of intentions (Kohn, 2013; Latour, 2007; Viveiros de Castro, 2013), we posit the role of female leaders as strategists and translators of world perspectives, cosmogonies, which they bring to national politics (Coba, 2017) challenging a State that keeps its colonial roots despite declaring itself plurinational. In turn, we observe their political strategies, which must overcome male chauvinist relations in homes, communities, and Indigenous organizations, as well as opposite the State and extractive companies. These female leaders have developed a capacity to interpret and link multiple semantic displacements, political strategies born at the very moment of translation. The *Kawsak Sacha* political proposal recognizes temporal and political overlaps extending from an ancestral past and a hidden present in which the living forest constantly experiences violence from national rentier capitalism and transnational capital.

Amazonian female leaders' strategies define forest-situated politics. They feed on national and global environmental and feminist support networks: networks in which they weave inter-class, inter-ethnic and urban-rural alliances, though not exempt from power relations. Their protest actions lead us to reflect on a definition of political action, sustained by daily experience facing the advances of patriarchal and colonial violence. "Resistance" as an Indigenous definition is experienced specifically by women. From a subordinate position, they exercise daily tactics to counteract gender subordination colonialism and weave political alliances. Permanent pressure on their territories has created a political culture of belligerence that poses the question: how do women construct Indigenous politics? What does the march mean in their political lives? What does the "living forest" mean from the women's point of view?

This research is the result of accompaniments, encounters, estrangements, political connections between subjects with very different histories, where we are united out of respect for the Amazonian rainforest and indignation for its destruction. As researchers, we have often visited Indigenous communities, interviewed leaders of the nationalities that make up Confenaie, and participated in different forums, marches, mobilizations in the territory, and community assemblies. There, we recorded their testimonies, trying to understand their political work, their strategies and world perspectives. Thus, it is important for us to state that the women interviewed are not mere informants, but thinkers and builders of knowledge who stimulate reflection.

The intimate politics of women. Between assemblies and family disputes

> And in an assembly I cut my hair in front of everyone, that is what we people live (Susana, young Kichwa, during a Saramanta Warmikuna workshop in Quito).

In the nebulous space of post-colonial and capitalist powers, in communities and *ayllus*, Catholic inculcation of strict gender roles with submission of women to men permeates the systems of community reciprocity. Some women state that they are left outside the community spaces of political participation because the dialogue with colonizing agents such as priests, military or multinationals' administrators is mediated by men. Nevertheless, the youngest women began to gain space in the federated associations of nationalities that in the 1990s formed the *Organización de Pueblos Indígenas de Pastaza* (OPIP, "Organization of Indigenous Peoples of Pastaza").[4] This organization was consolidated by means of the anti-oil fight.

In ancestral villages like Sarayaku, the struggle against oil has given a turn to Amazonian Kichwa women's position. The entry of the oil company CGC at the end of the 1990s and in the 2000s provoked the community's refusal but, together with pressure from the company, protected by the army, came promises and attempts to bribe the male leadership. Displaced from the negotiation and promises that oil offered, and faced with the certainty that only

---

[4] Amazonian Indigenous organizations were created with support from the Catholic Church, NGOs and other highland Indigenous organizations, especially the Ecuarunari, as well as Indigenous organizations from other countries. They gather together mainly with an aim of interlocution with the State and land titling claims, facing the massive impact consequence of the different periods of Agrarian Reform in the 1950s and 1960s. Regarding OPIP, see http://www.llacta.org/organiz/opip/

dependence, pollution and overwork were destined to them, the women went on a cross-legged strike. They would not perform any more housework or farmwork until negotiations ceased, and there would be no food, none of their traditional fermented drink *chicha* —or sex. In January 2003, the women sieged the army that had militarized the territory and requisitioned their weapons. When they decided to give them back to the army after calling on the national press, they stood in front of the colonel and, one by one, reprimanded him firmly before returning them. The women won this battle and Sarayaku became an emblem of anti-oil resistance.

Nevertheless, the Indigenous organization was fractured, largely due to pressure strategies by the State and transnational capital, in different periods. Starting in the 1990s, oil exploitation was privatized, and through successive bidding rounds new territories were granted. In the framework of the globalization process, with global-scale neoliberal policies deepening, the oil industry took a new turn: the era of Corporate Social Responsibility (CSR) began, with the arrival of community relations lobbyists in the communities. Although political organization in the Indigenous movement during those decades was very strong, the lack of organizations in several Indigenous nationalities led oil companies to create organizations that could sign agreements with them. The emblematic case is the *Organización de la Nacionalidad Waodani de la Amazonia Ecuatoriana* (ONHAE, "Organization of the Waodani Nationality of Ecuadorian Amazonia"), created as a result of the oil company Maxus's interested action. Later, various internal weakening and decentralization processes, added to frictions generated by interlocution with external actors such as the State and the companies, caused the multi-ethnic organization to break down: then, several other organizations were created: *Organización Interprovincial de la Nacionalidad Achuar del Ecuador* (OINAE, "Interprovincial Organization of the Achuar Nationality of Ecuador"),[5] *Asociación de la Nacionalidad Sápara de la Provincia de Pastaza del Ecuador* (Anazppa, "Association of the Sapara

---

[5] In 1993, https://es.wikipedia.org/wiki/Achuar.

Nationality of the Pastaza Province of Ecuador"),[6] *Organización de la Nacionalidad Shiwiar de Pastaza, Amazonia Ecuatoriana* (Onshipae, "Organization of the Shiwiar Nationality of Pastaza, Ecuadorian Amazonia"),[7] *Nacionalidad Andoa de Pastaza del Ecuador* ("Andoa Nationality of Pastaza of Ecuador", NAPE).[8] Parallel negotiations with the State for the recognition and titling of the space caused conflicts between the organizations. Many women who positioned themselves against oil and other State "development" projects were pushed aside in the assemblies by men, who favored extractivism.

This rise and fall of Indigenous organizations happened under a linearity of women's power displacement. However, various factors promoted the inclusion of women in leadership, progressively and not without difficulties. The inclusion of "women and family" leaders at all levels of organization, from first-degree organizations up to Conaie, was favored by a context in which the emergence of a left-wing, urban feminist movement and the arrival of development cooperation projects with gender equality as a central theme converged in Ecuador. In 1986, the First Conaie Congress of Indigenous Women was held, which triggered the first Women's Leadership, and between 1985 and 1986 women's leaderships were created in Ecuarunari and Confeniae.[9] Women's

---

[6] In 1998, http://www.llacta.org/organiz/anazppa/.

[7] In 1999, http://web.archive.org/web/20081221045326/http://www.codenpe.gov.ec/shiwiar.htm.

[8] In 2003, http://www.codenpe.gob.ec/index.php?option=com_content&view=article&id=130:andoa&catid=84.

[9] In 1980 the *Confederación de Nacionalidades Indígenas de la Amazonía Ecuatoriana* (Confeniae) was created, and in 1986, the *Confederación de Nacionalidades Indígenas del Ecuador* (Conaie), grouping peoples from the coastal, highland and Amazonian regions. See http://www.eurosur.org/FLACSO/mujeres/ecuador/part-6.htm.

leaderships were one of the first political spaces that Indigenous women managed to win within organizational processes, but some female leaders soon began to question their limits: they continued to be assigned logistical and family-related tasks, but were still denied access to decisions considered important, such as those regarding territorial issues. Despite their inferior position and naturalized gender roles, this provided spaces for training new women leaders, as well as the possibility of meeting with other women in national and international congresses.[10]

The Amazonian women who organize themselves must overcome different levels of violence installed in their lives and bodies. The gender role naturalization that burdens them with childcare work, as well as kitchen work and farmwork, implies difficulties for women's organization, requiring them to challenge traditional gender roles. Trying to reconcile women-assigned care work with political responsibilities when they take over leadership is a major source of concern for them. Mobilization efforts involve frequent and prolonged absences from home, often requiring permission from their husbands. In a context such as Pastaza, where 69.6% of women have suffered some kind of male violence (Consejo Nacional para la Igualdad de Género et al., 2014), submission to the husband is often based on violence and mistreatment: if women want to leave the house, violence increases. Women, usually women's leaders, who participate in workshops carrying their *wawas* (small children) are singled out as "patacaliente" (literally "hot-footed", wanderers) for leaving their houses and husbands for a few days. Therefore, when women get

---

[10] https://books.google.com.ec/books?id=wz17VuuWW24C&pg=PA62&lpg=PA62&dq=%22Congreso+de+la+Mujer+Ind%C3%ADgena%22+conaie&source=bl&ots=aZpREDkrhA&sig=S2NovUsWg-NYlpFSYzZk4yKC8Gs&hl=es&sa=X&ved=0ahUKEwjD77aSq__LAhVLqx4KHclhAOAQ6AEIIDAB#v=onepage&q=%22Congreso%20de%20la%20Mujer%20Ind%C3%ADgena%22%20conaie&f=false

organized, they face stigmatization processes that subject their private lives to social questioning.

During the marches that took place from the nineties onwards, women in charge of food and logistics put their bodies at the front lines, facing military devices during revolts; but, with some exceptions, they did not lead in public representation spheres (Sawyer, 2004). Political participation is a tortuous path, since male chauvinism naturalizes domination relationships and male voices as interlocutors in decision-making. Male hegemony in decision-making spaces is encouraged by State and corporate extractive actors, who develop their negotiation strategies with men. Being a female leader implies being strong enough to confront different violence scenarios, both in the intimate territory of the home and in public intimacy within community assemblies and federations, as well as in front of the State and corporate actors.

Throughout the 1990s and 2000s, specifically female organizations were formed in different Indigenous nationalities. However, gender discrimination is still visible in many assemblies, where oratory belongs to men. Some men try to convince them that "they are only useful at home", ridiculing their postponed, ignored, or silenced demands: "In my community they said I couldn't give an opinion because I was young."

The alliance forged with the national and international environmental movement is an important element in their position of strength. Support from Acción Ecológica ("Ecological Action") and the Fundación Pachamama ("Pachamama Foundation"), organizations also formed mainly by women, is strategic in the phases of greatest harassment by the CGC and the State. A lengthy trial before the CIDH, which showed Sarayaku to the world, was finally won in 2012. In recent years, in the Amazonia, women's firmness in the face of extractivism has been generalized with the support of Ecuadorian and international environmental organizations; thus they managed to gain legitimacy to lead struggles for territory defense against the government co-opting a good part of the traditional male leadership.

Bodies coming together: the Amazonian Women's march and the political perspective of the forest

> Our grandparents fought and defended our trees. That is why I have the huacamayo birdfeather, because animals are already in danger of extinction. And whose fault is that? Not our fault, we have been careful, we have conserved the territory. Now what do we want? We want the territory to be respected. We claim for our territory; it used to be immense, now the government is dividing it up more and more. Like a woman, I was born in the Yasuní. They talk so much about the Yasuní now: we Waorani don't agree with exploiting it. Because we are women who have been fighting, taking care of our forest, our rivers, our trees. Taking care of our children... All the old people don't agree. I claim for this as a Waorani woman. We have come to send out this message, so that they won't continue. So that there's an article saying that the Waorani spoke and that we don't agree. They can say that everyone is in favor of exploiting the Yasuní, but we're not. That's why we were born in Yasuní, as a woman. And there must be a consultation.
> Alicia Cawiya (Waorani female leader at the National Assembly, October 2013)

Conceptualization

> The *Kawsak Sacha* is the living space of all forest beings,
> from the most infinitesimal, to the greatest and supreme,
> including the animal, vegetable, mineral, cosmic and human worlds.
> It is a transcendental territorial space, destined to rehabilitate the emotional stages,
> psychological, physical, and spiritual, to restore energy, life
> and balance of the native peoples.
> Declaration of the South Central Amazonian Women, in favor of life (November 2013).

Little by little, alliances between the very diverse women of the Amazonian nationalities were articulated. The old Kichwa women are plant "yachags", expert horticulturists who plant biodiversity, recognize the multiple forest seasons, the creaking of branches after monkeys pass, the signs that indicate a storm is coming, the chonta tree maturation time. Women from different historical genealogies allied themselves to defend their territories because "men have stopped listening to the forests".

As connoisseurs of Amazonian ecosystems, dedicated and methodical observers of the appropriate seasonal cycles to carry seeds and diversify the forest's regeneration elements, they understand the intentions of forest dwellers (Kohn, 2013; Viveiros de Castro, 2013). The *Kawsak Sacha* names the concrete space in which substantial events occur for the community: life regeneration and the hidden violence that fractures and sickens them (Oslender, 2002).

The forest is not a mere resource: it has the intrinsic value of a fabric woven with the collective memory of the ancestral peoples who can keep existing only if the forest survives. For centuries, different family groups have developed ways of reproducing life, myths, stories, world views, and cosmologies that help guide them and reinvent life in complex ecosystems. Indigenous ancestry that supports the legitimate claim to their rights.

The spatial-temporal knowledge of forest regeneration cycles for the material and socio-cultural reproduction of *ayllus* life allows women a particular understanding of the political struggle. Disarming political economy based on GDP calculation means revealing the opacity of post-colonial relations in order to return the enchanted character to the world and recognize the violence of dispossession (Federici, 2004; Viveiros de Castro, 2013). Forest transformation into a natural resource, essential for national development and to feed the global economy's metabolism, hides the forest's social life and implies the reproduction of extractive political violence (Rose, 1993). The fetishism of commodities does not mean believing that they have a spirit, but attributing the character of something vainly interchangeable to them. In contrast, the *Kawsak Sacha* declaration appeals to the inter-subjective relationships with non-human beings that sustain all life. Interpreting the forest's point of view is a necessary exercise in the search for Indigenous and environmental justice: the attempt to defetishize the commodity-nature, to explain the forest regeneration processes, its interconnection for human sustainability.

The peak moment that led to the organization of the women's march in 2013 was related to the 11th Oil Bid Round, which granted concessions for 3.6 million hectares of central-southern Amazonia, at a time when the Amazonia region was also placed at the mercy of the approval for the first megamining concessions. In contrast to the fragmentation of Indigenous leaderships in a context of strong state interference in organizations, women embarked on a path towards unity for joint struggle. Recovering women's leaders' contacts from the 1992 march and workshops with the feminist and environmental movements, as well as visiting the headquarters of various Indigenous women's organizations in Puyo, the female leaders began to prepare for the 2013 women's march. With the women's organizations' meager resources and dwindling support from national and international NGOs, they managed to get a minimum that allowed them to reach Quito.

Although they marched as Confeniae women, they made up a name for the march, the Huangana Colectiva ("Huangana Collective"), referring to the wild pig herds that get organized to go in search of food. The crowd that climbed the hill had an implacable force, even though there were about 200 of them. The women's fight is aimed at politicizing the forest in the face of capitalist dispossession, politicizing the women's union against the violence that dispossesses their territories and also their bodies.

Conclusion. Fractured locus

Not all the nationalities' traditional leaderships looked favorably on this women's rebellion, in particular those leaderships co-opted by oil administrations and State investments. We face a fractured locus, a series of battles fought in the fields of everyday politics and all-powerful national politics, the delegitimization from male leaders who allowed themselves to be convinced, blackmailed, bought off by extractive businessmen. We face a scenario of generalized indolence. Getting organized requires great effort, breaking with geographical isolation between family groups, confronting different scales of personal and public male violence, overcoming inter-ethnic conflicts and violence from both the State and extractive companies.

In an act of political translation, the Women's Declaration[11] became an ethical appeal from those lives dispossessed and

---

[11] While it is true that the *Kawsak Sacha* proposal was created by the Sarayaku people as a whole and agreed on by organizations from all Indigenous nations in center-south Amazonia, it was

expelled from their territories, from the sustainability crisis of their lives (Pérez Orozco, 2012) as Indigenous people. The mobilization of Indigenous women towards Quito is part of a cycle of protests against the national regime, but also of a political culture of uprisings and rebellions that have historically taken place at times of great indignation.[12]

The politics of the young, adult, and elderly female leaders is a demonstration of physical and emotional resistance, strength of character, and political intelligence. In addition, their politics is an embodied warning about the dangers in oil colonization. The female leaders expose the forest's sacred character as a living place: they build a communal sense of their territories' defense in a context of inculcated misogyny, of internalized male violence at all levels. The Women's March favored the emergence of female political spaces in traditionally masculine places.

Their organization as Indigenous women places them in a specific site at the Indigenous nationalities' fight but also at the women's movements' fight, and decrees the forest as a model for life. The female leaders are translators of ontologies: they link overlapping understandings of reality, interpreting forest politics.

---

women who took responsibility for exercising representation of these collective Indigenous demands in front of external actors. This aspect implies a relevant turning point in women's political agenda regarding preceding mobilizations.

[12] Amazonian Indigenous uprisings have been recorded since colonial times. Supported by the Capuchin missions, family groups got organized into associations for land title claims in the late 1960s, starting with the agrarian reform and colonization legislation. In 1990, they took part in the first national Indigenous uprising called by the Conaie; later, some Indigenous leaders were incorporated into the State, which caused divisions among organizations. By then, the spirit of enterprise and risk and the self-regulating values of the market had spread; communications' globalization had energized the financial system (Ong); however, in 1998 the notion of *pluriculturality* was introduced into the Political Constitution.

They propose the fabric of reciprocities between human and non-human beings as a Plan for Living. The female leaders present the elements in the world as political subjects, but also manage to establish multi-scale alliances with ecologists' and feminists' voices. It is a multi-scale discourse among peoples' assemblies, social organizations, NGOs and global networks for environmental justice.

Multiple translations and geopolitical hierarchies succeed in displacing the territorial community struggle locus to the fabric of everyday anti-capitalist social organizations that endorse women as subjects of struggle. The capacity to mobilize resources to defend territories is a strategy of defense and construction of alternatives. The *Kawsak Sacha* is a reflection that displaces the market and the State as axes of desires, of collective needs and their solutions, giving way to an intersubjective utopia of world constitution.

Each society develops an *ethos* of values, a horizon of all that which deserves respect, which is not bought, sold, used, or abused, which is protected by ritual norms and defined as sacred: everything that is the most valuable in our world (Godelier, 2000). The *Kawsak Sacha* declaration is an attempt to return political balance to the forest's social reproduction, to denounce its destruction at the hands of the oil production kingdom, to raise the importance of restituting their souls to the bodies of the world. This small movement of women defenders of the territory positions a "politics of Indigenous women", a language of feminine political legitimization; in addition, it reminds us of the basics: life is produced in interrelationship and it has limits that require care.

There is no Indigenous territory without forest; people are part of the forest, the forest is part of their political organization. The territory is a political concept with porous borders that links history, geography, and body. Defense of the place is defense of existence; the forest has an intrinsic value. Expulsion from territories is a complex problem, which implies the impossibility of material and cultural continuity for these peoples, as well as the deterioration of inter-subjective relations between humans and non-humans. Great extensions of forests are destroyed, soil temperature increases, seasonal cycles of rains and droughts are altered, the beings' location coordinates in the world are disrupted.

Dismantling the Indigenous and the female as immanent qualities of care for nature is fundamental for a just anti-capitalist defense of the territories of peoples and women who inhabit them, as well as for criticism of violence happening at all levels. The aim is to transform the conflictive present into a territory of self-determination. A real plurinationality implies the return of authority to women in political organizations without this implying additional labor for them.

Women promote a utopia in the present, the restitution of their souls and bodies to the objectified world so that human beings can recognize themselves as part of it and can cure their ailments. The right to the forest is the right to (re)produce forests and bodies in territories which are freed from violence. This has meant decomposing liberal notions of rights based on isolated individualities, to move on to considerations of the world in interrelation. The defense of collective territory must take place together with sovereignty and personal autonomy of the bodies (Paredes, 2008).

Bibliography

Coba, Lisset (2017). Plurinacionalidad y sueños en un país petrolero: biografía de tres mujeres amazónicas beligerantes [under revision].

Consejo Nacional para la Igualdad de Género, Ministerio del Interior, Instituto Nacional de Estadísticas y Censos, ONU Mujeres (2014). *La violencia de género contra las mujeres en el Ecuador: análisis de los resultados de la Encuesta Nacional sobre Relaciones Familiares y Violencia de Género contra las Mujeres. Pastaza.* Available at http://www.elmachismoesviolencia.gob.ec/investigaciones/pastaza.pdf

Federici, Silvia (2004). Calibán y la bruja: mujeres, cuerpo y acumulación originaria. Madrid: Traficantes de Sueños.

Gibson, J. and K. Graham (2002). Beyond global vs. local: economic politics outside the binary frame. Forthcoming. In A. Herod and M. Wright (Eds.), *Geographies of Power: Placing Scale.* Oxford: Blackwell Publishers.

Godelier, Maurice (2000). Cuerpo, parentesco y poder: perspectivas antropológicas y críticas. Quito: Abya Yala.

Kohn, Eduardo (2013). *How forests think, towards an anthropology beyond the human*. Berkeley and Los Angeles: University of California Press.

Latour, Bruno (2007). Nunca fuimos modernos, ensayos de antropología simétrica. Mexico: Siglo XXI.

Oslender, U. (2002). Espacio, lugar y movimientos sociales: hacia una "espacialidad de resistencia". *Scripta Nova. Revista electrónica de geografía y ciencias sociales* VI(115). Universidad de Barcelona, 1 June. Available at http://www.ub.es/geocrit/sn/sn-115.htm [ISSN: 1138-9788].

Paredes, Julieta (2008). *Hilando fino, desde el feminismo comunitario*. La Paz: Comunidad Mujeres Creando Comunidad/CEDEC.

Pérez Orozco, Amaia (2012). *Crisis multidimensional y sostenibilidad de la vida*. Available at https://revistas.ucm.es/index.php/INFE/article/viewFile/38603/37328

Rose, Gillian (1993). Feminism and geography: The limits of geographical knowledge. Oxford: Polity Press.

Sawyer, Suzana (2004). Crude Chronicles. Indigenous politics, multinational oil, and neoliberalism in Ecuador. Durham: Duke University Press.

Secretaría Nacional de Planificación y Desarrollo de Ecuador (2013). *Buen Vivir: Plan Nacional 2013-2017 versión resumida*. Quito: Senplades.

Vicariato de Aguarico (s/d). *Ley de Tierras Rurales y Territorios ancestrales. Colonos: producción indígenas ancestralidad*. Available at http://www.vicariatoaguarico.org/index.php/documentos/achacaspi/810-34-colonos-produccion-indigenas-ancestralidad

Viveiros de Castro, Eduardo (2013). *La mirada del jaguar. Introducción al perspectivismo amerindio*. Buenos Aires: Tinta Limón.

Documentation

Conaie-UNFPA (1994). Memorias del Foro de la Mujer Indígena en el Ecuador. Available at https://www.yachana.org/earchivo/conaie/mujers1994.pdf

Declaratoria del *Kawsak sacha*-selva viviente de los territorios de las naciones originarias del centro sur amazónico, entregada a la Asamblea Nacional del Ecuador (2013). Available at http://www.wambraradio.com/declaratoria-del-kawsak-sacha-selva-viviente-entregada-a-la-asamblea-nacional-de-ecuador/

8. The Sepur Zarco Grandmothers and their fight for justice. Summary of a conviction[1]

Ana Lucía Ramazzini

Mujeres Transformando el Mundo ("Women Transforming the World", MTM) / Asociación de Mujeres para Estudios Feministas ("Women's Association for Feminist Studies", AMEF)

"We do not want what we went through to be forgotten."
"We do not want the historical struggle we put up to be forgotten."
"We want to let the new generation know what happened."
"... We want them to know, so that there will be no more violence against women."
"Everything will be written."
Abuelas de Sepur Zarco, Sepur Zarco Grandmothers.

Fifteen Mayan Q'eqchi' women, impoverished peasants and victims of sexual violence, sexual slavery and domestic slavery between 1982 and 1988, during the *Conflicto Armado Interno* (CAI, "Internal Armed Conflict") in the community of Sepur Zarco (El Estor, Izabal, Guatemala), had a long road ahead that would allow them to break the silence and get justice. After waiting for more than thirty years, in 2016 the trial was held against two of the accused: Lieutenant Colonel Esteelmer Francisco Reyes Girón, appointed to the Sepur Zarco Military Detachment,[2] and Heriberto Valdez Asig, military commissioner and municipal police officer.

On February 26 of that year, the First Court of Criminal Judgment, Drug Trafficking and Crimes against the Environment

---

[1] This article summarizes the terms of the conviction after the Sepur Zarco case and the reports produced by expert witnesses.

[2] Men from the different communities around Sepur Zarco were forced to build the military detachment in August 1982. The post remained for six years, until 1988, and then was dismantled. Many of the detachments in the region were built on private farms by men from the villages.

handed down a conviction sentence to the defendants: thirty years' non-commutable imprisonment, for having committed crimes against the duties of humanity in the forms of rape, sexual servitude, and domestic servitude, as well as humiliating and degrading treatment, as described in Guatemalan law. The crimes of murder of three women were also recognized: Dominga Coc and her two daughters (Anita, one year old, and Hermelinda, four years old), and the forced disappearance of seven men, husbands to seven of the surviving women, who had initiated applications to title land ownership in the area; all were deprived of their freedom without a competent judge's order, in clearly illegal detentions: actions which were witnessed by their cohabitants.[3] In addition, the Court recognized as victims[4] eleven Q'eqchi' women, seven disappeared men, three murdered women, the relatives of all of them, and the community of Sepur Zarco: 1. Felisa Cuc; 2. Vicenta Col Pop; 3. Candelaria Maas Sacul; 4. Manuela Bá; 5. Rosa Tiul; 6. Cecilia Caal; 7. María Bá Caal; 8. Carmen Xol Ical; 9. Demecia Yat; 10. Margarita Chub Choc; 11. Magdalena Pop; 12. Dominga Coc; 13. her daughters, Anita and Hermelinda.

The Sepur Zarco case sets an important precedent in Guatemala, because a national court tried and sentenced rape, sexual servitude and domestic servitude occurred during the CAI as crimes against the duties of humanity, which are crimes of

---

[3] In his role as an authority, Esteelmer Francisco Reyes Girón was found guilty of the murder of three women, and was sentenced to 30 years of imprisonment for each murder: that is, 90 years of imprisonment, which adds to the sentence for crimes against humanity to make a total of 120 years of incommutable imprisonment. Heriberto Valdez Asig was held responsible for the crime of forced disappearance, for which the Court sentenced him to 30 years imprisonment for each of the seven forced disappearances: a total of 210 years which, together with the 30-year-sentence imposed for crimes against the duties of humanity, bring it to a total of 240 years of incommutable imprisonment.

[4] We use the notion of "victim" as a legal term.

international importance. The violence exerted on the bodies of those who are now *Abuelas de Sepur Zarco* was part of a systematic plan carried out by the Guatemalan Army, which in turn was part of the military counter-insurgency strategy. The desecration of their bodies and the destruction of the position of Indigenous women was a war objective linked to the context of their husbands' land claims. The Sepur Zarco case is an account of the violence of a racist colonial patriarchal state against the bodies who have been historically most oppressed. But it is also a case that shows the constant struggle of these Q'eqchi' women for a dignified and transformative justice. "... I don't want a repetition of the violence as it happened in the war; everything we told is the truth, it was real and we lived it with our bodies" (Grandmother Antonia).

Guilty verdict, expert witness reports and the relationship between bodies and territories

Throughout the trial of the Sepur Zarco case, various testimonies and expert witness reports were presented that demonstrated that, in the Sepur Zarco Military Detachment, women were sexually and domestically enslaved, that sexual violence and inhumane, cruel and humiliating treatment were exerted on them, and that these acts were repeatedly executed. The facts recognized in the Verdict are the following:

- The women attended the detachment several days a week to cook and wash clothes for the soldiers and officers of the Guatemalan Army, with soap that the women themselves bought, without receiving any payment, and suffering sexual violations by several soldiers of the Guatemalan Army, every day that they completed the shift imposed during the years 1982 to 1983.
- Because their husbands had been captured and disappeared, their homes burned, their property destroyed, their crops razed, and their domestic animals killed, all by members of the Guatemalan Army, military commissioners and civilian self-defense patrols, some women were forced to move near the Sepur Zarco Military Detachment, and

- their status as "single women" was abused, placing them in a vulnerable situation. This place, where they resided with their minor children, consisted of improvised housing made of nylon pieces.
- When they were ordered not to work the "shift" any longer in the military compound described above, they were forced to carry tortillas made from their own corn, for approximately six years. Even when they did not have enough to eat for themselves and their children, they complied with the orders, without receiving any payment, until the soldiers and officers of the Guatemalan Army withdrew from the Sepur Zarco community.
- Guatemalan Army soldiers used rape, sexual slavery and torture as a "weapon of war", since these crimes were perpetrated in a repetitive and prolonged manner when women were under the control of members of the Guatemalan Army, in order to consolidate the results of their military operations within the framework of the counter-insurgency strategy.

> They were not paid to go to wash and cook. As a consequence of the rapes she suffered from hemorrhages. When she went to the Detachment her children stayed there, because she made a house out of nylon. [...] When she went back home, she prepared tortillas for the Detachment at home and sent them out. It was difficult for her to send the tortillas. They would send tortillas in the morning, at noon, and in the afternoon, she used to make an arroba (testimony).

The eighteen expert witness reports presented at the trial in the Sepur Zarco case had probative value on the part of the Court: Anthropological Gender Report, Rita Laura Segato; Forensic Psychiatric Report, Karen Denisse Peña Juárez; Military Report, Prudencio García and Martínez de Murguía; Report on International Standards of Credibility in Cases of Human Rights Violations, Arsenio García Cores; Psychosocial Report, Mónica Esmeralda Pinzón González; Report on Gender Crimes during the Armed Conflict in Guatemala, Paloma Soria Montañez; Cultural Report, Irma Alicia Velásquez Nimatuj; Anthropological-Linguistic Report, Mayra Nineth Barrios Torres; Sociological Military Report,

Héctor Roberto Rosada Granados; Historical-Registral Report, Juan Carlos Peláez Villalobos; Forensic Architecture Report, Gabriela Mendoza Mejía; Economic Report, Rafael Eduardo Bran Paz; Report on Reparations with a Gender Perspective, Dosia Calderón Maydon; Report on Racism and Rape of Women as a Weapon of War, Marta Elena Casaús; Ballistic Report, Helder Romelio Ajquiy Carrillo and Josué Benjamín López León; Photographic Report, Klaus Wilhelm Hengstenberg Morales, Luis Renato Mauricio Figueroa and Oskar Eduardo Aragón de Paz; two Forensic Anthropology Reports, FAFG multidisciplinary team: Daniel Alonzo Jiménez Gaytán, Mynor Adán Silvestre Aroche, Jaime Enrique Ruiz, Juan Carlos Gatica Pérez, Renaldo Leonel Acevedo Álvarez, Jorge Luis Romero de Paz, Oscar Ariel Ixpatá.

The verdict consists of 512 pages; a summary based on the analysis of the expert reports shows excessive violence against women's bodies as part of the appropriation of the territories.

The Sociological Military Report, by Héctor Rosada, revealed that the rape of women and their domestic and sexual slavery occurred within a situation of armed conflict in Guatemala, in the context of land claims in the area of Sepur Zarco, which is part of the ancestral territory of the Mayan Q'eqchi' people. This report states that the farmers in the region carried out actions that favored the denunciation to the military commissioners, so that people who were considered to be working for the guerrillas were persecuted. The motive was the fear spread in the landowning elite, who felt threatened by the request for land. Thus, people were regarded as alleged internal enemies and denounced to the authorities in the military detachments, which implied their murder. This expert report affirmed that, at the time of events, there was in Guatemala a Counterinsurgent Military State.

In connection to this, the Historical-Registral Report by Juan Carlos Peláez showed that the sexual violence and inhumane treatment suffered by women and men of the Mayan Q'eqchi' people of the Polochic Valley were consistent with the execution of a systematic plan of institutional state violence that sought to protect the interests of property owners with anomalous registry entries that would be reviewed. The report pointed out the existence of a relationship between land dispossession and the practice of slavery, degrading treatment and rape of women.

> The soldiers told her that she should not resist because they were in charge; they had already taken her husband, and besides they used to put a gun to her chest so that she would not say anything, that is why she was very afraid (testimony).

The Cultural Report by Irma Alicia Velasquez agreed that, beneath the violent deaths and forced disappearances, lies the land ownership issue. When the forced disappearances took place, the population was left without men; and the women, considered "alone" from the point of view of a patriarchal structure, were left in a situation of vulnerability.

In this same report, it was stated that the cruelty and fury in the sexual violence experienced by the Q'eqchi' women of Sepur Zarco cannot be understood without considering that they lived within the framework of a State that has exercised and reproduced a structural racism that still continues. Structural racism is historical; it is rooted in structures, institutions and the State, as well as in ideological frameworks. It has been fundamental for the consolidation of the country, working to control and exploit Indigenous peoples, and to make Indigenous women occupy the bottom step in the social pyramid and racial structure because, in the imaginary of the Criollo, the Ladino, the landowner, and the high military commands, they are assumed to be inferior and worthless human beings, only useful for servitude. The sexual violations experienced at Sepur Zarco are part of the continuum of crimes that have never been judged or punished in the history of Guatemala.

Along the same lines, Marta Elena Casaús argued in the Expert Report on Racism and the Rape of Women as a Weapon of War that racism in its diverse expressions, practices, manifestations and logics is a structural historical factor that has worked and still works as one of the main mechanisms of oppression, exploitation and, mainly, as the best justification for a system of domination. The State plays an important role in the formation of a racist, patriarchal, and authoritarian model of Nation. This report showed that, during the CAI in Guatemala, State agents employed violent practices such as sexual slavery, forced domestic labor and rape against Indigenous women. The rape of women reached its highest level and took place especially in militarized spaces such as military detachments. Moreover, such violence and rapes became a racist weapon against the Indigenous population in general and against Indigenous women in particular, not only because they were women, but because they were Indigenous women.

The Expert Report on Racism stated that the use of sexual violence during the CAI was due to four reasons: a) to physically and morally eliminate women considered to be internal enemies or social dangers; b) to physically and morally punish women considered to be loved ones of the internal enemy; c) to punish, through them, men considered to be the internal enemy; and d) to produce, as an aim towards women, guilt and shame in their bodies.

The Anthropological Gender Report, by Rita Laura Segato, showed that, from the victims' point of view, domestic and sexual slavery are inseparably linked. They are both part of the productive-reproductive microcosm in a family and community network that has marriage as its nuclear structure. From their perspective, women contribute to productive work through domestic labor; and to reproductive work, through sexual service. Nourishment, care and sexuality are perceived as strongly intertwined within the network of obligatory reciprocities that articulates the life of community members. Domestic slavery and sexual slavery affect this community bond and collective interest. Thus, one of the strategic objectives of the internal war was the degradation of productive and reproductive relationships.

The expert explained that, when Q'eqchi' women narrate their sexual and domestic subjugation, they all express the same anguish. For them, the slavery of their bodies was as strong as that of their labor: the food they were forced to take away from their families to give to the military, and the soap with which they had to wash their uniforms. They were forced to remove food from their homes and leave their children unfed to bring the food to the detachment.

> every three days I went to the Detachment, it was like doing the same patrol that the men did. She left her children at home, suffering from hunger (testimony).

This report also explained that women were forced to divert the sexual availability due to their husbands, as designated recipients by their community norms, in order to grant this access to the same troop who was responsible for their disappearances. In addition, the joint sexual access against the women generated a strong pact of male fraternity among the troop members.

> [...] they told the women that they were not alone anymore, that it was better for them to go to the Detachment, that they should go and look after the soldiers because they no longer had husbands, but now the soldiers would be their husbands (testimony).

The refusal of the productive and reproductive capacity of women to their husbands and their communities was a mortal blow to the female and maternal position within Q'eqchi' Mayan society; specifically, from the ancestral pattern of their value and their contribution to the continuity of their people. It meant social death and, in some cases, it translated into illness and physical death.

> As a result of the rapes she suffered from hemorrhages, her youngest son was four years old but still breastfeeding; but she did have heavy hemorrhages (testimony).

In this way, the expert pointed out, the damage to humanity was twofold: the woman was uprooted from her collective environment, and this environment was, in turn, severely damaged. This is not only the victim's suffering, as a private individual, but also the damage caused to all her community links, as she was uprooted from her relationship of marital reciprocity and her delivery of sexual and domestic services was diverted to her captors.

In this sense, the Expert Report on Racism also agreed that another way of establishing rape as a weapon of war against women was to subject them to forced domestic work, which was generally accompanied by sexual slavery of girls and women. These practices constitute a form of submission and control over women who are forced to contribute their relations of production-reproduction. If this happens under conditions of forced and massive abduction, forced domestic work and sexual slavery of Indigenous women not only have repercussions in the individual sphere of their lives, but they also affect the entire community's social life, since the community is being dispossessed of the labor force that is indispensable for life reproduction. Indigenous women were used not only as prisoners of war, but also as a force whose labor was lucrative for military domination.

In turn, the Anthropological-Linguistic Report, produced by Mayra Nineth Barrios, revealed that rape in q'eqchi' can be said in several ways: Muxuc; Xexmuxlin-yu'am; Xi ne'xchapy, Xi nexxbatz'unle'; numsink, jot'oky maakob'k. The term most often used by the victims was Muxuc. This term has deep connotations within the Q'eqchi' cosmogony. It means that the woman was *desecrated, pierced through, soiled.* Consequently, as the report pointed out, she was no longer a woman worthy of her community, of remarriage; she was a woman who lost respect for herself, for her community and from her community. Her social and spiritual world was destroyed, broken up in all areas of her life.

> She felt a sort of rejection, they said they were the soldiers' lovers or toys (testimony).

Likewise, the Anthropological Gender Report remarked that, for Q'eqchi' women, desecration means destruction in their dignity, in their sacredness; the sacredness of their own capacity and continuity of lineage, the sacredness of their own capacity to give continuity to their people. When their bodies were desecrated, this relationship was broken and interrupted. They themselves declared that they became exiles even though they continued to live within the same space of the community: that is, social death.

This report states that the desecration of their bodies resulted in the moral and physical destruction of the community, because the woman's body represents the social body. In addition, the expert Rita Segato emphasized that in Guatemala there was a *contemporary war* in which the desecration of women's bodies was also a way of preventing them from giving continuity to their people. The people were torn apart by the transmission of the fear that produced the internal exile of the women, stigmatized in their own community.

Further in this report, it was explained that a feature of contemporary wars is no longer the rape of women as spoils of war, or their annexation as a part of conquered territory, but their desecration or moral and physical destruction by sexual means to affect the dignity of the subjugated people. Woman's body symbolizes the social body; and domination over it, power over a territory. The expert argued that this no longer means collateral damage. Today, what can be observed is destruction, the direct attack on that body. Sexual assault was a strategic motive for war. The State used woman's body as a way to morally destroy its enemy, to destroy the community's articulation. Through the sexual violations of women, the exercise of power over the people was demonstrated.

> It was four men who sexually abused her. The soldiers were armed. They grabbed her, threw her down and didn't say anything to her. She indicated that her house was surrounded by soldiers. She said that, when they raped her, she was pregnant and due only a few days later (testimony).

Rita Laura Segato argued that the destruction of the Indigenous woman's position was a war objective. This action was intended to destabilize social relations, reciprocity, and trust in social members. The victimization of women was part of a set of actions of war that occurred in obedience to higher military orders and, therefore, of sexual domination to which women were subjected. Sexual violations did not occur in the form of spontaneous rapes, resulting from the "loss of control or disarray in the troops". They were routine and not isolated acts by undisciplined soldiers, which is demonstrated by the fact that they injected women so that they would not become pregnant.

The Report on Racism stated that the systematic use of contraceptive methods engraved in women's memories and bodies the imposed message of "no reproduction of the group". And it confirmed that the acts of cruelty and brutality applied by the State, military leadership, commissioners and landowners against the

Indigenous communities surrounding the Sepur Zarco detachment were not isolated acts of violence or excesses committed by the troops, but rather followed a behavior pattern of sexual violence and sexual slavery of women that was repeated in almost all cases, and responded to a counter-insurgency policy that was designed, planned and executed by the Military High Command, with involvement from all the intermediate bodies and patrols, with the aim of destroying the ethnic community.

> She stated that they gave the women injections; they wanted the women not to get pregnant. They told the women that the government had sent them and that they were in their hands (testimony).

Rape, sexual slavery and domestic slavery were a strategic war objective. Rita Laura Segato, in charge of the Anthropological Gender Report, argued that in Sepur Zarco there was a "femigenocide". For her part, Marta Elena Casaús, Expert Witness on Racism, pointed out that, although in this trial the defendants were not accused of feminicide, it is necessary to point out the systematic and massive use of sexual violation with the political intention of subduing and massacring women, just because they were women, related to their being Mayan and poor, a population that was mostly considered an "internal enemy". For the expert, this shows the relationship between the racist State, feminicide and sexual violation as crimes of war or against duties to humanity. Through the Cultural, Racism and Anthropological Gender Reports, it was possible to establish the oppression and disproportionality of the force used against the women of Sepur Zarco.

The Cultural Report explained that the systematic sexual violations and servitude produced cultural breaks in the communities; that is, they damaged the victims themselves and their family nucleus, but also affected the entire community, preventing them from recovering their culture and returning to a normal life. These cultural breaks modified or destroyed communities, extended families, systems of organization and authority, property, production, construction and reproduction of solidarity, medical, and spiritual knowledge.

> She said that what happened to her really hurts; all that happened to her because she was a woman. She was 22 years old when all that happened to her. When that happened to her, people hated her and mistreated her, saying, "Soldiers rape you all the time". They said she smelled bad (testimony).

The Psychiatric Forensic Report, by Karen Denisse Peña, showed that the victims' submission to a methodical and systematic violence caused the tear in their social fabric. Furthermore, this is proved by the Psychosocial Report produced by Mónica Pinzón, since the Indigenous women victims and their communities could no longer carry out their ceremonies for celebrations or events such as births, weddings, illnesses or deaths, nor request permission from Mother Earth to sow or harvest. Therefore, one of the strongest consequences of this tear in the social fabric is the feeling of defeat and despair, since it was not only material goods that were destroyed, but also all the social links and references that generated community cohesion.

> A week after giving birth to her son, she decided to leave; and it was in the mountains where she found other neighbors. She took her eight children with her, but three of them died in the mountain, and one more died in the community. She does not remember how old each of her children was, only that the eldest was 9 years old and the youngest one, one week old. All they ate was fruits from the trees. [...] She was in the mountains for six years. [...] Her children died of cold and hunger because it was raining very hard, and because they didn't find any food (testimony).

Since then, they have suffered physical discomfort, weakness, psychological suffering and "frights", nightmares, great anxiety, and are unable to dissociate themselves from the suffering of what they went through. Clinically, they present post-traumatic stress.

> The war left me with a stomach ache and my heart is affected. I live in fear and anything that bursts or breaks frightens me (testimony).

The Psychosocial Report showed the way in which their quality of life was impaired, their integrity was damaged, and the deprivation of essential aspects and values for the life of a human being was inflicted on them. The life project of the 15 women was seriously damaged, causing insecurity, disorientation, grief and lack of control over their own lives, preventing the realization of their dreams and desires until today.

The Expert Report on Racism noted that many of the survivors refer to this period as a time that "marked my life", "destroyed my marriage and my family", and "changed my life forever".

> Before they went to the mountains, they and their children were fine; when they went to the mountains, their children began to suffer from diseases and so began to die [...] She returned without any of her children [...] she returned with nothing [...] It was many years, it was six years that she was in the mountains, when she returned her house no longer existed, she had domestic animals, there was nothing left... (testimony).

The Cultural Report argued that in Sepur Zarco there are two clearly identifiable losses that are impossible to separate: human loss and cultural loss. Cultural loss includes social, spiritual and material elements. Specifically, among the spiritual cultural elements is the loss implied by being unable to practice the religion with which each of the victims identified herself, and also the loss of self-worth and self-esteem. As part of the social losses, it was noted that the retention and disappearance of their husbands meant the breakdown of the family hierarchy with which the community functioned. It meant a loss of income, leadership, companionship, and support.

> Once she got her courage up, she went to complain to the lieutenant and the response he gave her was, "Maybe you wanted it too, you got them used to it", which she finds painful, because it was an animal treatment since her husband was not there (testimony).

Material losses, such as the house, animals, supplies, crops, clothing, were also a cultural loss, because these goods were part of the social, economic and coexistence practices within their communities.

> When she was raped, she was three months pregnant. As a result, she suffered from hemorrhages and had a miscarriage on the third day. She had to leave the house where she lived with her husband. She said she only saw the smoke from her house as it was burning. She was not given time to take anything away, there were her chickens and pigs. It was the soldiers who burned her house and killed her husband (testimony).

Irma Alicia Velásquez Nimatuj, in charge of this expert report, also emphasized that with these events there was a loss in the transmission of universal knowledge such as weaving, which was a fundamental loss in the communities. Their skills were limited and they could no longer transmit and practice their culture. Not only were people killed, but a fundamental part of the Q'eqchi' culture was destroyed. There was a cultural loss that goes beyond Sepur Zarco: there was a cultural loss for the country.

The Anthropological Gender Report noted that women are a symbol of power in the community, since they are the life bearers, which explains their elimination. That is to say, when the damage to the women of Sepur Zarco occurred, humanity was also damaged; not only in the victims' suffering, but also in the injury to the entire humanitarian bond.

The leading role of the Sepur Zarco women and the future

The women of Sepur Zarco were protagonists along the path to justice. They were accompanied along this path by several organizations. In 2009, the Equipo de Estudios Comunitarios y Acción Psicosocial (ECAP, "Community Studies and Psychosocial Action Team"), the Unión Nacional de Mujeres Guatemaltecas (UNAMG, "National Union of Guatemalan Women") and Mujeres Transformando el Mundo (MTM, "Women Transforming the World"), formed the Alianza Rompiendo el Silencio y la Impunidad ("Alliance Breaking the Silence and Impunity"). In 2011, UNAMG and MTM constituted themselves as plaintiffs in the process and, in 2014, the women survivors also constituted themselves as *adhesive plaintiffs*, participating in all phases of the process, organizing themselves into the Jalok 'U Collective, which in Q'eqchi' language means "transformation or change".

The Court that presided over the trial unanimously declared the petition for dignified and transformative reparations requested by Abuelas de Sepur Zarco to be successful. This figure implies generating the conditions so that the same structural situation of violence and discrimination is not repeated. Among the measures for dignified and transformative reparation are: the installation of a bilingual high school that guarantees the right to education for girls, adolescents, and women; the granting of scholarships; the incorporation of the case of the Sepur Zarco women into school texts; the translation of the Verdict into different languages; the installation of a health center in the community; and the continuation of the land titling process initiated by their husbands.

They express that surely they will not see much of this anymore, because of their age, but they want to make sure that their children, grandchildren, boys and girls are guaranteed these measures by the State, because they are convinced that this will prevent a repetition of the conditions of vulnerability that they experienced: "My message is above all the fight I made, which is for those who are coming. It is not only for my children and grandchildren, but for everyone, that is what I have fought for. My person ends, but the fight I started does not end" (Abuela Rosa).

In the process of demanding justice, the grandmothers of Sepur Zarco faced the death of one of the youngest group members, Magdalena Pop, four months after she gave her testimony at an anticipated evidence hearing in a national court. Magdalena's words still resonate with them: "I've done my part, now it's your turn to follow the path of justice".

The Court

Tribunal Primero de Sentencia Penal, Narcoactividad y Delitos contra el Ambiente (First Court of Criminal Sentence, Drug Trafficking and Crimes against the Environment): presiding judge: Dr. Iris Yassmin Barrios Aguilar; vocal judge: Patricia Isabel Bustamante García; vocal judge: Gervi Hionardo Sical Guerra; secretary: lawyer Sonia Elizabeth Paniagua Ocampo. Prosecutors of the Public Ministry: Hilda Elizabeth Pineda García, Carmen Lucrecia Morales Ruiz, Paula Yesenia Herrarte Chajón. MTM Legal Team: Paula Marcela Barrios Paiz, Jennifer Marinez Bravo Flores, Esteban Emanuel Celada Flores, Enma Rubí Hernández Castro, Norma Lissette Herrera Mijangos, Wilson Camacho. Adhesive Plaintiffs: JALOK'U Collective (CJU), legal representative: Demecia Yat de Xol;

MUJERES TRANSFORMANDO EL MUNDO / ASOCIACIÓN DE MUJERES PARA ESTUDIOS FEMINISTAS

Asociación Mujeres Transformando El Mundo (MTM), legal representative and president: Paula Marcela Barrios Paiz; Asociación Unión Nacional de Mujeres Guatemaltecas (UNAMG), legal representative and president: Ada Iveth Valenzuela López. Court translators: Carolina Yaxcal and Arturo Haroldo Chub Ical.

Source

Verdict in the Case of Sepur Zarco. Ruling C-01076-2012-00021 Of. 2°.

PART 2: METHODOLOGICAL APPLICATIONS AND PROPOSALS

9. From the body: Art, politics and transformation. Sharing *Magdalenas Uruguay-Teatro de las Oprimidas*

Lorena Rodríguez Lezica, Norina Torres Paz, Cecilia Durán Jaurena, Agustina Araujo, Noe Spinillo, Lucía Baffigo, Gabriela Núñes de Moraes[1]

In these times of struggle against pain and anger, but also times of joyous rebellion, we embrace the collective need to meet, to give ourselves the space of a circle full of experiences and knowledge. Here we share our fabric woven by creative, sustained, contained women, our effort for sorority among ourselves and in the mutual construction with others.

Magdalenas Uruguay[2] is a collective of ten female companions of diverse ages, coming from different neighborhoods, some of us migrants from the interior of the country. We each come from our different life paths, occupations and experiences, working with the method of the Theater of the Oppressed and specifically through the Laboratorio Magdalena (Magdalena Laboratory) since May 2012.

Magdalenas is an international movement within the methodological proposal of the Theater of the Oppressed, which works specifically on the oppression of women in our patriarchal societies. It is a proposal promoted, created and systematized in 2010 by the theater directors and multipliers of this methodology Bárbara Santos and Alessandra Vannucci. This Laboratory[3] has as

---

[1] Colectivo Magdalenas Uruguay-Teatro de las oprimidas.

[2] Available at https://www.facebook.com/magdalenasuruguay/

[3] By Laboratory we mean a process of research and artistic creation. It is not a workshop that is multiplied without

its starting point the research on women's bodies, bodies that have been kept enclosed, protected and censored by male power for centuries, and that today, in contrast, play a central role in the media. In the Laboratory we explore female bodies, naked bodies, exhibited for the enjoyment of others on magazine pages and in all media, bodies used to feed the consumer culture of a capitalist market.[4]

Some of us have been members in this group of women from the beginning, since the multiplication of the Laboratory in Montevideo in early 2012, and others have joined us since then. The group was formed as a collective once the methodology had been appropriated by all members and as we politicized our work, permanently seeking and testing horizontality and another way of finding ourselves, which we call *sororal circularity*. Some members decided to leave, as well, and this has been part of a painful learning process in addressing the differences between us.

For a long time we prioritized sharing our collective creations, Teatro Foro (Forum Theatre)[5] plays, with unions, high schools, neighborhood, social and popular organizations, as well as with women in prison, and multiplying the Laboratory with others, in different parts of the country and in Montevideo. The first play deals with different forms of violence within a couple, and the

---

modifications over and over again, but a modifiable proposal of continuous research for the design of exercises and games that allow us a greater possibility for creation and enrichment.

[4] Available at http://kuringa-barbarasantos.blogspot.com.uy/2010/08/laboratorio-magdalena-teatro-de-las.html

[5] Teatro Foro (Forum Theater) is a play based on real events, where a female oppressed and her (male or female) oppressors come into conflict in a clear and objective way, in defense of their desires and interests. In this confrontation, the female oppressed fails, and the audience is invited by the *Kuringa* to enter the stage, to substitute the oppressed protagonist and look for alternatives to the staged problem.

second with sexual harassment and male violence in the labor and union environments. Several of the members whose stories were central to the creation of these works decided to leave, and new ones joined the collective. Over time, we put into words the need to give closure to the presentation of these plays, since many did not feel these stories were theirs. We shared the need to create something new. At the same time, the dynamics of weekly meetings made the use of words a priority and that began to wear us down. This is why some time ago we decided to prioritize turning our gaze, our thinking and our feeling "inwards", in our collective need to intensely work again from the body, its memory, its sensitivity, its emotions.

An awakening

Most of us who came to Magdalenas didn't know what it was all about; a few of us knew a little about the existence of the *theater of the oppressed*, but not in this form. What was this *theater of the female oppressed*? Magdalenas was an awakening for many of us, a (re)discovery, an act of (re)cognition of our bodies and our histories. Little by little, that initial curiosity turned into an individual and also a collective search:

> [...] the day I dropped by the Laboratory, I knew about the Theater of the Oppressed, but I didn't really know what Magdalenas was about, just that it was something specific to women and something about gender issues. And as I gave in to the dynamics of that type of specific games, I felt how from the body I was heading towards certain searches, a search for my womanhood, a backwards search for women, and a search for my female peers. And then, as it became more complex, it was like an awakening. If something was clear to me before, it was either very basic, or common sense, or anger, or things that happened to me which I didn't understand. It kind of made me wake up, an awareness of gender construction and consciousness of my being in the world and specific things that I wanted to change about my being a woman. I took on that outlook from that day. And now it's like a monster, now you feel that it doesn't stop.

Some of us approached it seeking to express ourselves through art, enthusiastic about doing theater; others, in search of a political tool, or from the need to think of ourselves together with others.

> [...] undoubtedly I arrived without knowing what this Theater of the Oppressed was about, I didn't bring any theoretical or university background, just a housewife with all her issues, two children, a lot of things. And when I went, I said, "What's this?" And I stayed. Because when they explained to me what it was, I didn't understand. But I stayed anyway. I liked what I saw. I think the first thing was the people, I fit in well there.
>
> [...] I was coming from a separation, leaving behind an extended puerperium, carrying around many things in my body. So, I don't know whether my need was to find the theater of the female oppressed, but to think of myself as a woman and with other women.
>
> I approached it [...] in search of a tool for activism. I wasn't thinking about exploring myself at all. And I thought, "This will be a tool that will allow me to work with other groups, collectives, organizations, not to work on myself." And, in fact, that isn't so far back in time, it's still in me. And it keeps adding to that armor that I put on, to that shield that I create around me so that I don't work on myself from my body. It's still hard. That workshop on Theater of the Oppressed called for activists, social educators, people who worked with neighborhood groups, etc., and I found myself working on myself, starting on a path to recognize my own oppressions.

Recognizing oppressions on our female selves has not been an easy path. Most of us did not recognize ourselves as oppressed. Violence was something we could identify in others and hardly ever in ourselves. Our conception of violence in many cases was reduced to the most visible forms of physical aggression.

> When we were asked "do you have any oppression", I said "I don't". Because I had understood that the oppression was physical. I understood beating, domestic violence, I didn't understand the rest. And I started to follow the process and it wasn't until we did a cartography[6] recently that my drawing was full of garbage and I thought, "Either I've moved forward, or that was wrong." So, lucky me, because I recognize them; and by recognizing them, you know how you can face them, and you can handle them. So along that path, I have achieved something.
>
> When I started to do theater of the oppressed, I also thought that I didn't have oppressions and the first one who told me "Hm, you are a woman:

---

[6] An adaptation of the body-territory mapping in the context of the course "Women, social movements and feminisms", School of Psychology, 2017. Available at https://psico.edu.uy/ensenanza/formacion-permanente/curso/mujeres-movimientos-sociales-y-feminismos-1

because of your physique and whatever else, you have millions" was Boal. And then I thought: "Well, maybe..."
During the exercises in which we had to close our eyes, I couldn't do any of them without feeling huge discomfort. I tried to walk with my eyes closed and I tensed my body, frowned, and put my hands in front of me as if to protect myself, and I couldn't do it. Until at one point I went into a corner and started crying, and I couldn't stop. And several years went by before I could do that kind of exercise; it was only at Magdalenas that I was able to "open my eyes" *(laughs)*. I mean, close my eyes. And well, also "open my eyes", in that other way, in that awakening. And if it was so hard for me, it was because it's an exercise of trust in others, but also trust in yourself. Because, when you close your eyes, what you see is yourself, your experiences, and it's really hard to do that.

Through the different games and exercises that are part of the methodology, and in the constant exercise of looking at ourselves, we recognized those oppressions, exploring ourselves as women, mirroring each other, and the body taking on a leading role in the creation and recreation of ourselves.

With the theater of the oppressed itself, it meant to find myself inside a body that I hated, because that's what it is, a body that I hated; and I thought that the responsibility of hating that body was mine. This journey has made me notice the structure that not only makes me hate my body, but that we all at some point hate the body we live in; and that is a structural issue in this culture, not feeling comfortable in your own skin, in your own experience, and not finding yourself, not finding yourself between what you feel and what you should be. And for me the theater of the oppressed people, especially Magdalenas, has been a journey: it has transformed me in body and soul, so I can experience my sexuality, from my tastes, my desires, many things. I have gone from denying myself a lot, from my body, from my experience, to accepting myself and being a happier person, which is the main thing.

I remember one of the first questions in the Laboratory, which will stay with me for the rest of my life: "What are your oppressions?" And I replied: "Right now, I have none" (laughs). And from then on, with the point of view of my companions, I was able to start making my body the protagonist, and even up to the point of changing my diet, and the way of thinking my body as a woman, and exploring it and taking it to the game inside Magdalenas to be able to complement myself and mirror myself in others.

The body's memory

The exercise of "las ancestrales" (the ancestral females) is one of the most powerful exercises of the Laboratory, through which we activate corporal, emotional and sensitive memories of our daily life and our ancestral history.

> When investigating our *ancestrales*, we follow the corporal path of the mother and the grandmother, and so on until the most distant one. [...] We switch the day, the hour and the century. We continue to work on the imaginary body of our ancestral women as well as on our own, yesterday as today. [...] We continue to investigate the bodies of those women who are remembered, known and/or imagined, creating conditions so that they can find themselves in a space of trust and confidence in the unutterable, even if only to see themselves in an imaginary mirror.[7]

The exercise of *las ancestrales* activates the body's memory, it invokes those other women who are part of our history. We revive their pains, their fears, their secrets; we bring them to our daily life, we recognize them in our own pains and fears to be able to transform them, and we recognize them in our more hidden secrets, to unveil them.

> [...] I've done *las ancestrales* many times, and I sort of recognized myself in my mother, and began to realize how many things I reject even today, and where they came from.
> [...] it was very hard for me, the first time I did it. I remember that I stood still. I really couldn't, because that meant going to the mother, and my mother's mother and... it was tough. [...] it took a lot of effort. I think I stopped at the grandmother, after that I couldn't imagine or embody anything else.

First, starting from body movement, women are brought into contact with the activities that they go through every day in their daily lives, with who we are, through what we do, territorially located in the region of the world where we were born or where we live today. Then, we invite them to make contact with the tasks and movements that accompanied our female ancestors: one by one we recognize the body-movement and place of origin of our mother, grandmother, great-grandmother... until we reach *the first woman* who inhabited our land. This exercise closes by forming a tree of

---

[7] Bárbara Santos, 2010. Available at http://kuringa-barbarasantos.blogspot.com.uy/2010/08/laboratorio-magdalena-teatro-de-las.html

women: the amalgamated bodies become the trunk, our legs become the roots that connect with the earth, earth that has nourished us from the most ancient of our ancestral women, our arms on the branches, our fingers on the leaves, and each one rests, holds and is held by the others. The tree is the total image of what we are, where we come from and where we want to go.

We live this exercise as a ritual, a ritual that is lived in different ways each time, and that empowers and challenges us in each Laboratory that we share with others.

> about the body, I felt that doing the exercise of *las ancestrales* I really felt that memory. Later, in another body expression workshop, outside the Magdalenas, I identified it with that name.
> The first time I experienced it, reviewing my women, my female ancestors, which was not something conscious, nor was it present in my personal construction, that day I saw how all my mother's ways of doing were recorded, what I believed might be her desires and the things I did not even know. You realize that there is a silent memory, but that memory still exists in the body.
> I started to go through the history of my female ancestors, my own, and I finally saw that in fact it wasn't me who facilitated the exercise right then, but actually I was giving myself over to the power of all those bodies that were in synchronicity with that energy, looking for what resonated in that moment: how one moves and thinks through those things that our mothers, our grandmothers taught us.

Embodying: tensions between feeling and thinking

For more than a year we gave ourselves several instances to think about ourselves as a collective of women practitioners of theater of the female oppressed, to discuss what form of organization we wanted to give ourselves, and to decide what problem we wanted to work on, in dialogue with the rest of society. At a certain point we began to feel uncomfortable with the excessive use of words, expressing our feelings from our thoughts, which we felt were disconnected from the sensitivity of our bodies and their memory, their emotions, their fragility, and also their strength. The need for the body to be more present and to put aside the centrality of the word resonated with us.

> I arrived in Magdalenas as a feminist activist, I wanted to do theater of the oppressed and I found that this group of women who do theater of the oppressed, and I said, "Everything I'm looking for, in just one collective!" [...]
> I came from this hyper-rationality, which made me feel something that only today I can read about: it was my impossibility to work from the body, because it was and it is hard for me to work on myself, to be unable to talk much about myself, about the violences, and to embody them from that body memory.
> I need to embody the work, but I also need to think about my body. I feel that one way to embody is to think of myself in that body.

As we continue to exchange around this tension, we come to the conclusion that the body is always present, no matter how much we don't appeal to ourselves or make an explicit invitation to put it into play. It is always there and it is challenged.

> I believe that sometimes the need may arise for the body to be more present, but I believe that in Magdalenas there has been a commitment placed into games, into exercises; even in standing in front of other women and being able to give away that knowledge in the multiplication of the Laboratories. If it doesn't go through your body, through your experience, it is very difficult to transmit it.
> For me the body is always there, even if we say: "What will we do today? Will we work the body or won't we? The body is there, the mind is body, too.

We recognize that "the word" as such is fundamental, and it is not opposed to the body, although there is undoubtedly a hierarchy of thought above the emotions and sensations that make up the body's memory. The methodology uses the body to destructure what has been acquired, to give new meanings to our words, images and sounds.

> It is by possessing the word, the image and the sound that the oppressors oppress, before doing so by means of money or weapons. We must react against all forms of oppression. And this struggle must also take place on the three important battlefields of Sensitive Thought. We must reconquer the Word, the Image and the Sound (Boal, 2012, p. 57).

The word is one of the aesthetic means used by the oppressor, along with other languages: sound and image.

> [...] through art, culture, and all media, the dominant classes, the oppressors, with the clear purpose of forcing illiteracy on the whole population, control

and use the word (newspapers, stands, schools), the image (photography, film, television), sound (radio, CD, musical shows) and monopolize those channels to produce an aesthetic anesthetic —allow me the contradiction—, conquer citizens' brains to sterilize them and program them for obedience, mimetism and lack of creativity (Boal, 2012, p. 25).

There is a need to resignify the word and, above all, to take it, to re-appropriate it. Historically, women have been condemned to silence; and today we are together on this path towards recovering the expropriated word. This is how it is stated in the slogan of #NiUnaMenos (#NotOneLess) from the Coordination of Feminisms of Uruguay, during the intervention in which we participated from Magdalenas Uruguay as one of our concrete and continuous actions in articulation with others and as part of the feminist movement: "Let the pain become rage, the rage become struggle, and our voice become a yell!"[8] The proposal from the aesthetics of the oppressed is the reappropriation of our word, sound and image in order to recover our body. It is a work that implies constantly going back and forth between mind and body, inseparably, where both are constantly re-signified.

Reviewing those exercises that most question the rationality that obstructs the sensible language, we brought one of the exercises in the Laboratory as an example. It is the "Dance of the four elements", which invites to the immersion of each woman into herself and in the environment that is generated in the shared space. Those of us who dynamize the exercise use different musical instruments (recognized as such, or created specifically for this instance from common elements made from metal, glass, paper/cardboard/wood and plastic) to awaken and accompany the intensities that each element entails, while one of us as the guide. It is an intimate exercise, with closed eyes, that appeals to the sensitive and liberating movement from a passage through the four elements. We accompany the women on a journey through contact with the water, earth, air and fire that inhabit them.

---

[8] Zur y Rebelarte, Porfiadas, June 2017. Available at http://zur.org.uy/content/porfiadas

> There's something there that I don't know how to put into words. I can really embody when I connect with something else, I don't know how to explain it, the fact that the word doesn't predominate, but the vibration does, even with my eyes closed; listening to the sounds of those elements, those sounds are what makes me move, dance, loosen, feel, feel and feel, and block the head which is what overpowers me.

Since the body and its memory regained the center, we began the aesthetic process of creating a new forum theater play. There have been many instances of asking ourselves what is the oppression that we are experiencing at each moment, instances in which we set out to share, to reflect and to create. What are the violences on our bodies? And how is our erotic desire conditioned? These are some of the premises on which we have been building, and through which we propose to explore and reflect on women's oppressions around our sexualities. Working on sexuality in our collective would have been unimaginable two years ago. We did not talk about it, it was not the focus of our shared stories; or, at least, we thought so.

> Before, in Magdalenas, first off, we didn't talk about sexuality. It wasn't even mentioned. During a meeting in Buenos Aires in 2013, along with other Magdalenas collectives from Argentina, I remember that we did an exercise in which we had to make animal couples. And we said, "We can't do this with our female partners!" We had to form pairs, touch each other, establish a relationship from the body. We were really far from reaching that point!
> The fact that we are talking about sexuality in our new play, I feel that it has to do with things that all women are vibrating with. I went to a Minervas[9] consciousness-raising group a little while ago, where we talked about orgasm. So, that also talks about being perceptive through our minds and bodies, attentive, because that's what's challenging us. Like other issues in context, what happens to us. And that I can't think of myself without other women who are also thinking about this.

The personal and the political

We discussed around "the political" in our collective, a sensitive absence for some, while for others it was always present. The slogan

---

[9] Minervas, feminist female collective in Uruguay, https://www.facebook.com/minervascolectivofeminista/.

"the personal is political" took shape in the heat of the debate, as we questioned ourselves about what each of us expected from the collective in terms of our actions inwards (our individual and collective interior), or outwards (in articulation with other females and males).

> I was missing something that is fundamental in theater of the oppressed: art and politics. I felt that the art was there, and I lacked the political. And then somehow Magdalenas took a turn, and maybe today we're clearer on the political. And we have both things together, because we have a strong "political art", with a strong presence in the streets, in performances, as well as with forum theatre plays.
> For me, the political aspect was like: "Here you were, I found you!" It was the great discovery of the whole process that I had been doing with my history as a woman, mirroring myself with other women [...] when the political aspect appeared in Magdalenas, for me it meant: "This was the angle that I was missing", and I felt that it will never go back. But today it gives me a lot of anguish because I can have a wider view of humanity, of the global, and that generates in my body a lot of pain, a lot of anguish. And not knowing what the Magdalenas or all the women in the world will do, how we'll manage to make all those oppressions on women stop happening. For me it was fundamental that I was still in Magdalenas when we began to think from that place.

In the context of the World Women's Strike and the demonstration on March 8, 2017, we shared a street intervention as Magdalenas, in articulation with the Coordinator of Feminisms, expressing some of the oppressions we perceived and their treatment by the media, specifically the press. During the creation process we embarked on a search for the news that had most outraged us in recent years, and used some tools from journalistic theater[10] to transform them into a demand through art. This somehow led us to link this to another type of symbolic violence experienced in our childhood, children's song-games. The main themes that emerged were: the moral

---

[10] Journalistic theater is a technique within the Theater of the Oppressed method, the oldest technique, created in the seventies in the context of the Brazilian dictatorship. In it, press news are used: and from an aesthetic proposal and from the perspective of denouncement, an issue that is badly treated in the media is approached.

censorship of women who have abortions, the blame placed on adolescent victims of sexual exploitation, the invisibility of violence experienced by women in the streets. Recalling this and other actions, the idea of political bodies and the questioning of this split between the personal and the political appear.

Some of us associate politics with thinking of ourselves as a collective, searching for alliances, asking ourselves whether or not we are feminists.

> I like to think about political bodies, because it seems to me that politicizing is really important. And I think that in discussing whether or not we are feminists as a collective, it is also really important to politicize the tool even more, but from feminism. I feel, with many of you, that the experience of March 8 this year was vibrant, and I could not get out of that emotion of embodying, of feeling the body vibrating, pulsing in a historical 8M, and feeling it as a tool for struggle, by placing it in the street, in a mobilization.

We give ourselves the time to disagree. This is how the idea arises that the political has never been absent, but that we are focusing on different things.

> understanding politics as any act that you do, where you express your opinion or your view about something that is happening. And that is very clear from the matrix of Boal's theater of the oppressed, the idea that "I stand as a citizen when I am doing something in reference to what is happening to me" [...] what we did with our body before was totally political, because it is searching for yourself and finding yourself.

We question ourselves like this, in our bid to distance ourselves from political discourse without a transformation of ourselves.

> If in some groups you start from the previous discourse, from the political discourse, which doesn't mean that you don't have it, you put up a barrier. Because there is something to deconstruct first, which is finding your own voice. If you don't find your voice, you won't know what to say. So, before you take a stand from a political discourse, that is, we now have this discourse because we found out what there is inside us and what needs to be said, we found out where we could unite our voices, but everything was political, from the beginning it is political.

At the same time, we bring up profoundly political decisions that took us time to discuss collectively.

> When I say political, I mean questioning how we stand, define ourselves, or question ourselves when invited by different institutions, organizations. And as I said, I made a whole exploration of myself by mirroring myself in other women and then in a way achieving the questioning.
>
> Today I can read that perhaps my emphasis on working on "the political" more, the need for this to be more present in the collective, may have been a certain blockage. I was afraid and I still am, because if I work from the body, violences will emerge —violences that I don't remember, but that are there, things that I am not ready to work on will come out. So from there I can explain the reason for my emphasis on the "outward". My hurry was not so much that the collective pronounced itself feminist, but that we questioned things, such as which invitations we accepted and which we didn't, who we articulated or didn't articulate with.

We are back to the old slogan: the personal is political in this circular thread of thought, trying not to let any discrepancy escape us, looking for agreements, while also respecting the times and processes of each one of us. We conclude that the political is also manifested in the revision each one of us makes of our lives, problematizing the upbringing, eating habits, reproduction, or the break with a patriarchal culture.

> The idea that the personal is also political was also something that made me stop looking outwards, and realize that how I stand and move around in the world is my politics. And to become an activist of my own life, to be a protagonist. And that for me means a before and after, because it is often difficult for me to be the protagonist of my own life.
>
> Maybe I don't speak very well, or I haven't studied much, or I don't have a lot of theory, but what I did learn is that I have to incorporate this, and I think I mostly try to get it into my house, which is what I was explaining to them. I don't know if I'll ever be that full-blown woman and whatever, and maybe I don't know if I'll ever be a feminist. But I do know that if I want to change things, I have to change them starting from my home. And I have to begin with my children, so that they can replicate it outwards, so that my daughter can be a free woman, without conditions, and wherever she wants to stand she can, without anybody telling her not to. And my son, the same thing, to know that tolerance comes first, and to know that he is a man and the fellow man is to be respected, and above all things the fellow woman is to be respected. I know what I want to teach them, I don't know if they will manage to understand along this road. I think that, in some positions with my children, I am trying to leave my grain of sand.

This is how discrepancies are expressed, different readings of the political within the collective, which respond to different needs, urgencies, processes. But there are also agreements when processing discrepancies, agreeing that, parallel to the need to politicize our actions with others, it is essential to politicize our daily lives, to recognize ourselves as protagonists of our own lives: to revise, deconstruct, and rebuild each and every one of us fundamentally together.

Sororal circularity

In previous pages we narrated our need to "look inward", to embark on a creative process that places our body at the center. This process also involved "looking inward" inside our group. The first multiplication of Laboratorio Magdalenas, in 2012, led to the formation of a group where there were differentiated roles: workshop instructor-Kuringa, and participants. The internal movements of the group, the departures and new integrations, the self-education in feminism and the exchange with other feminist collectives in Uruguay allowed our collective to process diverse changes in its structure and functioning, going from a group that is "organized and facilitated" by a Kuringa-workshop instructor to a collective, where what happens in the time-space of our meeting is the responsibility of all of us.

To do this, we had to unlearn the patriarchal forms of organization, participation and direction, the times of dialogue and listening, decision making, our bodies' disposition in space. Rather than finding ourselves in the linear design that horizontality proposes, we preferred to find ourselves in what we call sororal circularity. In this political-methodological-organizational design "there is no top or bottom", nor are there sides or margins. Each one of us is a fundamental part of that circle: together we create new links, care networks, and strategies to resist patriarchy.

Based on Marcela Lagarde's (1997) conceptualizations of sorority, we understand sororal circularity as the only possible way of being, of meeting and organizing ourselves, which calls us to immerse ourselves in the experience of questioning our relationships with other women and creating new forms of relating. Sororal circularity is shown in the recognition of one in the other, which is part of a path from the individual to the collective. The only way we can find ourselves is with others. This is how one of our companions describes it in her testimony:

> For me it was also like a learning experience to embody alongside other women. Holding, hugging, it's not something that I often do, or did at that time, with everyone, embracing, looking into each other's eyes, maybe it wasn't much of a daily life thing, this force, the circle. For me it's healing, it's liberating, it focuses me in another place, in my bond with other women, and if I think about what Magdalenas has given me all this time, it is that. I also think about how we involve our bodies into embodying, that way of organizing ourselves that we also discuss, in a way. That movement of working with everyone, embodying, changing places, unlearning certain forms that we bring with us. I receive and I give, too. Being more circular, because the word is not horizontal, I think it's circular. And caressing each other, and finding closeness in it, the recognition of a body that is the same or different from mine, that closeness [...] I see it as a support, as a possibility of finding affection, love, listening.

Sororal circularity is powerful. It does not admit asymmetries; in it each one takes her place, each one contributes to the collective from her potentialities, and the collective is enriched by diversity and differences. We take Audre Lorde's words "without community, there is no liberation", a statement with which the writer reminds us that women have been taught to ignore their differences, or to see them as a reason for separation. "In our world, divide and conquer must become define and empower" (Lorde, 1984, p. 112).

Sororal circularity is powerful, as each one is a mirror of the other, each one brings the weaving forward by adding her own stitches to the blanket in which we catch each other if we fall, or we get shelter in the cold. Sororal circularity is powerful, as it is healing, transforming, nourishing, loving, a space for care and listening. It is a magical circularity, of companions, sisters, friends, witches and warriors. It is a form of struggle and resistance against capitalism and heteronormative patriarchy.

Closing words in this circular writing

To write this text, we gave ourselves a time and a space to meet, and we put together the questions we wanted to share with each other and our readers. We agreed to start with our experience from the first Laboratorio Magdalenas. We turned on the recorder, we looked at each other, we listened to each other, we questioned each other as a collective and, as we went along, with all its successes and all its mistakes, we saw differences but also agreements. We have shared testimonies of our journey from and about our bodies, the changes that we identified in this process of walking together, how we have tried to name the experiences of our oppressions and to express our desires: testimonies of the form that we have given ourselves to appropriate our histories and above all our bodies.

Bibliography

Santos, Bárbara and Alessandra Vannucci (2010). Laboratorio Magdalena-Teatro de las oprimidas. Available at http://kuringa-barbarasantos.blogspot.com.uy/2010/08/laboratorio-magdalena-teatro-de-las.html

Boal, Augusto (2012). *La estética del oprimido*. ALBA Editorial.

Zur and Rebelarte. Porfiadas, June 2017. Available at http://zur.org.uy/content/porfiadas

Lagarde, Marcela (1997). *La política de las mujeres*, Madrid: Cátedra.

Lorde, Audre (1984). *Sister Outsider: Essays and Speeches*. Trumansburg, New York: The Crossing Press, 1984. Spanish edition: *La hermana, la extranjera*. Madrid: Horas y Horas.

10. Reaching out, feeling and getting involved: reflections on an investigation into emotions

Jonatan Rodas[1]

Introduction

Taking an interest in emotions seems both an attractive and a mad idea. In social analysis, interest in their importance in different areas of life has grown, so that paying analytical attention to them is striking. On second thought, questions blurring that initial charm arise: what emotions? Whose emotions and about what or who? Who expresses them and what for? Who listens to them and what is done with them after they are heard? Concerns like these have accompanied the process of my doctoral research from beginning to end.[2]

In this text, I would like to share some of the concerns that questions like these generated in my positioning in front of the reality that I approached for research purposes, mainly because my focus demanded moving from an interest *in* emotions to a posture

---

[1] PhD in Social Anthropology for the Centro de Investigaciones y Estudios Superiores en Antropología Social (CIESAS, "Center for the Research and Higher Studies on Social Anthropology"), Southeast site, Chiapas, Mexico. The reflections presented in this text were written during work in the mentioned PhD Program, between the years 2015 to 2019.

[2] The research project focuses on the role of emotions in the articulation of resistance practices of a group of inhabitants of two municipalities in the department of Guatemala, in the same country. Preliminarily it was entitled "Affectivity and resistance: a review from the experience of the Movimiento de Resistencia de La Puya ("Resistance Movement of La Puya") in Guatemala".

from emotions. What I propose is to offer some episodes of my own experience with the Movimiento de La Puya to highlight discussion points that may result from that step towards an investigation on the very forms of feeling. The argument that I aim to support is that a movement of such nature requires a transit from the methodological posture of participant observation, as the closest way to subjects' experience, towards opening to a posture of *involvement* in which one must assume and position oneself with one's own circumstances.

The first questions

The economic policy promoted in Guatemala in the years after the signing of the peace agreement in 1996 generated a revitalization of the social struggles in the country, which had decreased since the 1980s (Figueroa Ibarra, 2006; Yagenova and Veliz, 2011). This revitalization, however, does not share the same characteristics of previous eras. The mobilizations in resistance to the current economic model, which includes the promotion of the extractive industry, were characterized by having as their main protagonist the *community subject*, i.e., Indigenous peoples and peasant communities articulated under the slogan of the *defense of the territory* (Yagenova and García, 2009). In addition, this *community resistance* operates under a logic that, rather than opposing the State, as classic peasant- or Indigenous-based organizations would do at other times, seeks to force the State to fulfill its duties to protect natural resources against the particular interests of companies (Bastos and De León, 2014). Part of these new forms of struggle has been their displacement to the judicial field, where the communities not only seek to have the judicial bodies resolve their demands, given the legal irregularities with which mining projects are often promoted, but also find themselves forced to confront the State and the companies due to the criminalization of several of their members. It is therefore an antagonistic situation in which discursive frameworks of different significance come into play, in a struggle for a definition of reality. The success of their struggle in the various fields in which it takes place will depend on the effectiveness of this process of defining reality.

In this context, the year 2012 witnessed the public emergence of an organization of residents of several villages in the municipalities of San José del Golfo and San Pedro Ayampuc, located in the department of Guatemala, who demonstrated against the imposition of a mining project on their territory. The group became known as the Movimiento de Resistencia Pacífica de La Puya ("Movement of Peaceful Resistance of La Puya"). One of the main characteristics of this group was their interest in promoting peaceful resistance; that is, a strategy that did not fall under the provocations of the State security forces and the mining company. But in addition, their struggle became more notorious due to the manifestations of faith and spirituality that accompanied their forms of action, mainly on the part of the women. Thus, the group was soon identified as an "exemplary" resistance. The latter was what initially drew my attention and led me to approach their experience.

In July 2016, on the occasion of a press conference given by the movement in a well-known café in Guatemala City, I met Dani, a religious friend whom I had known for years. She told me that she was accompanying the group's actions, and I, in turn, told her of my interest in approaching the group for research purposes. Thanks to that meeting I had the opportunity to present my project to one of the best-known members of La Puya, but the meeting was no more than an exchange of ideas and some information. The meeting was simple and without major disruption. However, I found out that it was through the project they directed that the first information had been spread about the installation of the mining project and the consequences it would have on the environment and the lives of local people. Months later, I contacted Dani again with the aim of having another meeting; this time, hopefully, with the "leading group" in the movement. Until then, I did not know that in La Puya there was no such leadership structure. So the meeting did not turn out to be what I expected.

It had taken me an hour to arrive at Dani's house, located in a village in the municipality of San Pedro Ayampuc, in the department of Guatemala. A truck had tried to turn on the road and caused chaos on the narrow, winding road leading to the village. I was nervous: I thought my tardiness was not a good letter of introduction to the group. In my experience with communities in the northwestern Guatemalan highlands, I learned that when a community assembly opens itself to outside visitors, it is necessary to observe the conditions they pose. It is also true (and I had completely forgotten) that in many communities time runs inversely to the troubled life of the cities, and that on many occasions it is necessary to wait a long time until the issue under discussion is clarified. Fortunately for me, that day the people summoned were also caught up in traffic.

These details are not meant to be mere anecdotes. On the contrary, they attempt to inform about the emotional conditions that shape this field work and research in general. In my particular case, those first moments were lived with anxiety, since I was well aware of the criticism that many organized communities currently have with respect to "academics" and researchers, who they view with a certain distrust, since they only arrive as extractors of information, a perception that is largely justified.

Finally, we met Miriam and Ana, two members of the group, at Dani's house. I introduced myself by digressing into my journey through social organizations and research projects, until I arrived at the personal reasons that led me to become interested in emotions as a topic and in the Movimiento de Resistencia Pacífica de La Puya as a "research subject". But, as I wrote at the beginning, although talking about emotional life seems to be an attractive subject, it also turns out to be problematic. This became clear to me when I finished talking and Miriam took the floor to tell me, among other things, "We won't talk to you about emotions". The motives she gave were significant: 1) many people in the group still resented the effects of the aggressions they had suffered in the different episodes in which the State and the company had tried to enter the mine, in addition to other forms of aggression experienced individually: defamation, slander, physical aggression, among others; this meant that questioning them about it could open up wounds that I, in my role as a researcher, was not prepared to close;

2) talking about their moods or the feelings they experienced could be counterproductive to the group's action, since they also ran the risk that by becoming public they could be used against them; and 3) because what was being asked for research purposes was a somewhat daring, strange request: people's intimacy, something that could not be done with just anyone, without a previous bond.

Although I understood and shared these concerns myself, at the time I was overcome by worry: what would become of the research then, if its main focus was not possible? Dani intervened to point out that many people within the group needed to talk about their feelings and that, in any case, doing so meant talking about personal motivations rather than group strategies. But Miriam intervened again, pointing out that precisely what I was looking for, to talk about emotions, ran the risk of falling into the hands of the company and showing them what La Puya was as a group, also adding a criticism of the role that academics have had in the dissemination of information that is often wrong or misleading, thus undermining the movements' struggles.

Once the meeting was over, we returned with Ana and Miriam to the capital city. During the trip, Miriam surprised me again, telling me that it was possible to work on people's emotional lives, but that it required patience, the creation of trust, and above all, plenty of commitment. I remember that, more cordially, she told me that I could not ask people to talk to me about something as important as their emotions and then leave them without closure. The criticism I had made of the academics' approaches and the use of the information they obtained, as I could understand later, was not directed at my work in particular but at a way of doing research that the group had already faced and that, despite the expressions of commitment and good will of those who came, continued to reproduce hardly ethical practices based on the researcher-researched dichotomy.

Being a matter as intimate as people's emotional lives, these criticisms took on other dimensions. During the preparation of the research project I had noticed something that had also been noticed by scholars in this field, that in the evolution of the field of study of emotions within the social sciences there has been a preponderance of theoretical developments over empirical research and the appropriate methodologies and research techniques (Ariza, 2016). Now, in addition to the theoretical-methodological challenges that I already knew, my conversation with Miriam raised new ethical and political questions that I had not previously considered. This raised a new question: how is it possible to carry out research that attempts to highlight the relevance of affective aspects in sustaining a resistance struggle without, at the same time, violating the integrity of those who participate in that resistance?

My initial confusion decreased when I understood that the phrase in which Miriam had said that they would not talk about their emotions did not represent a total closure to my purposes, but rather an invitation to consider from the beginning the implications that my research could have both for the members of *the resistance*, and for their work as a whole. In light of this, Miriam had pointed out that it was necessary to always keep in mind what was written and who was going to read it. It was not just a question of negotiating interpretations of reality, I believe, but a concern for the people in the movement, a form of "self-care", as they said.

That first meeting had left me with many concerns about the work of social research, or to put it in the terms that resonated in my head: "what is the point of all this?" Over time I have considered that such a question helps to think about at least two things: 1) The role of social research in the face of the social and political processes that take place in our countries today. It is not a simple subject, nor is it limited to individual reflection, but the experiences in the field where researchers encounter criticism and demands for their work continue to indicate the urgency of continuing to deepen the relationship between academia and society. 2) That at the same time, a discussion on the social uses of science inevitably leads us to rethink the already traditional methodological approaches which, with more or fewer declarations of good intentions, do not go beyond the use of the interview and participant observation as basic techniques for gathering information.

This made me rethink the way I was trying to account for people's emotional experience, as I present it below.

The first feelings

After meeting with Dani, Ana, and Miriam, I followed their recommendation to approach the resistance to meet the people who were participating in the surveillance shifts. When the camp began in 2012, residents of several villages organized themselves into groups that monitored the entrance to the mine, in order to prevent the company from resuming the activities it had begun without consulting the population. These shifts began at 5 in the afternoon on one day and lasted until 5 in the afternoon the next day, in a continuous six-day cycle.

The first time I arrived at the resistance, I met the El Guapinol village shift. It was mostly made up of women who talked very pleasantly around a table in the resistance's kitchen. I approached them to introduce myself and inform them of my purposes and my intention to stay there for the rest of the day. This did not seem to disturb them, so after my introduction life continued on its daily course. A good part of the afternoon was spent sitting in the same place where they left me after offering me some food. They moved from one place to another, alternating in small groups where they talked about anything. Eventually we exchanged some words and I talked a little more about what I wanted to do but still didn't get any feedback. At times I thought (perhaps as consolation!) that the fact that they did not object to my presence and continued with their daily activities placed me in a privileged position to observe as much as I wanted. This happened on a few more occasions in other shifts. I could write and record whatever I wanted, but something else was going on inside me as I took the bus back to the capital, feeling that nothing was happening, that I did not understand anything and, in the worst case, I came to consider that the matter of "seeing emotions" was just a post-modern whim of mine. At times I argued with Miriam in my head, I agreed with her and ironically replied to myself that, for everyone's peace of mind, there would be nothing to read on the subject, because I was not writing anything. I was furious.

Fortunately, recognizing one's own emotional experience has therapeutic effects, and back then it also had methodological effects. Recognizing that I felt frustrated, angry, and lost in front of my project was the starting point for reconsidering that, if my interest went beyond the study of emotions in politics to the politics of emotions, this could only be through a change of position from the study *of* emotions to the study *from* emotions. But how to do this?

One of the advances in the study of emotions from the social sciences is to consider that these do not only correspond to states of mind of an internal and individual nature, but to forms of relationship. This first idea serves to outline an answer to the previous question. Starting from the emotions as a form of knowledge implies the involvement of the researcher with reality. But it is precisely in this part that I felt it was necessary to say something about the method of participant observation.

In general terms, the method of participant observation outlined by anthropologist Bronislaw Malinowski in his well-known work *Argonauts of the Western Pacific* (1986) is characterized by the anthropologist's involvement in people's lives, observing and participating, so that he can have access to first-hand information. It is an ethnographic model that was very successful, not only within anthropology but also in other social science disciplines. The methodological position of participant observation can be summarized as *being there*, so that by living with people on a daily basis it is possible to understand their logics of action. For me, "being there" was not giving the expected results; I had been visiting the resistance for many days and was no more than "that one doing a study", who sat down to eat and witness daily life without feeling that he understood anything. On the other hand, it was necessary to remember one of the basic principles of ethnographic work outlined by Malinowski: that it is less a question of concrete prescriptions than of placing oneself in a position in which one can have a very specific type of experience (Stocking Jr., 1993, p. 85). I will try to show how this led me to think that, in the inquiry of emotional experience, an attitude of *involvement* is necessary, and what that entails. I will propose two examples to start with.

In the conversations of the early days when I began to visit the resistance, some of the members were interested in knowing details about my economic conditions. About the reasons and conditions of my work, although there could be curiosities, the what and how to develop it seemed to be clearer: like many others before, I got there to do my university study. But the economic aspect, that is to say, the remuneration I received for doing that work, was the cause of somewhat timid questions. My answers, besides being evasive, were also shy. As I got to know details of their experience, I noticed that the question had a reason to be anchored in the discomfort that at one time caused the arrival of "researchers who only went to get information" and who made good profits from the work they did on them. I tried not to discuss it, I did not want to justify or condemn the actions of other researchers, especially since I did not have the elements for judgment at that time. But what I did have to understand was that, if what mattered was to establish bonds of trust, it was better to start talking clearly. So, on one occasion, in conversation with one of them, I explained to him my concern about the insistence of the question and, at the same time, I explained the economic conditions of my research. It was a relief, since in doing so I could understand that I was uncomfortable with the comparison against the economic conditions of other researchers, especially since mine at that time were not optimal.

On another occasion, we were talking about religion with a group of women. They were all fervent practitioners of Catholicism and I kept asking them about their experience until one of them, with her firm and direct tone, asked me, "Anyway, what about you? Do you believe in God or not?" As well as the questions about my economic condition, these also had a background that was based on the knowledge that many activists who approached them from the early days of their struggle did not profess any religion, and used to participate in their religious acts respectfully, but without their belief. In such circumstances, it seems, I had two paths: either I lied and tried to make myself look good by saying I did believe in God, or I told the truth. I opted for the latter, despite my fear of suffering some blockage in what we were talking about up to that point. I was scolded for my lack of faith, but sincerity acted as a gesture of trust, to the point that on my first visit to the village to which these ladies belonged, they took me to the parish to see the image of the local patron virgin. For my part, I felt I had to tell them something, do something, so I got down on my knees and gave thanks for the opportunity to be there. It didn't take long, I once professed Catholicism myself, and what was left for me to do was to acknowledge that I understood the meaning of faith very well.

And feeling involved

As I mentioned, to this day, participant observation continues to be the preeminent working methodological posture of social research. Techniques may vary, from interviews, focus groups, to simply being there, but the premise is always the same: to understand reality from the point of view of those who live it.

My idea of *involvement* tries to problematize this issue, but it coincides with what was said before about the ethnographic method being more the possibility of having a certain type of experience than the observance of a certain scheme.

I have borrowed the notion of implication from an analysis that Axel Honneth makes of Martin Heidegger's and Georg Luckács's philosophical projects in relation to the reification of reality and the subject-object schema. The point that interests me is how, in these philosophers, the *praxis of implication* is understood as a link with reality resulting from an existential interest and not only with cognitive interests. In particular, Luckács considered that the establishment of a relationship by a subject who knows, without this supposing a degree of implication, only "reifies" reality, that is, takes it as a thing. Luckács conceived reification thus: "the habit or custom of a simply observant behavior from whose perspective the natural environment, the social environment and the potentials of the personality are conceived in an indolent and dispassionate way as something that has the quality of a thing" (Honneth, 2007: 30).

Since reification constitutes a posture towards the world, a posture that sees it as a thing, getting involved could be thought of as a posture that blurs this distinction through existential involvement; that is, a posture that not only participates in the lives of others, but also recognizes the self in that world with one's own circumstances. This is what I meant when I showed the emotions and feelings I experienced, and the accounts I gave about myself at various times during the work. From this experience of my own feelings I had to recognize that I was not the sober and rational researcher for whom every event was the object of analysis, but just another person who was uncomfortable with certain things and attracted by others. This may seem contradictory to the innumerable indications we receive before going out in the field, about distancing ourselves from our "object of study". For me, this is not a "conversion into a native"; several times I tried to make it clear that I did not intend to assume that I was a member of the resistance or a privileged observer who understood more than others could. My idea of involvement assumes, as Honneth (2007, p. 75) puts it, not a position as an epistemic subject but as an existentially involved subject. Such existential involvement, even if it is within the framework of an investigative action, is an ontological displacement that helps us to break the objectifying relationship that we, as traditional rational epistemic subjects, establish with people and their world. It is allowing oneself to feel affected.

Bibliography

Ariza, M. (2016). La sociología de las emociones como plataforma para la investigación social. In M. Ariza (ed.), *Emociones, afectos y sociología. Diálogos desde la investigación social y la interdisciplina* (pp: 7-36). Mexico: UNAM-Instituto de Investigaciones sociales.

Bastos, S., and Q. De León (2014). Dinámicas de despojo y resistencia en Guatemala. Comunidades, Estado y empresas. Guatemala: Serviprensa.

Honneth, A. (2007). Reificación. Un estudio en la teoría del reconocimiento. Buenos Aires: Katz.

Malinowski, B. (1986). *Los argonautas del Pacífico Occidental*. Barcelona: Editorial Planeta.

Stocking Jr., G. W. (1993). La magia del etnógrafo. El trabajo de campo en la antropología británica desde Tylor a Malinowski. In H. M. Velasco, A. Díaz de Rada and F. J. García Castaño (Eds.), *Lecturas de antropología para educadores. El ámbito de la antropología de la educación y de la etnografía escolar* (pp. 43-93). Madrid: Trotta.

Yagenova, S. V., and R. García (April 2009). Guatemala: El pueblo de Sipakapa versus la empresa minera Goldcorp. *OSAL*(25): 65-77.

11. Living Mesoamerican methodologies: body, earth and feminisms

Elvira Cuadra Lira, Mauricio Arellano Nucamendi and Rosa H.G. Govela Gutiérrez (†)[1]

To the memory of Rosi, who bequeathed to us her experience, knowledge and
rural feminism

Introduction

The challenge of writing this chapter was significant because of the distances that separate our regions and countries: Nicaragua, southeast and central Mexico. However, once we agreed on the points to be addressed, we wrote from our experiences, making an effort to present them in a clear and summarized manner, establishing common points: the feminist commitment to land, territories and bodies of and from women, and the actions of women in the face of the patriarchal, colonial and capitalist reality.

---

[1] Elvira Cuadra is a sociologist, Associate Researcher at the Centro de Investigaciones de la Comunicación (Cinco, "Center for the Research on Communications") and the Instituto de Estudios Estratégicos y Políticas Públicas (IEEPP, "Institute of Strategic Studies and Public Policies") in Nicaragua. Mauricio Arellano is a researcher at the Centro de Estudios Superiores de México y Centroamérica (Center for Higher Studies of Mexico and Central America) of the Universidad de Ciencias y Artes de Chiapas (Cesmeca-Unicach) and a doctoral student in Rural Development at the Universidad Autónoma Metropolitana Xochimilco. Rosa H. G. Govela Gutiérrez collaborated with Comaletzin A.C. and the Centro de Estudios para el Desarrollo Rural (Cesder, "Center of Studies for Rural Development"). She did doctoral studies on Rural Development at the Universidad Autónoma Metropolitana, site Xochimilco. Rosi, as we called her, passed away while the book was in the process of publication.

Then we read each other and exchanged ideas (electronically) to formulate conclusions.

Elvira presents the experience that the women of Xochilt Acalt, in Malpaisillo, Nicaragua, have built for 27 years, based on the facilitation of reflexive processes and the systematization of experiences. Mauricio, from his work in Cesmeca-Unicach in collaboration with the Centro de Derechos de la Mujer de Chiapas (CDMCH, "Center for Women's Rights of Chiapas"), shares the struggles of Indigenous and peasant women for their right to land, in *ejidos* (shared lands) and communities of Chiapas. Rosa discusses her experience with women defenders of their territories in a process of more than 30 years of work by rural feminists.

We hope to contribute to the reflection on methodologies of accompaniment of peasant and Indigenous women, rethinking the patriarchal and capitalist relations that seek to dominate our bodies and territories as we, who wrote this essay, and the subjects who appeal to us, have lived it.

The body, the earth and feminism: the experience of the Xochilt Acalt

In 2001, the rural women's organization of the Xochilt Acalt Center in Malpaisillo, in western Nicaragua, approached the Center where she worked (Cinco) and asked us to systematize the experiences of their empowerment process for women. Although there was a fairly close relationship with the leaders of the feminist movement in the country, such processes had never been facilitated. My colleague, Sofía Montenegro, and I accepted the challenge, which meant for us a continuous and enriching process of questioning and searching that took us from the reality of women and our own to the theory, and back, to understand that much of what we had experienced, both them and us, was not in books. From there, a perspective and a framework of analysis for the empowerment of rural women arose: later, as researchers, we had the opportunity to test and improve it by systematizing the experience of other women's organizations in Nicaragua.

Later, I had the chance to return to Malpaisillo and systematize other processes derived from that first experience of empowerment, so that over the course of almost seventeen years I have closely observed the changes that this group of women generated in their lives, in those of their families and in their locality, in the subjective, economic, social and political spheres. The methodological route of their experience has been full of achievements and difficulties, without recipes. Along the way, they built their own route, a core of experiences and knowledge. It is worth sharing the experience, in addition to personal learning, with other women who are trying to change life, their lives.

From the body to the earth

The Xochilt Acalt Women's Center was born about twenty-seven years ago in a town in the country that was once an area of massive cotton cultivation and mining; when the cotton boom ended, the town was impoverished and the soils damaged by the excessive use of agrochemicals and over-exploitation of the land. Water sources were scarce and many were polluted. People throughout the town languished because of high levels of poverty and unemployment; women suffered from kidney disease and cervical-uterine cancer, children suffered from chronic malnutrition. In addition, women experienced high levels of violence, especially from their partners. Faced with this situation, a group of women leaders in the town decided to create a clinic that would attend to cases of cervical-uterine cancer and provide preventive gynecological care to the women of the town. With some scarce cooperation funds, they founded the clinic, began providing care to the women of the communities and gave workshops on sexual and reproductive health. The clinic continues to operate to this day.

Some time later, by their own means, they carried out a survey to learn more about women's situation; among the results, one of the most critical aspects had to do with food security for the women and their families. Thus they founded the productive programs of the Centro Xochilt Acalt (Xochilt Acalt Center), which are basically backyard crops within family properties. The backyard crops gave way to goat farming. In a short time, the women were able to ensure their food and that of their families. During the systematization some expressed that leaving the space and domestic chores to take care of their yards had given them a new identity and a new sense of the land's importance and potential, as well as their own potential as social subjects.

The second milestone was to improve access to water by means of the construction of wells and water pumps. The women were responsible for their construction and installation; they all recognize the change in their lives brought about by having clean water near their homes. Land ownership is the third and greatest milestone for them: it completed a link that began with backyard cultivation; a dialogical relationship in which the land got care from the women and rewarded them with food, while they grew day by day with new knowledge and a deep understanding of the times and conditions of the land. It was difficult for their families and communities to understand that this group of women was defying adversity and building a new way of life. The process of recognizing the capacities and potential of the women, and of the land, was slow and, in most cases, an open dispute between the women themselves and the rest of the world. One of the most important achievements came about when, through effort and evidence, women managed to get their partners to title the land with their names. This was one of the breakthroughs in the system of unequal power relations that usually deprives women of land ownership, and it introduced a new element of change into couple and family relationships.

The process has been long; most of the women who participated in the productive programs were able to ensure their families' nourishment, integrate the family collective in productive tasks and recover the fertility and richness of soils damaged by cotton cultivation and over-exploitation. Production levels have sufficient surplus and they can offer their products in the local market, thus contributing to the town's food security with quality products and low prices.

From land to policy

The closeness to the land allowed women to build gender identity and awareness. They learned to re-learn themselves and to understand that individual conditions were similar for the whole group; they also began to wonder why those were their living conditions and how they could transform them. The paths they found were twofold: a) promoting women's leadership and political participation from a feminist perspective, and b) becoming actively involved in the town public affairs to demand the sustainability of local development processes, the protection of natural resources and living conditions in the communities. Women became actively involved in the political processes of citizen participation and decided to run for representative positions both in their communities and in the town; this led to the emergence of a group of women leaders later on, the Organización Autónoma de Mujeres (OAM, "Autonomous Organization of Women") and the Red de Jóvenas (Young Women Network).

OAM was born about nine years ago; its origins are in a school of community leadership in which they raised the need for a space, strategies and actions of their own to claim women's rights. They created their own form of organization in each community where there were women willing to take part, and decided to differentiate their activities from the productive and social programs promoted by the Centro Xochilt Acalt. The drive and strength of OAM allowed women to gain recognition in their communities, both in their leadership and in the incorporation of women's own demands and proposals in community plans and initiatives. They also developed a school of feminist learning and mobilization actions linked to feminist movement rallying cries in Nicaragua, such as the decriminalization of abortion, the passing of Law 779 to prevent and punish violence against women, public mobilizations against violence and the commemoration of important dates for the movement. One of OAM's most important actions in conjunction with the Centro Xochilt Acalt was the creation of the Red de mujeres defensoras contra la violencia (Network of Women Defenders against Violence), which provides accompaniment and advocacy for rural women who are victims of violence; this involves everything from going to physically defend women during episodes of violence to accompanying them to carry out procedures at police stations or other public institutions. In turn, the Centro provides medical and psychological care to victims.

Along with the OAM, the Red de Jóvenas was also formed, composed mostly by daughters and granddaughters of the founders of productive programs of the Centro Xochilt Acalt or the OAM. The Red de Jóvenas aims to promote the participation of young women in spaces and processes of political participation with a clear feminist orientation. One of its main areas of work is related to women's sexual rights, early prevention of violence against women and the empowerment of young women. They have organized their own spaces for meetings, training, action and exchange with adult women. It is worth stopping at this point to emphasize that the processes developed by the Centro Xochilt Acalt and the OAM made it possible to exchange knowledge from one generation of women to the next, so often three generations of women from the same family can be found participating at the same time.

Another dimension of women's political participation is their involvement in local public affairs, such as the processes of electing public officials at the community and municipal government levels, and their active participation to prepare municipal budgets and local development plans. Women's conditions and rights are central to their demands and proposals, as is the sustainability of development processes linked to the preservation of natural resources and soil recovery. In the last few years, women have been very active in the preservation of water sources, threatened once more by extensive cultivation of peanuts and sugar cane; they have also contributed to forming brigades or groups in the communities for the care of the forests and reforestation; and they have strongly opposed mining exploitation in some of the town's communities.

Back to the body

Some months before, in the work sessions on the systematization of experiences with the women of Malpaisillo, it was interesting to listen to them reflect on their new senses of being and on how they went from re-knowing and re-defining themselves individually as women, peasants and feminists, to re-knowing and re-defining themselves as political subjects, organized women, protagonists of their own transformation. As they related their personal processes, it was evident that the body, previously conceived as its physical attributes, is now endowed with a subjective dimension in which new identities, consciousness, knowledge and abilities are interwoven. That subjective dimension of the body transcends them as individuals and becomes collective subjective through affection, bonds and interaction with other women and with their communities.

This new conception has had as its central axis the land, the direct contact with the soil, the water, and other living beings that inhabit it. There is an awareness that this would not have been possible if they had not lived the experience of re-learning to cultivate and care for the land. The body is the land and the land is life. Such a process, with the intensity and richness with which the Xochilts experienced it, inevitably refers to a feminist epistemology and political positioning. In the end, and without intending to, they constructed an alternative proposal for the development and empowerment of rural women from a feminist perspective. Their personal and collective achievements have exceeded all their individual and collective expectations, and those of anyone else who has the opportunity to get to know them. The process is still underway and, like so many other experiences, it constantly faces difficulties and obstacles, but the Xochilt of Malpaisillo really want to change life.

ELVIRA CUADRA LIRA, MAURICIO ARELLANO NUCAMENDI AND ROSA H.G. GOVELA GUTIÉRREZ (†)

The body-territory and the struggles of Indigenous and peasant women in defense of the land in *ejidos* and communities of Chiapas

In the years immediately following the 1994 armed uprising in Chiapas, the deployment of counter-insurgent forces to break up the social support bases of the Ejército Zapatista de Liberación Nacional (EZLN, Zapatista Army of National Liberation) turned Indigenous women, their families and their territories into war targets. In this scenario, towards November 1999, indignation for the territorial violence, expressed in forced displacements, sexual violations by the military, the Acteal massacre by paramilitaries (1997), among other crimes of State, was embodied in the city of San Cristóbal de Las Casas by more than three thousand Indigenous and non-Indigenous women, who were present in the meeting "Reclamo de las mujeres ante la violencia, la impunidad y la guerra en Chiapas" ("Women's Claim in the Face of Violence, Impunity and War in Chiapas"). The multiple denunciations documented in this space about human rights violations against women revealed the need for a civil organization that would address gender violence based on the international human rights framework (CDMCH, 2017). Thus, in 2004 the Centro de Derechos de la Mujer de Chiapas, A. C. (Center for Chiapas's Women's Rights) was created with the political objective of working with women, paying special attention to the Indigenous regions of Chiapas, its agency in the defense of their individual and collective rights.

Very soon, the exclusion from the possession, use, usufruct and decision making over land in their *ejidos* (shared lands) and communities, as well as the violation of their rights by the State's neo-liberal policies, became demands from the Indigenous and peasant women linked to the CDMCH: "Land is the root of our rights", "we need a campaign because as women we are crushed by bad governments", "I do not have part of the land, only the men, only they have it; but I also suffered it, I also fought it" (CDMCH, 2006). Thus, in its feminist practice *from below and to the left*, in a permanent collective process of researching, analyzing strategies and experiencing changes, the CDMCH has been designing and adapting political strategies against all patriarchal and capitalist ways of seeing and living life, for the full exercise of the rights of women and their peoples to land/territory. Two moments configure the above:

1) *Campaña Mujeres sin Tierra y sin Derechos Nunca Más* (Women without Land and Rights Never Again Campaign, 2006): a strategy that proposed the defense of the rights of women and their peoples to land/territory, centered on the rejection of policies that privatize social property (*ejidos* and communities) resulting from the imposition of the constitutional reform to article 27 (1992); it was implemented with a lot of pressure upon *ejido* holders, from 1993 to 2006, through the Programa de Certificación de Derechos Agrarios (Program for the Certification of Agrarian Rights, Procede) for the establishment of the regime of Full Ownership (end to the *ejido*). This regime was decided in the *ejido* assemblies in which women, most of whom were communal farmers, could not participate and decide, since they were not recognized as subjects of agrarian rights. Acceptance of this program resulted in the land, a family asset, being individually titled in favor of men, reproducing exclusion.

2) *Movimiento en Defensa de la Tierra, el Territorio y por el Derecho de las Mujeres a Decidir* (Movement in Defense of Land, Territory and Women's Right to Decide, 2015). This movement was promoted after attending to more than 100 cases of land dispossession of Indigenous and peasant women by their families and assemblies, documenting cases of internal regulations that violate the human rights of women in Chiapas' *ejidos*, legally endorsed by federal government agencies;[2] as well as attending to complaints of threats or consummated acts of dispossession of

---

[2] The case of the internal regulations in the Bellavista del Norte *ejido*, registered in the National Agrarian Registry on October 15, 2001, is paradigmatic; Article 37 establishes that "Women of the *ejido* who join in marriage or in free union with men outside the *ejido*, must reside outside the *ejido*, being able to visit their family when they so desire" (Padilla and Vázquez, 2017, p. 77).

women's territories by neo-extractivist projects. At first, the demand was for land co-ownership (2016) and now, family land tenure (2017), a conceptual change with political implications in the struggle to transcend individual and commercial land tenure, two of the material bases of male power and the patriarchal and capitalist structuring of life (cf. CDMCH, 2015).

The defense of women's rights from the CDMCH[3] in Indigenous regions has the peculiarity of operating in the context of three overlapping legal systems in Chiapas: traditional Indigenous (customary) law, autonomous (Zapatista) law, and positive (state, national and international) law. This poses great challenges in the understanding and action of individual and collective women's rights. In this wide-reaching reality two great strategies are posed: legal and formative. Both start from a methodology of *participative defense,* a subjectivation process by which women whose rights have been violated identify themselves not only as victims but also as agents in the construction of their self-determination and the breaking of the patriarchal relations in their culture. The CDMCH's work is based on the use of participatory methodologies in the formation and defense of women's human rights (Freire, 1975).

Another important aspect in the methodology is the collaboration that we have established between Grupo Tierra del Cesmeca-Unicach[4] and the CDMCH since 2009, to carry out

---

[3] The CDMCH is made up of a multidisciplinary female team of bilingual promoters, lawyers, agroecologists, sociologists and anthropologists articulated to women's collectives in *ejidos* and communities in the Altos, Norte-Selva and Fronteriza regions.

[4] This group has its antecedent in the research "Impact of the global crisis on the situation, position and participation of marginalized women in Chiapas" (Olivera, Bermúdez and Arellano, 2014), where among others Mercedes Olivera Bustamante (founder of the CDMCH) and I, Mauricio Arellano Nucamendi, participated. In 2014 we were joined by Amaranta Cornejo Hernández, and in 2016 by Araceli Calderón Cisneros,

research that is socially committed to rural women: the basis for the reformulation of our already-mentioned formation and defense strategies (Olivera, Bermúdez and Arellano, 2014; Olivera, Hernández and Arellano, 2016). In a self-critical sense, we point out that during this time we have given greater importance to the objective relations of Indigenous and rural women with the land and little importance to the subjective nature of those relations, despite the importance they have in the strategies to promote their participation in the transformation or disappearance of their subordination, in all areas of their existence. Thus, in our actions we also identify the gap in the knowledge of the tendencies of young women's relations with the land, caused by the fact that in general we work with adult women.

Emotions and symbolic expressions have been a fundamental part in uprisings and social movements. The connection between the human body and the cosmos in pre-Hispanic societies constitutes a philosophy that we should take up again (López Austin, 1989). Fortunately, we observe that the sacred meaning that Indigenous peoples or groups marginally confer on their relationship with the land (with the sacred tierra-*ch'ul lum kinal*, in the Tseltal language) is still latent. We consider that if we wish to have an integral vision of the genesis and dynamics of the relationships that peasantry and women hold with the land, it is necessary to include the individual and collective emotional dimension that, as Bourdieu (2000) proposes, in-corporates and energizes all social relationships, and in the case of the peasantry, gives it its specific character. Thus, in the mobilization in defense of the land and territory that Indigenous women carry forth, it is important to know and acknowledge that emotional part.

The body-territory and feminism approach brings us to the study of the transformation of relations of subordination and oppression from and with Indigenous and peasant women in Chiapas; to the design of strategies to achieve the exercise of

---

both Conacyt Chair researchers commissioned to Cesmeca-Unicach.

women's right to land tenure and to decide on land/territory. It is very important to acknowledge how women, in their daily lives, bodily question patriarchal and capitalist structures and relationships by, for example, challenging their authorities, refusing to give land tenure to their sons to protect their potentially widowed daughters-in-law and grandchildren from a possible land sale, and how to live their individual problems as a social problem, in the struggle for an Indigenous-peasant life that is free of patriarchal and capitalist violence.

Learning communities, a way to land rural feminism

Since December 2016[5], work has been done to promote and establish three Learning Communities with peasant and Indigenous women, who defend their territories in three rural communities in the municipalities of Zautla, Ixtacamaxtitlán and Cuetzalan, located in the Sierra Norte of the state of Puebla, Mexico, where they have faced threats from mining and hydroelectric projects.

Rural feminism[6] frames this work experience with peasant and Indigenous women, a feminism that has been built on sharing, learning and walking with these women. It is based on the search for the well-being of these women, their families and rural communities. This commitment includes working together with rural women in their recognition as food producers and generators of an ancestral food culture, leading to an impact on food sovereignty, as well as on the well-being of the environment and territories, the space that we inhabit and that provides us with what

---

[5] As part of a doctoral research on women and territories.

[6] Rural feminism exists at least in Spain, Brazil and Mexico, with political commitment from the Red Nacional de Asesoras y Promotoras Rurales (National Network of Rural Advisors and Promoters) and its member organizations and women (in which Comaletzin A. C. stands out). This feminism was born from its roots in the countryside and the daily coexistence with the ways of life of peasant and Indigenous women.

we need to live, such as water, soil, air, and especially food (Govela, 2017). The cross-cutting methodological axes are: gender, interculturality, and class, which correspond to three of the systems of oppression in which peasant and Indigenous women are immersed: patriarchy, colonial thought, and capitalism. In addition to the thematic axes, which correspond to the strategic interests that we want to defend and build: Rights of Peasant and Indigenous Women, Food Sovereignty, and Environment and Territory (Carmona, Govela and Velásquez, 2017).

The methodological axis of gender leads us to question patriarchal power by recognizing the differences between women and men, as well as the way in which, based on these differences, social inequalities have been constructed. It is recognized that this is not "natural" but a social construction and, therefore, that it can be changed. As part of the axis of interculturality, the diversity of cultures is recognized and valued at all times; it is analyzed how, based on these differences, social inequalities have been constructed, and relations of subordination have been established, both among Indigenous peoples and between them and the hegemonic culture. In the face of this, it is necessary to work on valuing and strengthening identities in order to establish authentic intercultural relations, based on mutual respect and recognition. It is essential to question and reflect on the power structures in which all people are immersed. Without a doubt, capitalism is a system that keeps us immersed in consumerism, while a good part of the world's population lives in poverty. So, from this methodological axis of class, we question capitalism, analyzing the place occupied by the peasant life within this system and reflecting how peasants are now considered *poor*, erasing their role as producers of food.

These methodological axes are not worked separately, but used and practiced simultaneously: "... starting from the needs of women, it is necessary to take up again the subjective and objective aspects that conform the condition of women and cover particular experiences to collectivize them" (Aguirre *et al*, 1993, p. 11). These axes run through the work of the Learning Communities, whose methodological proposal has as its antecedent the experience of the Centro de Estudios para el Desarrollo Rural (Cesder, "Center of

Studies for Rural Development")[7] and the Coordinación Interregional Feminista Rural Comaletzin ("Comaletzin Rural Feminist Interregional Coordination")[8]; in which they are understood as "spaces for relationships between people who share meanings and senses of the world of life, brought together on the basis of shared interests to resolve learning needs that give rise to a practice of transformation of their reality" (Berlanga, 2005).

Once the participants recognize themselves as a community of people who share aspects of their life worlds, the process of knowledge construction begins. Each cycle of collective learning consists of three moments: the first moment consists of narrating what is happening to me/us, to put oneself in the world from one's own experience, to move on to a second phase, "the *in front of* phase", which consists of putting oneself *in front of* what is happening: what is happening to me/us? Once we understand what is happening to me/us, we enter the phase of empowerment, which basically consists of answering two questions: what do we want to happen to me/us? What do we need to learn to achieve it? And of course, what do we do so that what we want can happen to us? (Berlanga, 2005). In the case of the Learning Communities of women defenders, gathering the methodological axes of rural feminism, this process is translated into the narration of what happens in the territories and in the defense processes; there is analysis of why it happens to us, from a critical look at capitalism, as well as the power relations between genders, cultures, ages, that are lived in the different communities.

In this sense, the Learning Communities of women defenders of life are spaces where they can express their feelings and thoughts

---

[7] A social organization located in the municipality of Zautla, Puebla, Mexico, which has as one of its main objectives to offer quality education for rural and Indigenous people.

[8] A social organization formed by rural feminists working in different regions of Mexico. Currently its work is focused on formation processes for the Culture of Good Treatment, which addresses and opposes violence against women.

about life in their territories. In doing so, they build knowledge about their participation in movements for the defense of life. They begin by reconstructing their experience as defenders of life, the environment and their communities; they dialogue, share knowledge and reflect on what they think and feel about the spaces we inhabit, as well as the knowledge of *other* peasant and Indigenous women who participate in other movements, generating dialogues where the practices that give us life are located, in order to maintain and strengthen them; and those that do not allow it, in order to transform them by finding new forms of life and *r-existence*.[9]

Taking into account all these methodological aspects, we have been accompanying the three Learning Communities, which have their own characteristics, times and rhythms that must be respected. These have been spaces of meeting and conversation, where women of different ages, experience and cultures have been listened to. Through simple questions, we were able to bring up topics that ground our participation in the defense and care of our communities and territories: the environment, food production, culture, our children, those who come after us: life. One of the themes that has already emerged in reflections is the care for territories as an important part of their defense. In order to address this issue, it has become evident that women take care of their territories, which includes a reflection on the place occupied by reproductive work in people's lives and how it is functional to the system, since it makes it possible for productive work to be done, with the consequence of women's workload. However, the importance of this work by women is also valued and it is recognized that the knowledge they have generated must be rescued.

On the other hand, as part of the process we have gradually addressed self-care, so that women do not forget that it is not only

---

[9] *R-existing*, that is, reaffirming oneself by reinventing one's cultural existence (Porto and Leff, in press, cited in Escobar, 2012).

about being for others, but that we must be aware of our own needs. We cannot fail to recognize that these processes have also faced difficulties. The most important one so far is for women to have time to carry out the Learning Communities sessions, as they not only have workloads in their families and communities, but also have to attend to responsibilities in their groups and organizations, as well as in the defense movement in which they participate. In the case of the Learning Community of Ixtacamaxtitlán, the process has been slower, as women, due to the little organizational history in the community as well as the division and fear generated by the threat they face, expressed interest in carrying out other types of activities such as learning how to prepare preserves, as it is difficult for them to understand that women can meet to talk about the issues that interest them.

At the time of writing, Learning Communities are entering the second stage, which consists of asking and reflecting on what is happening. Questions have been generated that help us to understand their reality and to continue contributing to the defense of the territories. Some of these questions are: why do companies come to make their projects of death? Why do the authorities hand over our territories and pass projects that damage the environment without consulting the citizens? As for the role of women, do men and women defend the territory? Why? Do they do so in the same way? Do men take into account the work of women in the defense of the territory? And to continue in our processes: how can we continue to stand firm so that they cannot return, how can we continue to have support from the communities?[10]

With what we have worked on so far, we can see how the Learning Communities proposed here are spaces where the methodology of rural feminism is lived and rescued, where we propose to learn from our experience and strengthen the organizational processes of rural and Indigenous women. This in turn becomes a relevant space for research, where not only

---

[10] These questions were elaborated in the Cuetzalan and Tlamanca Learning communities.

information is found but where it is systematized and reflected upon, building knowledge.

Conclusions

The three experiences, in Nicaragua, Chiapas and Puebla, built and developed from the everyday life of women in resistance, constitute living methodologies that relate the body, the earth and feminisms. Each one, with its dynamics, rhythms, and specificities, shows key aspects that are important to highlight. One of them is the breaking point in the relationship between body-territory and feminisms. In each of the experiences, reflection on the individual and collective life trajectories of women in relation to the body and the land has facilitated another reflection that questions the causes for their situation and their resistance, leading them to transcend towards a feminist perspective. Furthermore, it made it possible to question women's situation from the intersectionality of relations between gender, class and ethnicity, to understand the forms of appropriation of land and territory in terms of realities but also of resistance actions.

In each experience, women formed their own spaces of encounter, recognition, dialogue and collective construction. It is in these spaces where they have constructed their own views, links and resistances, which little by little have given life to living methodological routes, incarnated in daily practice and from all dimensions of life. Each experience is unique and yet their features are similar. They are spaces of personal and collective empowerment. Another element present in the methodologies is the approach to the body and the relationship with the territory. In all three experiences, the reflection processes allowed to transcend the image and recognition of the female body as a set of differentiated physical attributes. The bodies are now recognized as corporeal spaces-territories where the physical attributes are interwoven with the subjective dimension of being; that is, knowledge, emotions and perceptions.

The relationship with the land and territory constitutes another key element in the methodologies. As processes advance, the land-territory is transformed from an object into a dialogical entity with which women establish a relationship that is not limited only to the extraction of resources for survival and well-being, but instead is part of life itself.

Thus, the Indigenous and peasant women who stand up individually and collectively to their male authorities, who enunciate their rejection of extractive plundering and feminicidal violence, challenge us; they call on us to imagine new frameworks of interpretation and new political strategies to eliminate the subordinations and oppressions that have colonized our bodies and our territories; they teach us that it is possible to denaturalize inequality and social exclusion, both within the communities themselves and outside of them. The experiences narrated here constitute different paths in which rural women seek to transcend the difficulty of listening and the devaluation of their word and their work, the closure of male privilege in power structures, and the structuring violence that in daily life seeks to strip us of our humanity and the material and subjective conditions that make it possible.

Bibliographical references

Aguirre et al., (2015). Saberes para sentir, pensar y hacer el buen trato y el bienestar. Conversando entre géneros, generaciones y culturas diversas. Puebla: Comaletzin AC.

Aguirre, Irma Estela et al. (1993). De la teoría a la práctica del feminismo rural. Sistematización de los encuentros de la Red Nacional de Promotoras y Asesoras Rurales. México: RedPAR.

Ávila et al. (2015). Comunidades de aprendizaje como práctica creativa de transformación y buen trato. In Aguirre et al., Saberes para sentir, pensar y hacer el buen trato y el bienestar. Conversando entre géneros, generaciones y culturas diversas. Puebla: Comaletzin AC.

Berlanga, Benjamín (2005). La educación como relación pedagógica para la resignificación del mundo de vida: la propuesta educativa de comunidades de aprendizaje. México: Cesder.

Bourdieu, Pierre (2000). *La dominación masculina*. Barcelona: Anagrama.

Carmona, C. Velásquez, R. Govela (2017). *Propuestas metodológicas del feminismo rural*. México: RedPAR: Mimeo.

Centro de Derechos de la Mujer de Chiapas, AC (2017). Cumple 13 años de lucha feminista, *Boletín de prensa* (4). San Cristóbal de Las Casas, April 26. Available at https://vocesfeministas.com/2017/04/27/centro-de-derechos-de-la-mujer-de-chiapas-ac-cdmch-cumple-13-anos-de-lucha-feminista/ (15 May 2018).

— (2015). Construcción del Movimiento en Defensa de la Tierra y el Territorio y por la Participación y Reconocimiento de las Mujeres en la Toma de Decisiones. San Cristóbal de Las Casas: CDMCH.

Cruz, T., R Govela and C. Velásquez (2016). El Feminismo Rural, la apuesta de la Red Nacional de Promotoras y Asesoras Rurales. México: RedPAR-Mímeo.

Escobar, Arturo (2014). Sentipensar con la Tierra. Nuevas lecturas sobre desarrollo, territorio y diferencia. Medellín: Ediciones UNAULA.

Federici, Silvia (2013). *Calibán y la bruja. Mujeres, cuerpo y acumulación originaria*. 1st ed. México: Pez en el Árbol.

Freire, Paulo (1975). *Pedagogía del oprimido*. Madrid: Siglo XXI.

García Padilla, Alma and Vázquez Cruz, Claudia (2017). Las mujeres que se unan con hombres ajenos al ejido deberán radicar fuera del ejido. In Gisela Espinosa Damián (Ed.), *Mujeres rurales en lucha por sus derechos y su ciudadanía*. México: Red Nacional de Asesoras y Promotoras Rurales. Available at <http://redpar.org.mx/> (15 March 2018).

Govela, Rosa (2017). Feminismo Rural, 30 años de experiencia de la Red Nacional de Promotoras y Asesoras Rurales. México: Mímeo.

Instituto Nacional de Estadística y Geografía. *Anuario estadístico del estado de Chiapas, edición 2010*. Aguascalientes: INEGI.

López Austin, Alfredo (1989). Cuerpo humano e ideología. Las concepciones de los antiguos nahuas, t. I. Mexico: IIA-UNAM.

Mejía, Susana (2010). Resistencia y acción colectiva de las mujeres nahuas de Cuetzalan: ¿Construcción de un feminismo indígena? PhD Thesis, Rural Development Postgraduate Course, UAM-Xochimilco.

Olivera Bustamante, Mercedes; Flor Marina Bermúdez Urbina and Mauricio Arellano Nucamendi (2014). *Subordinaciones estructurales de Género: Las mujeres marginales de Chiapas frente a la crisis*. México: CDMCH/Cesmeca-Unicach/Juan Pablo Editores.

Olivera Bustamante, Mercedes, Cornejo Hernández Amaranta and Arellano Nucamendi, Mauricio (2016). Movimiento chiapaneco en defensa de la tierra, el territorio y el derecho de las mujeres a decidir. Directorio de organizaciones campesinas y de mujeres de Chiapas. San Cristóbal de las Casas: Cesmeca-Unicach.

Elvira Cuadra Lira, Mauricio Arellano Nucamendi and Rosa H.G. Govela Gutiérrez (†)
Video

Centro de Derechos de la Mujer de Chiapas (2006). *Mujeres sin tierra y sin derechos. ¡Nunca más!* Available at <https://www.youtube.com/watch?v=HKeqauWqMZw> (Accessed 3 May 2018).

12. Collective views and walks. Experiences of rural extension and feminist action-research in eastern Uruguay

Rossana Cantieri Cagnone and Lorena Rodríguez Lezica

Our views

Being able to write this article together is an opportunity to systematize and share our experience from rural extension, particularly concerning work with rural women: family producers (cattle, horticulture and beekeeping) and artisanal fisherwomen in the eastern region of Uruguay, women who build and dispute their territory daily from their farms, from their houses and from the groups and organizations they form. We feel it is an opportunity to pause and look at ourselves, think about ourselves, and encourage our walk.

At first we approached the territory of the department of Rocha[1] from our university insertion, both from Montevideo and

---

[1] In Rocha, one of Uruguay's 19 departments, livestock is the second most important industry, with a predominance of family livestock farms that in some cases include sheep and pigs and on natural fields. Rice production and forestry (eucalyptus plantations) also compete for this territory. Rocha is the department with the largest extension of oceanic coast and coastal lagoon systems in Uruguay, with an important development of artisanal fishing. It is also the department with the largest number of territories integrated by the Sistema Nacional de Áreas Protegidas (SNAP, National System of Protected Areas), to which most of the organizations mentioned are linked culturally, socially, geographically, economically and productively.

from the recently created regional university centers.[2] We have given continuity to the bond in and with the territory in multiple ways: starting from a series of concerns initially raised by some groups and organizations, incorporating others that have emerged in the concrete historical development of work in the territory, and more recently from the construction of a formation plan, supported by a feminist methodology and action research. This construction has meant recovering activities and works that preceded us, in integration and dialogue with the collective thought of this specific formation. We consider it fundamental to start from this acknowledgement, since it is not a question of disembarking in a vacuum, but rather of a conscious intervention, articulating with other actors in the territory, respecting previous processes.

It is from critical extension, linked to popular education and action-participatory research that we position ourselves in a careful intervention in the territory together with organizations and/or groups of women and mixed groups. We understand that critical extension distances itself from technical-professional training and from a commitment to the transformation of society "[...] it proposes to contribute to the processes of organization and autonomy of the subaltern popular sectors, trying to contribute to the generation of popular power" (Tommasino and Cano, 2016, p. 10).

It is an experience that has meant instances of exchange, growth, learning and challenges that enrich and feed back into the proposed practice itself. The Investigación Acción Participativa (IAP, Participatory Action Research) proposal puts forth a horizontal relationship between researchers/teachers/technicians and the communities, a careful intervention in the territory and in the link with their organizations or groups of women, an experience of mutual growth and collective learning. Along with activist research, community-based research and militant research, IAP shares some fundamental axes. We highlight some that have guided us in our practice: breaking the distance between subject

---

[2] Centro Universitario Regional Este (Rocha) and Facultad de Agronomía (Montevideo)-Universidad de la República.

and object and instead building a horizontal relationship, of mutual growth and joint learning; questioning the separation between research and action and instead researching from the commitment to transformation; a real participation of the communities involved in all the steps of research-reflection-action, with the communities as the ones who define the agendas and the ones who decide what, how and what for research is done; researching to know more about the processes that determine the problems; knowing to understand, and understanding to transform.

Building a proposal for participatory methodologies implies an initial reflection on what we understand by participation. From our practice, we choose to distance ourselves from the imaginary of creating participation. In agreement with Rebellato and Giménez, we consider it "at least, ignorant of the complicated networks that sustain human collectives and assuming in fact an ethical perspective that is not very respectful of local peculiarities, frequently derived from an ethnocentric and authoritarian vision" (Rebellato and Giménez, 1997). It is not uncommon to confuse it with mere presence, leaving its conceptualization reduced, limited to the claim for the mere fact of being present in a particular place, space and time. However, if we understand participation as a collective construction, participation is not only reduced to presence and consultation; rather, it goes beyond that: multiple activities are shared and thought of from, by and for the communities.

> It happened to us that, from the beginning, when they came to propose the funds and all to us, we were presented as not having much confidence. Not knowing whether to take a risk or not. There weren't many of us, there were five or six of us. Later, we started to see the reality, we started to see that we were part of this. It wasn't like other times when people came, worked, supposedly for us, and we didn't participate much more than seeing what was going to be done. And they decided everything, what to buy, what to leave, what to take away (B. B., artisanal fisherwoman).

When we talk about participation, we understand that communities are part of it, and in that sense they belong; communities also have a part in fulfilling a function, a role, a position in what they are part of, and they take part, that is, they decide, they become aware that "one can and should influence the course of events, based on the critical analysis of needs and problems" (Rebellato and Giménez, 1997).

From the perspective of feeling-thinking sociology, Fals Borda (1981) points out several crossroads and dilemmas. Among them, he proposes to move away from intellectual colonialism, affirming the need to bring disciplinary/academic practice closer to the work with communities, transcending isolated practices by "experts", without moving away from methodological and epistemological constructions of critical social science. He proposes an approach based on know-how, on thinking and being, on thinking and acting; which leads us to reflect on the generation of knowledge, on learning and grasping knowledge, and the situation in which this learning takes place. Each collective, each community deserves to know and say more about their own conditions of existence in order to defend their interests from those classes that have monopolized knowledge, stories and resources.

> We organized ourselves gradually, participating in the meetings and deciding how we were going to do it. Finding out the best way. Working out how we could save money; because it was our money and we had to see how we could, beyond the help, see how we could manage. Like our own things, like the house (B. B.: artisan fisherwoman).

We believe that developing a training plan based on IAP methodology contributes to generating knowledge for/with women and the collectives involved, in relation to the methodology itself and the process of development, training and research. In this way, we can learn, grasp and generate new knowledge based on our historical and concrete practices. We return to Freire when he states that

> Knowing is a task for subjects, not objects. And it is as a subject, and only as a subject, that man can really know. This is why, in the process of learning, those who truly learn are only those who appropriate what they have learned, transforming it into what they have grasped, with which they can, for this very reason, reinvent it; those who are able to apply what they have learned-grasped to concrete existential situations (Freire, 1984, p. 28).

We are also nourished by a feminist perspective, which, together with the participatory perspective within the critical tradition of social sciences, shares the explicit idea that research should have a political objective as well as a purely knowledge-generating one.

> Today there is agreement in considering feminism as a political proposal that goes beyond the different orientations [...] it proposes to change the subordinate condition of women, in such a way that the social, political, cultural and subjective obstacles that prevent them from exercising their freedoms and from having full access to human dignity are eliminated (De Barbieri, 2002, p. 120-121).

It is from this theoretical and political perspective that we decide how and for what to investigate, guided by some criteria like carrying out excavation work that reveals the perspectives of all women, in plural, and aiming to make visible that which has been ignored or has not been regarded as important because it is about interests, concerns or desires of women. A feminist methodological approach seeks to carry out research that is useful for women, oriented towards action and social change (DeVault, 1999; Teresita De Barbieri, 2002; Baylina Ferré, 2004). And it is from this perspective that we question previous theoretical conceptions with which we arrive at the territory.

Our walks

The formation plan on gender and territorial integration[3] (from now on "the Plan") arises from the concern to reflect on accumulated experiences of intervention and research in a specific territory, as well as to address some issues of interest raised by the community. The IAP proposal is drawn with the objective of

---

[3] In this *formation plan* we work with several collectives: Grupo de mujeres Flores del Este-Sociedad de Fomento Rural Ruta 109; Sociedad de Fomento Rural de Rocha in Cebollatí; Cooperativa de Apicultores del Este (Cooaade); Asociación de Mujeres Rurales (AMRU) in Rocha; La Cocina de la Barra-Asociación de Pescadores/as Artesanales de las Lagunas Costeras (Apalco).

addressing one of the main problems identified by some of the women in the territory: the invisibility of reproductive and care work, and of the productive work of many of them, family agricultural and/or livestock producers and artisanal fisherwomen.

The Plan was discussed and elaborated collectively, proposing to address the following areas of reflection and work: i) sexual division of labor and invisibility of productive and reproductive work; ii) being women; iii) collective processes and participation; iv) violence against women; v) body and territory; vi) formulation of projects with a gender perspective and a territorial approach. We proposed to work around these axes contemplating integrating instances in the territory, in which only women could participate and exchange in some cases, and in others, the different groups and organizations in relation to the issues raised. We will focus on one of these encounters, from a feminist view of the territory, a view that takes into account the perspective of women over their place in the world.

Addressing gender issues, particularly in family agricultural production and artisanal fishing, means recovering processes and visions of a relevant sector that proposes other forms of life, production and access to natural resources, often in opposition to the hegemonic model that prevails today in the territories, articulating factors such as land, work and family on varied original forms, exposing internal power relations and domination in family production (especially gender relations). The latter take on particular relevance since they make the social subject (rural women) vulnerable, strongly influencing the ways in which work is organized within the family production project (Blixen *et al.*, 2013; Gallo and Peluso, 2013).

One of the challenges posed has been to strain some concepts that are naturalized in day-to-day relations between family, work and production. We find it necessary to problematize and discuss the extended conception in which the family accompanies the producer, assuming the pre-eminence of the male role, and where the sphere of social reproduction is made invisible. To address this, we agreed on the first work axis. The proposal was materialized in a workshop within the framework of the Formation Plan, specifically dedicated to addressing this issue, entitled "Me, a producer?"

Women: in the production, reproduction and sustainability of life

We chose to focus here on analyzing what was experienced and reflected upon within the framework of the first axis, in one of the workshop instances, in which we proposed to work from the elaboration of "daily routine clocks". The idea of this workshop came up in the framework of a meeting of one of the women's groups, in which they questioned the convenience (or not) of appearing as her husband's "collaborator" instead of his "employee", when thinking about the contributions for her retirement. It has become a custom in the countryside for women to appear as employees of their husbands, and this began to generate some discomfort. The discussion about its implications in legal terms led to visualize the deep implications at a subjective level. Likewise, in other instances, there was unease with the invisibility of their work and with the fact that they did not receive any kind of recognition as "producers", either symbolic or economic. One of the problems identified is the (in)visibility and devaluation of women's reproductive and productive work linked to family agricultural production and artisanal fishing, which hides the fundamental role they play in life sustainability.

In Uruguay, as in the rest of Latin America, it is common to find a sexual division of labor in the rural world in which women specialize in reproductive work: unpaid, invisible and unvalued work on which capitalist exploitation is based (Dalla Costa, 1972; Galcerán Huguet, 2006; Federici, 2013). In many cases, we also find the invisibility of those tasks considered productive, performed by some women.

> The problem of rural women is that [work] is never finished: there's no Saturday, there's no Sunday. When it's not the house, it's "help me with the cow" [...] there's always work to do (C. P., Family producer: beekeeper).

In this same sense, in many cases, in addition to the fact that reproduction tasks are made invisible, productive tasks are dismissed, minimized or devalued, and with them, decision-making or the possibility of occupying spaces of power. These depend on women procuring and earning their own space.

> But just as we are good at herding, or just as we were good at holding the flag so that the fumigation could pass and we were the first ones to have toxic products fall on us, we have to be called to think, to decide, to make decisions, we have to be there. And the place we earn depends on us women (C. P., Family producer: beekeeper).

The workshop was an explicitly convened instance to address the identification of women as "producers". As in the other workshop events, the day began as a corporal dynamic that allowed to feel-think from the body. Once they found a comfortable place, with their eyes closed, they started to go through their day, bringing to their memory and reviewing in their body movements all those activities they had done. They were remembering with whom, how, with what effort, with what desire, for whom, since they started their day, until they arrived at the workshop. This led them to think about all those other tasks that remained to be done on that day. They also brought to mind all those other tasks that fall upon them, out of desire or obligation, in their daily life. After this exercise, each one worked with their "daily routine clock", identifying that the responsibility of reproduction and life sustainability falls on them.

Following Silvia Federici, we understand by *reproduction* all those daily activities and those relationships that make life possible and the development of people's work capacity. It is a job that is not visible as such, a domestic job that goes beyond cleaning the house.

> It is serving those who earn the salary, physically, emotionally and sexually, having them ready for work day after day. It is raising and caring for our children —the future workers— by looking after them from the day they are born and during their school years, making sure that they too act in the way expected under capitalism (Federici, 2013, p. 55-56).

Each one draws their own clock, capturing in the drawing all the activities brought from the body's memory in the previous exercise.

In a following moment they share them, exchanging about them. Some continue to complete their clocks from what they see or hear from a partner's clock, drawing or writing that task they forgot to draw. That task that the routine itself has kept invisible even to itself. A discussion is generated about which tasks are work and which are not, and why. Which ones are considered "productive" and which ones are not, and why. We visualize that leisure/recreation activities are scarce in their clocks, and in some cases the clocks are also overloaded with community-social activities.

They note that the partner who works outside the domestic sphere does so as an extension of her work "in the house" but in a paid way, a job learned in her socialization as a woman, daughter, wife, mother and/or grandmother. We ask ourselves about reproductive work, about care, about tasks in the field; they calculate how much it would cost to pay someone for all the tasks they do; and the question of who controls the money that comes into the home is put forth for discussion. They compare their drawings and notice that the clocks are overloaded when there are younger children who need more care: then there is little or no time for rest. They recognize themselves as housewives, caregivers, nurses, laborers and administrators at the same time. One of them, who has taken the longest time to come to recognize and name herself a "producer," writes in her drawing: "I grab the horse, help in the corrals, get firewood, ration calves, help with wires, do sewing, sweep the yard, do errands in Rocha, illness: help in care" (taken from M. N.'s clock). From a Marxist analysis of economy, the work done by women has not gained importance, it appears as a personal service external to capital, and by not receiving remuneration for their work, the exploitation of women remains hidden (Federici, 2013). From a critical view of Marxist political economy, Silvia Federici seeks to unmask the process of naturalization of reproductive work, which, as domestic work,

> has not only been imposed on women, but has been transformed into a natural attribute of our female psyche and personality, an internal need, an aspiration, supposedly coming from the depths of our female character. [...] In turn, the unpaid condition of domestic work has been the most powerful

weapon in strengthening the widespread assumption that domestic work is not work [...] (Federici, 2013, p. 37).

Making visible the reproductive work done by women shows the specific role of women in the capitalist division of labor and, at the same time, Federici continues, "the specific forms that our revolt must take" (Federici, 2013, pp. 57-58). In working with rural women, some guiding questions arise in this action-research experience: the first revolves around the recognition or non-recognition of their reproductive work as labor; the second deals with the recognition of themselves as producers; and the third takes the form of Federici's provocation, which has to do with the strategy to be followed, with the forms that will be given to the struggle as organized women and within the family nucleus.

In turn, Amaia Pérez Orozco proposes to go beyond the efforts made by feminist theorists to rescue and revalue the economic in areas where women are the protagonists, efforts that have resulted in the distinction between production and reproduction, between visible wage labor and invisible domestic work. From a feminist critique of political economy, she proposes to transcend the dichotomy between the economic and the non-economic, between work and non-work, and instead seeks a term that contemplates and contains the idea of care for life. For the author, "to continue dividing production (of things) and reproduction (of people) is a harmful analytical strategy that does not allow us to see what matters to us, which is, ultimately (and in the first instance) people, their well-being, the transversal" (Pérez Orozco, 2006, p. 233). She refers to the concept of life sustainability, proposing it as a central analytical category. It is a concept that, from feminist economics, includes the different activities and the different processes developed to guarantee the satisfaction of people's needs, activities and processes that constitute the base of the economic system. Another perspective to think about social organization, making visible what is hidden, naming and making explicit what is implicit

[...] also makes it possible to highlight the priority interests of a society, to recover all the work processes, to name those who assume responsibility for the care of life, to study gender and power relations and, consequently, to analyze how the work and life times of the different population sectors are structured (Pérez Orozco, 2006, p. 244).

From feminist economics it is thus proposed to start from the diversity of women's experiences, in the plural, while paying attention to their specificity as women's experiences. Instead of focusing on the exploitation of women's work, and on images of oppression and discrimination, their experiences are revalued and the focus is placed above all on resistance to the processes of hierarchization and commodification of society.

From this workshop we highlight the chance to discuss the multiple tasks that they brought to their clocks, and to identify which tasks are essential for the reproduction of life, indispensable for allowing the work that they define as productive and, therefore, as work: washing clothes, washing dishes, cooking, sewing, sweeping the yard, gathering firewood, watering plants, caring for the sick, buying food and other items necessary for the daily functioning of the home, doing school work with the children, walking around the fields, helping in the pens, vaccinating animals, rationing calves, helping with wires, curing animals, fertilizing land for the farms, feeding the chickens, cleaning the bird cages, visiting the veterinarian, buying medicine, taking care of the family relations, running errands locally and going to the city, taking care of planning, organization and group meetings, participating in projects, receiving the "technicians" who visit them with a clean house and cooked food. Those are the same rural extensionists who often accentuate inequalities by not seeing them as producers, thus perpetuating their exclusion from discussion areas.

Women: their place in the world

When we talk about territory, we consider on the one hand what Mançano worked on, in terms of the confluence of material territories (physical space) and immaterial territories (social space: relations, thoughts, concepts, theories and ideologies). For this author both are inseparable, because there is no one or the other (Mançano, 2008, p. 7). For his part, Urruzola (2002) considers that its inhabitants "transform the territory into a place: they humanize it, they load it with meanings and stories". But this is not enough when we focus on the relationships between those who build it, shape it and inhabit it; relationships that are often profoundly unequal. A feminist view of the territory is necessary, one that contemplates these inequalities but that also takes into account a first dimension, one that many theorists have forgotten, but that feminist geographers have made visible: the bodies.

In a review of the literature on female bodies and territories-spaces as separate but articulated categories, Delmy Tania Cruz Hernández takes up the proposal of feminist geographers, asking about the place occupied by women's bodies in territories, finding that "femininities and masculinities are produced and reproduced together with everything that symbolically links subjects to their place" (Cruz, 2016, p. 5-6) and placing social relations and interactions at the center for the conceptualization of social space. This allows visualizing the gender inequalities and therefore the power inequalities that occur in the spaces.

In such biogeographically diverse territories (as there are in the department of Rocha), the presence of conflicting interests is frequent among the actors (also very diverse) that construct it. Addressing the issues from a holistic approach and from participatory methodologies such as social mapping allows for respecting this diversity and seeking appropriate alternatives "aimed at the recognition of experiential and symbolic elements of the territory, which favors the co-construction of a common view on the potentialities, assets and difficulties, present in the same territory" (Carroza, 2007, p. 105). Problematizing these questions at the community level offers the opportunity to contribute to the strengthening of the collectives, who are active actors, coexisting, disputing and building their own territory.

In exchange with women from different groups, within the framework of the course "Territories, Feminisms, Ecologies and an approach from the cartography"[4], the students proposed to work with cartography. In response to the question "What is the territory we inhabit?" the women mapped their territory, pointing out the changes in the landscape, changes that speak of a territory in dispute, a land-territory threatened by the rapid expansion of extractive activities, which endanger the survival of family production. The current landscape is described as a hell crowded with wild boars, surrounded by eucalyptus plantations. The concern is that the fields have dried up due to the expansion of forestation and the impossibility of being able to engage in agroecological production when surrounded by agrochemicals. In relation to this, they comment that, in the past, women used to be assigned the task of flag bearers. While the men (husbands, male children) operated the machinery to fumigate, women put their bodies forth to mark the field, indicating where to throw the poison. In the exchange, they discover that this does not seem to be a thing of the past, when one of the women present shared that she continues doing this task. This exchange generates a discussion about caring for others (getting protection for those responsible for "curing" the field: husband or male children) and not caring for themselves (complete lack of protection in the task of flag-waving or cases of poisoning due to exposure to the products used). As a snowball, one by one they narrate similar situations, as well as the actions they took in this respect: requests to the Minister of Livestock, Agriculture and Fisheries for the prohibition of fumigation which has affected their production and health.

They all agree that they are attached to the countryside, and that it is "their place in the world," and they share a concern for their children's and their own futures in the countryside, in the face of field sales to foreigners and the migration of small producers while the large ones expand. The dispute for common goods and the care of water, soil, palm groves, native forests, native fauna, the

---

[4] Continuing education course presented at the Centro Universitario Región Este (Rocha), Universidad de la República, Uruguay, in the second semester of 2017.

landscape as a cultural and historical identity, agricultural production as a basis for economic sustenance, and family production as a way of life, as an exercise of sovereignty and rights, among others, come up as emerging issues.

Closing and opening words

> A lot of things changed for us. Not only this, coming here, spending a lot of hours [...] that's incredible. For us, it's value. We know we can do it. For our house and our family, it's all right. Everything we did, cooking, and not just that. Everything else. We were used to fixing things. But doing it this way was an adventure, realizing that we could. Even being in a group. We weren't that close... and this group for us is very strong (B. B., artisanal fisherwoman).

For us, who transcribed and made our own many of these words, plenty of things also changed. It changed the way we approach, look, think and plan our work in the territory, together with the collectives and communities that live there. We share these words as a trial, as an experience that initiates and at the same time motivates us to continue moving forward. We do know and firmly maintain that we question the hierarchical ways of building knowledge, that we choose to distance ourselves from diffusionism, from non-critical extension, from practices that do not take the time and place to think about themselves. We wish to build and rethink the processes in the territory, with women, with the different collectives and communities, contemplating and accompanying their worlds (in dialogue with ours), integrating and sharing interests, challenges, projections. At the center, we place their concerns, women's concerns, their experiences, their ailments, their fears, their dreams, their worries, their desire to build collectively. At the center, we place, at the same time, our concerns, our desires and these words that are the input to continue thinking about us.

Bibliographical references

Baylina Ferré, M. (2004). Metodología para el estudio de las mujeres y la sociedad rural. *Revista Estudios Geográficos* 65(254), pp. 5-28.

Blixen, C., R. Cantieri, I. Malán, V. Menéndez and I. Peluso (2012). Cuando se es abeja y se tira como un tractor. Reflexiones en torno a la formación de productoras/es familiares con perspectiva de género y generación. In D. Piñeiro, R. Vitelli and J. Cardeillac, *Relaciones de género en el medio rural uruguayo: inequidades "a la intemperie"* (pp. 63-80). Montevideo: Programa I+D-CSIC/ NESA/FCS-UDELAR.

Carroza, N. (2017). Metodologías de trabajo de experiencias de vinculación con el medio en universidades chilenas: entre lo convencional y lo emergente. In B. González, P. Saravia, N. Carroza, F. Gascón, C. Dinamarca and L. Castro, *Vinculación con el Medio y Territorio. Heterogeneidad de modelos, prácticas y sentidos en las universidades chilenas* (pp. 93-114). Valparaíso: Observatorio de Participación Social y Territorio-Universidad de Playa Ancha.

Cruz Hernández, D. T. (2016). Una mirada muy otra a los territorios-cuerpos femeninos. *SOLAR, Revista de Filosofía Iberoamericana* 12(1), pp. 35-46.

Dalla Costa, M. R. (1972), *Las mujeres y la subversión de la comunidad*. Mexico: Siglo XXI.

De Barbieri, T. ([1998] 2002). Acerca de las propuestas metodológicas feministas. In Bartra, Eli (Comp.), *Debates en torno a una metodología feminista* (pp. 103-140). 2nd ed. Mexico: UAM-Xochimilco, UNAM-PUEG.

DeVault, M. (1999). *Liberating Methods: Feminism and Social Research*. Philadelphia: Temple University Press.

Fals Borda, Orlando (1981). La ciencia y el pueblo. In *Investigación participativa y praxis rural. Nuevos conceptos en educación y desarrollo comunal* (pp. 19-47). Lima: Mosca Azul Editores.

Federici, S. (2013). Revolución en punto cero. Trabajo doméstico, reproducción y luchas feministas. Madrid: Traficantes de Sueños.

Freire, Paulo (1984). ¿Extensión o comunicación? La concientización en el medio rural. Mexico: Siglo XXI.

Gallo, Alejandra and Irene Peluso (2013). Estrategias sucesorias en la ganadería familiar: un enfoque de género. *Revista de Ciencias Sociales* 26(32), pp.17-34. DS-FCS.

García Roces, I. and M. Soler Montiel (2010). Mujeres, agroecología y soberanía alimentaria en la comunidad Moreno Maia del Estado de Acre. *Investigaciones Feministas 1*. pp. 43-65.

Galcerán Huguet, M. (2006). Introducción: Producción y reproducción en Marx. In *Transformaciones del trabajo desde una perspectiva feminista. Producción, reproducción, deseo, consumo.* Madrid: Tierradenadie Ediciones, S.L./ Ciempozuelos.

Mançano Fernandes, Bernardo (2008). Territorio, teoría y política. In *Actas del Seminario Internacional "Las configuraciones de los territorios rurales en el siglo XXI"*. Bogotá: Pontificia Universidad Javeriana.

Pérez Orozco, A. (2006). La economía: de icebergs, trabajos e (in)visibilidades. Laboratorio Feminista. In M. Galcerán Huguet, *Transformaciones del trabajo desde una perspectiva feminista. Producción, reproducción, deseo, consumo.* Madrid: Tierradenadie Ediciones, S.L./Ciempozuelos.

Urruzola, Juan Pedro (2002). *Escritos urbanos*. Montevideo: Montevideo.

Rebellato, J. L. and L. Giménez (1997). *Ética de la autonomía*. Montevideo: Roca.

Tommasino, H. and A. Cano (2016). Avances y retrocesos de la extensión crítica en la Universidad de la República de Uruguay, *Revista de Extensión Univesitaria Másquedòs* (1), pp. 9-23. Buenos Aires: Unicen.

13. The map as a guide: mapping feminicidal violence and feminist progression

Melissa Moreano and Iñigo Arrazola

Colectivo de Geografía Crítica del Ecuador

1.

The idea of mapping violence against women had been around for some of us at the Colectivo de Geografía Crítica for a long time. This idea arose from the violence experienced by women themselves, from the feminism that appeared as a political option. An idea that progressively gained strength in the accompaniment of collectives and communities involved in processes of defense of their territories. For years we could see how the consolidation of certain types of agro-industrial, extractive and urban expansion projects produced clearly differentiated effects on women: pollution, forced displacement or community divisions are experienced differently by those who generally occupy the central positions of care and preservation of collective identities. In territories affected by mining projects, for example, the arrival of companies is associated with the installation of camps and brothels, with the consequent increase in insecurity and sexual violence.

How did we start? It was after seeing Sonia Madrigal's work in Mexico that the idea took shape. It fitted perfectly with the counter-mapping work we had been doing in the Colectivo de Geografía Crítica. In general, in the Colectivo we have regarded maps as very powerful tools of communication and construction of counter-hegemony. Maps have the potential to show realities in the territories from the point of view of those who suffer violence, using codes and representations strongly internalized by the population. They are a legitimized instrument of counter-information that we have learned to exploit over time.

At the same time, new geographic tools, and the power of what they now call "democratization of geography" (Ordoqui, 2008), through mapping applications to which we all have access from a telephone or a computer, appeared to be the best way to do it. Thus, it became evident that the first map could be assembled as a Google Map, also inspired by the work of the Mexican Sonia Aguilar and her project "Death comes out of the East". Currently, Sonia collects information sent by organizations in Mexico, Argentina and Ecuador, and invited organizations from all over Latin America to contribute to the map under construction.[1]

---

[1] Although it was the first work we saw that prompted us to do our mapping, it is not the only initiative. Other experiences: María Salguero also in Mexico: https://feminicidiosmx.crowdmap.com/; Ivonne Ramírez also in Mexico: http://www.ellastienennombre.org/; in Rosario, Argentina: https://www.google.com/maps/d/u/0/viewer?mid=17tuG Td-crQ3vCa429uh6W7D_eNk&ll=-30.755724265796925%2C-61.299816568749975&z=6. In La Plata, Argentina, the group Mapas de lo efímero (Maps of the Ephemeral) created a map of street sexual harassment: https://www.google.com/maps/d/viewer?mid=1r4BGL3O Wz2WlYhL8kc760k4pUfI&ll=-34.88207488334351%2C-57.98196374999998&z=12 . In Honduras, the Centro de Derechos de mujeres (Women's Rights Center) created a map of different forms of violence against women: http://gruponahuiik.com/temp/cdm/mapa-de-las-violencias-contra-las-mujeres-honduras-2013-2/.

Figure 1. Artistic interventions by Sonia Madrigal, 2015.

Source: http://lamuertesaleporeloriente.tumblr.com/

The need was also circumstantial. In the vortex of denunciations of feminicide throughout the continent[2], with a frightening intensification of the form of violence exerted on our bodies, the *Ni Una Menos, Vivas Nos Queremos* march also rose like a tide. It was September 2016, and the march would be on November 25. It seemed like the ideal time to present a map, a contribution from geography that would denounce what we sensed was happening: that we were being systematically and silently murdered. Our aim at that time, more than systematizing a geography of violence against women, was to make *the number of cases* visible. It was the

---

[2] In 2014, CEPAL's Observatorio de Igualdad de Género de América Latina y el Caribe (OIG, Gender Equality Observatory for Latin America and the Caribbean) reported that 1831 women were victims of feminicide in 2016 in 16 countries (https://oig.cepal.org/es/indicadores/feminicidio). This figure excludes Brazil, which reported 2925 cases of feminicides that year (https://www.efe.com/efe/espana/sociedad/brasil-registro-al-menos-ocho-feminicidios-diarios-en-un-ano/10004-3359907).

map as an instrument of communication of an aberrant situation that, like everything else, would present many silences.

Since we were new to these issues, we did not know where to look, so we consulted. Those of our companions who have been in this struggle for years are rightly suspicious of official sources. Often, these are hermetic and inaccurate, recording only what the hegemonic power is interested in. That is why feminist organizations have long been counting the beaten, abused, and murdered. But that is a source we would come to later, after gathering the initial figures.

In our first exercise we opted to review the written press. It was a source of quick access and we counted on journalistic morbidity to play in our favor to attenuate under-registration. Alisson reviewed *El Telégrafo*, Sara *El Comercio*, Iñigo and I reviewed *La Hora*. The first two, national newspapers. Understanding the political moment Ecuador is going through and the political dimension of our search, we decided to review a public-state newspaper (*El Telégrafo*), and a private newspaper (*El Comercio*). We would then expand the search to a newspaper that, in addition to having national circulation, has coverage in several provinces (*La Hora*), something that the others lacked. We are often asked why we do not review the best known red chronicle newspaper (*El Extra*). This newspaper exploits this type of events with morbidity and truculent images. The truth is that we do not work with *El Extra* in self-protection. If reviewing the other newspapers had already upset us deeply, we did not want to even imagine what it would be like to do archive work with this other newspaper. We decided to recognize our limits, to respect them, also taking into account that this first analysis had an exploratory character. We also learned later that this newspaper does not keep archives of its issues for more than a year.

With the press review work we had two objectives: on the one hand, to approach a figure that, without being systematic or pretending to be so, could give us an idea of the magnitude of this drama. On the other hand, we sought to understand the ways in which violence against women is narrated in the country. In this last part, which is more qualitative, we wanted to understand the mechanisms of naturalization of violence. We already knew that violence against women appears as a natural phenomenon, which is related as isolated accidents resulting from acts of unpredictable madness, and we wanted to evaluate the role of the media in this regard.

How did we proceed? We prepared an Excel table to record the data: who is the victim (man, woman, girl, LGBTI person), who is the aggressor (partner, ex-partner, father, stepfather, friend, acquaintance), the type of aggression (domestic violence, sexual harassment, rape, feminicide), the State's response, the geographical location. In the column "observations" we would write the name of the victim. We also left other fields to note the qualitative aspects that had caught our attention —omitting the subject of the action, mentioning irrelevant details such as the victim's clothes, deliberately using morbid headlines, details of the perpetrator's grievous harm to the victim's body, etc. The review took two months and covered two years of press reports. A total of 1800 copies of newspapers, hundreds of news items with all sorts of details and silences. The press review exercise initiated the feminist progression, with the empirical verification of the violence that women live and the systematic way in which the media hide it, disguising it as crimes of passion. As one of the authors wrote at the time:

> Finding the first case, its lurid details, trying to discern if it is gender violence. "She was stabbed by her partner in front of her five-year-old son." It is feminicide. Recording, filling in the table, moving on. Next issue. More cases. Rape with mutilation. Girl. Raped. Slashed woman: "he was assailed with jealousy". Feminicide. Pamela, Dyladis, Rosa, Diana, Joselyn, Eva, Angelica, Lenny, Nancy. Little by little I was concentrating on the police section or the red chronicle. Although the news I was looking for was sometimes distributed in other sections, most of it was there (Moreano, 2016).

In the midst of an evident absence of analysis by the media, the shocking data was drawn: between November 2014 and November 2016, the media reported 299 cases of violence against women, from sexual harassment to aggravated feminicide, the name used when a feminicide perpetrator is particularly vicious against the woman or girl's body.

Of those 299 cases, 97 were of feminicide, aggravated feminicide and attempted feminicide and the aggressor was someone close to the woman or girl: her partner, ex-partner, father, stepfather, friend or neighbor. Couples and ex-couples were responsible for 81 cases. The headlines were repeated: "Love blinded him" or "He killed her because she left him." Behind these headlines that naturalize feminicidal violence, the media narrated murders that often ended with the suicide of the feminicide perpetrator. Gruesome stories in which the daughters and sons of the murdered women were present, were the ones who found the bodies or were killed as the first "example" to the woman. Another finding was the level of viciousness applied to the women's bodies: feminicide was often accompanied by rape and mutilation.

The responsibility of the media was evident in the language and graphics used. The naturalization of "crime of passion" and "loves that kill" only stimulates the permanent need of men to exercise their power over those they consider *their* women, spreading the idea that "normal" men, in a moment of madness stimulated by passion (or alcohol, or drugs), murdered their partner.

Geographical localization was useful to place the points on Google Maps.[3] We associated the information in the table to each point. The map constructed in this way presented some geographical gaps. For example, the cases were concentrated in Quito, Santo Domingo, Guayaquil, and Durán, which we thought was not necessarily linked to the fact that there was more violence in those cities, but rather to the representation of those urban centers in the newspapers. There was also a striking class bias: most of the cases reported were victims from the working and lower classes, which also cannot be attributed to greater violence in those

---

[3] The Google Map is available at our website: https://geografiacriticaecuador.org/2016/11/23/violencia-feminicida-en-el-ecuador-lo-que-la-prensa-revela/

strata, but rather to a lack of violence visibility in the higher strata, with women who are likely better able to protect their privacy.

Google Maps helped us to systematize the information. But, as we had been doing, we produced a map of protesting Ecuador (Figure 2), with an aesthetic of denunciation, which we distributed in the *Ni Una Menos, Vivas Nos Queremos* march.[4]

Figure 2. Feminicides in Ecuador: what the press reveals.

Source: *El Comercio*, *El Telégrafo* and *La Hora* newspapers. Design: Colectivo de Geografía Crítica del Ecuador.

2.

The impact created by the map of violence against women constructed from print media data was unexpected. The map — numbers placed over Ecuador's provinces with female outlines, in pink, the color of the march— would be the first trial to be repeated later with the maps we produced on official information on

---

[4] In Ecuador, this march is organized by the Plataforma Vivas Nos Queremos: https://www.facebook.com/VivasNosQueremosEcuador/

violence, the bi-monthly maps of feminicide, and finally the maps on the criminalization of abortion. The idea of putting numbers on a map, as simple as it seems, was a shock. We had no idea what it would do, how it would bring together the outrage and rage that many women already felt.

For us, critical geographers, producing maps had always meant the appropriation of a tool that power had used for territorial control and war (Lacoste 1990 [1976]). Our position is, in the end, that the map is not a faithful copy of reality, it is only *a representation* of it, a simplification for various purposes. For us, the purpose was to reveal, in shades of pink and lilac, "what was covered up": that violence against women has been systematically and historically denied (Femenias and Rossi 2009, p. 54).

Thus, although the map attempts to represent the dimension of the problem through the assignment of figures that symbolize the number of women murdered per province, it does not nearly capture all the complexity and pain of the situation. In any case, the risk of the map being taken as a truth was latent. For example, the need immediately arose, from those who saw the maps, to know if there was a national emergency in which women *were being murdered in greater numbers than before*. This was a response that we could not give from the maps, even after having access to official figures and those of feminist and women's organizations.

However, there are voices that claim that there is an upsurge in violence against women in Latin America. Femenias and Rossi attribute this to the fact that "men —as a result of changes in the labor market and culture in general— are attempting to discipline with violence those 'autonomous' women they see as the axis of their ills" (2009, p. 44). In an effort to understand violence against women in a broader historical-social framework, they analyze the precarization of employment conditions and reproduction of life with the evolution of capitalist globalization, which has also reversed many of the previous labor conquests, "widening the margins of exclusion, destabilization and crisis of the traditional models of the male provider" (Femenías and Rossi, 2009, p. 48). The authors put forward the interesting hypothesis that violence has been intensified by men who have become precarized and lost in the face of the "irruption of women" into the public sphere. Frustration with the new conditions of exploitation would cause men to attack women who are just as exploited as they are, but who they consider dangerous or competitive, instead of directing their anger at men in privileged situations. Disciplining women would create the illusion of somehow recovering their status, "masculinity — in terms of belonging to the male set— [is] recognized in terms of the subjugation and subalternization of women" (Femenías and Rossi, 2009, p. 58).

However, "it is difficult to understand rape, mutilation and torture as modes of punishment or discipline" (Femenías and Rossi, 2009, p. 58). In this sense, it became urgent for us to unveil the sharpness of the violence and the political recognition of the feminist struggle.

3.

What we thought would be the end of this process was not the end. The information extracted from the newspapers was too valuable. As our companion Cristina Burneo would tell us in a forum: we had done a translation exercise. From the red chronicle texts to reflection and political denunciation, we decided that the gaps found in the press review should be filled. In addition, we had an overwhelming desire —in our bodies— to talk to the journalists who wrote about these atrocities, and we wanted to compare what we had found with official information.

Alisson Molina, a fellow intern at the collective, who reviewed the newspaper *El Telégrafo* describes this second moment:

> In the second part of the process, after the information was collected, an analysis was made contrasting the data obtained by the Colectivo with the data from official reports. The results of this comparative analysis were crucial in sustaining the process that followed. After an extensive study by the members of the Colectivo, and thanks to the theoretical contributions of colleagues with knowledge of gender issues, violence against women, feminist and women's collectives, it was possible to expand the research and prepare a document that would contribute to the struggle to eradicate gender violence. With the document ready, an informative booklet was elaborated on "The role of journalism in the eradication of violence against women", which was distributed to journalists in different cities of the

country (Cuenca, Quito, Guayaquil, Puyo, Portoviejo and Ambato) (Molina 2017).

In effect, we decided to map the "Route of the Denunciation", with the interest of evidencing *the amount* of violent events that occur and how violence indicators vary considerably depending on the source of official information used. As we investigated, it also became evident that underreporting levels are very high and that women in situations of violence are absolutely helpless. For the elaboration of this Route, we used the data available from the 2011 National Survey on Violence against Women by the Instituto Nacional de Estadísticas y Censos (INEC, National Institute of Statistics and Censuses); but also data by other state institutions to which we specifically addressed requests. Among them are: (1) the emergency call system ECU911, (2) the Department of Domestic Violence in the National Police, (3) the Prosecutor's Office and (4) the Judiciary Council.

The following is a preliminary analysis[5] of the information gathered from various public institutions, a geography of violence against women that is censored, that we all feel is wrong, that has raised anger and indignation throughout the world, throughout Latin America. This analysis would then allow us to make the connection with what we consider feminicidal state violence that is not considered as such: the criminalization of abortion.[6]

---

[5] A preliminary analysis of this information was presented in the *Manifiesto geográfico contra la violencia hacia las mujeres* (Geographical Manifesto of Violence Against Women), available at https://geografiacriticaecuador.org/2017/08/08/manifiesto-geografico-contra-violencia-hacia-las-mujeres/. Part of this information has also been discussed in S. Zaragocin, M. Silveira and I. Arrazola (2018).

[6] In this article we do not address the mapping of the criminalization of abortion. The main findings will be soon published in S. Zaragocin, A. Yépez, V. Vera, G. Ruales, G. Falanga and I. Arazola, "Mapeando la criminalización del

According to the INEC (2011), at least 6 out of 10 women have suffered from gender-based violence in Ecuador. In fact, Figure 3 expresses the percentage of women by province who declare to have suffered any type of gender violence. The design of the map allowed us to add additional information: in the vast majority of cases, violence is caused by the victim's partner or former partner. Likewise, the data from ECU 911 is chilling: during 2015 and 2016 there were 564 daily calls reporting domestic violence.

Figure 3. Map of violence against women according to INEC data (2011)

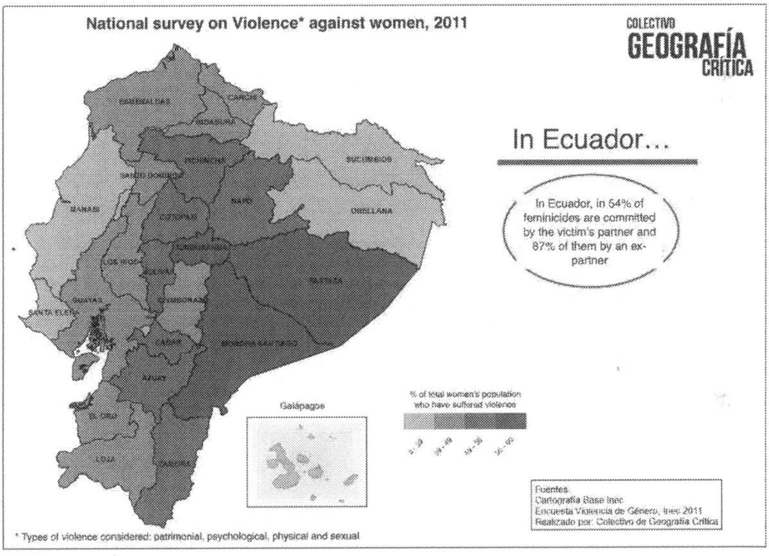

Source: Cartografía Base Inec. Design: Colectivo de Geografía Crítica del Ecuador.

As a group that questions the legitimacy of the State when it comes to ordering and administering the territory, we have to be careful with the use we make of this information. What do the surveys and the rest of the data collected by the official bodies tell us?

---

aborto en el Ecuador" ("Mapping the criminalization of abortion in Ecuador", in press), *Revista de Bioética y Derecho*.

Throughout numerous internal debates and with other feminist colleagues, we have discussed the degree of validity and reliability of this INEC survey. Our concerns with the survey data relate both to the bias of its own application —although it is representative of the provinces, the survey was conducted primarily in urban centers— and to the type of instrument itself. As it was applied throughout the country, we believe that the survey has difficulties in focusing on the different contexts where gender violence occurs, given the heterogeneity of the women who are violated —urban women of the upper middle class, urban women in popular neighborhoods, rural and Indigenous women in territories hit by megamining, peasant women who defend their autonomy in the face of agro-industrial chains, etc.

In spite of the above, we believe that the survey data are useful when taken as a first diagnostic image, of course keeping in mind its biases and limitations. First of all, we are struck by the high rate of violence in the Central Sierra and the Amazonia. Although the Amazonia region is one of the areas with the lowest population density in the country, the results make us wonder about the reasons why, in relative terms, violence against women shows such high rates. One possible cause of this lies in the very process of territorialization of State and business actors in Amazonia. For decades, the Amazonia region has been seen in the collective imagination as a space of extraction and colonization (Colectivo de Geografía Crítica del Ecuador, 2014). Oil exploitation and the advance of the agricultural frontier caused great tensions in the territories of Amazonian communities, undermining their livelihoods by polluting and displacing these peoples. As we have already argued, the increase in violence against women is also related to these processes. Having said this, we wish to make it clear that, far from starting from an ideal conception about equity and harmony of the communities prior to the arrival of these conflicts, what we are saying is that the reproduction of gender violence has, as an unrenounceable element of explanation and of political intervention, the environment of generalized violence caused by these projects in their territories.

THE MAP AS A GUIDE

In the following map (figure 4) we show the data on complaints of violence against women between the years 2014 and 2016 according to the Prosecutor's Office. The provinces are colored according to the relative rate between the number of complaints and total women in each province. This map, read in relation to the previous map, raises important questions about women's access to official reporting and assistance. Why is the relative rate of reports not among the highest in the Central Sierra and the Amazonia, areas with the highest rates of violence? What is the reason for this under-representation of violence constructed from the data of the Prosecutor's Office? This type of question is an invitation to reflect on the unequal distribution of State institutions throughout the country and on the particular ways in which violence takes place in spaces shaped by such different histories and cultural patterns.

Figure 4. Violence against women according to data from the State Attorney General's Office.

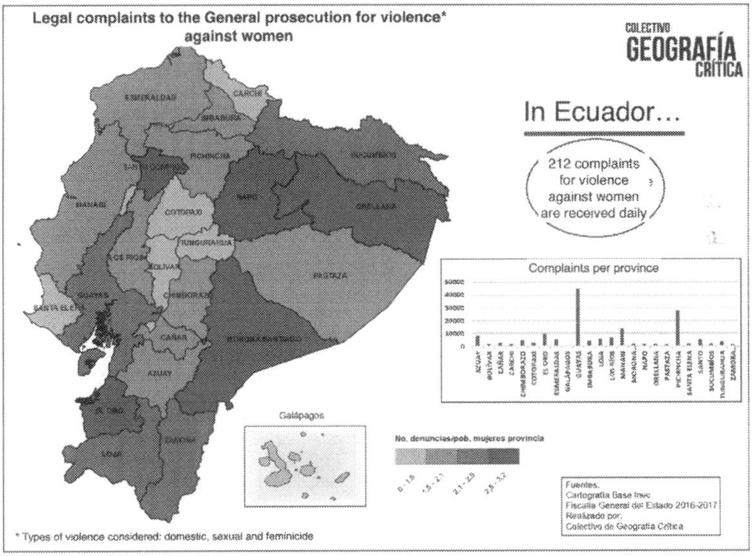

Source: Cartografía Base Inec. Design: Colectivo de Geografía Crítica del Ecuador.

Another central axis for understanding gender-based violence in Ecuador has to do with the ineffectiveness of the judicial system, as mentioned in the manifesto submitted to the National Assembly:

229

> [...] impunity with respect to violence against women has reached intolerable levels. The justice system is inefficient and generates greater vulnerability and helplessness for women who are victims of violence. [According to INEC data] only 20% of women who are victims of violence turn to the justice system, but less than 50% finally report it. Of those who do report, only 5% of cases are sentenced and less than 1% of women receive a sentence in their favor (Colectivo de Geografía Crítica del Ecuador, 2017, p. 1).

The INEC survey (2011) offers some clues to understand the reasons why women do not report. Both for cases of violence in the social, school and work environment and for cases of sexual violence, women mentioned fear or threats as the main reasons for not reporting (31% and 45% respectively). Given that in most cases women are subjected to violence by partners, ex-partners or people from their family environment, it is more than likely that this fear and these threats come from that same environment. On the other hand, when asked about the reasons why many women withdraw their complaints and do not continue with the trials, the same INEC survey shows that, for cases of sexual violence, 35% of the women reported having withdrawn the complaints due to lack of money.

What kind of measures can we think of when it comes to tackling these problems? A central aspect has to do with the training of the judicial system's personnel. As a feminist lawyer who is an expert on these issues told us, "lawyers, judges and prosecutors now know about laws on gender violence, but still do not understand well what gender violence is" (Arévalo 2017, personal communication). Therefore, there is no point in having adapted legal codes if those in charge of enforcing them on a daily basis do not have the necessary skills to do so.

On the other hand, the creation of spaces and institutions in which women can trust and feel safe is another aspect that cannot be ignored when talking about actions that address the problem as a whole. As we have already pointed out, according to data from the same INEC, most of the aggressions come from the most immediate family circle (parents, uncles, but above all partners and former partners). The State must therefore guarantee the material conditions of women and their children when they report and follow up on the judicial process. However, we are still faced with a judicial labyrinth that favors the re-victimization of women who have been subjected to violence, and discourages them from following a process that is already long.

4.

The elaboration of the countermaps of violence against women pushed us, at that moment without knowing it, towards a theme in which we would end up deeply involved. This is how it has always happened: the production of the map with very instrumental purposes of counter-hegemony leads us to represent a reality that, already denaturalized, impels us. As geographers, the map is only a starting point. But also, in this case it meant, in some way, the beginning of the feminist evolution of the Colectivo de Geografía Crítica del Ecuador.

We chose to reveal the figures of violence, but in that journey we also revealed the inscription of that violence in our own bodies. We, reading such news, the women of the aid networks, the lawyers, the members of the platforms that demand justice for feminicides, the women's organizations, the November marchers, all women who have suffered violence in our bodies as a result of the violent patriarchal structure, feel those deaths in our own bodies. As a companion from the Colectivo de Geografía Crítica said, "It hurts in the womb."

We had said that, as geographers, the map is only a starting point. In this case, it was also a guide to the growing militant commitment that would involve not only working to highlight the alarming figures on violence against women, for example, through the production of bi-monthly maps that would account for the growing number of feminicides in the country, but also to try to understand the different dimensions of that violence. We would then map the criminalization of abortion and try to integrate the gender violence dimension into our longstanding work on territorial conflicts.

However, this is not just a story of mourning. Behind the evidence of our dead stand organized women, among whom we are now. As Nela Martínez, an Ecuadorian feminist, says: "in search of a story: telling it, writing it, singing it is necessary. First, we must rescue it" ([1985] 2010, p. 119).

Bibliography

Arévalo, A. (2017). Personal communication. Guayaquil: Centro Ecuatoriano para la Promoción y Acción de la Mujer.

Colectivo de Geografía Crítica del Ecuador (2017). *Manifiesto contra la violencia hacia las mujeres desde la Geografía Crítica*. Available at https://geografiacriticaecuador.org/wp-content/uploads/2017/08/Manifiesto-geogr%C3%A1fico-contra-violencia-hacia-las-mujeres-FINAL.pdf (Accessed 10 September 2017).

— (2014). *Manifiesto en defensa del Yasuní*. Available at https://geografiacriticaecuador.org/wp-content/uploads/2014/04/colectivo-geografia-critica-en-defensa-del-yasuni.pdf (Accessed 14 August 2017).

Femenías, M. L. and P. Soza Rossi (2009). Poder y violencia sobre el cuerpo de las mujeres. *Sociologias* (21), p. 42-65.

Instituto Nacional de Estadística y Censos (INDEC) (2011). *Encuesta nacional sobre Relaciones Familiares y Violencia de Género contra las Mujeres*. Available at http://www.ecuadorencifras.gob.ec/violencia-de-genero (Accessed 10 January 2017).

Lacoste, Yves (1990 [1976]). *La geografía: un arma para la guerra*. Barcelona: Anagrama.

Martínez, N. ([1985] 2010). En busca de una historia: contarla, escribirla, cantarla es necesario. Antes hay que rescatarla, Quito, 1985. In Francesca Gargallo, (Ed.), *Antología del pensamiento feminista nuestroamericano*, t. II: *Movimiento de liberación de las mujeres* (pp. 119-124). Caracas: Biblioteca Ayacucho.

Molina, A. (2017). *Informe de prácticas pre-profesionales*. Ecuador: Escuela de Gestión Social-Pontificia Universidad Católica del Ecuador (unpublished document).

Moreano, M. (2016). Queremos todos los nombres. *Revista Digital La Barra Espaciadora*. Available at http://labarraespaciadora.com/aqui-y-ahora/feminicidios-queremos-todos-los-nombres/

Ordoqui, J. M. (2008). La Geografía, los geógrafos y la gestión. Aportes para la democratización del Territorio. *Boletín geográfico* (31), p. 269-287. Departamento Geografía. Edición especial: VII Jornadas Patagónicas de Geografía. Neuquén: Universidad Nacional del Comahue.

Zaragocin, S., M. Silveira and I. Arrazola (2018). Construyendo una geografía del feminicidio en el Ecuador. In *Género y construcción del espacio: de la exclusión a la reivindicación del derecho a la ciudad*. Observatorio de Antropología del Conflicto Urbano (in press).

14. Subverting the geopolitics of sexual violence: a proposal for (counter)mapping our bodies-territory

Giulia Marchese

Universidad Nacional Autónoma de México.
GeoBrujas-Comunidad de Geógrafas

Introduction

> My feminism is based not on embodied abstractions, but on bodily realities. The material body is the center and central. The body is the land of thought and imagination... Our task is to imagine Coyolxauhqui, neither dead nor headless, but with eyes wide open. Our task is to illuminate the darkness.
> Gloria Anzaldúa

The female or feminized body experience is historically infiltrated by actors from the most diverse backgrounds, where silenced women become witnesses to a dynamic of contention between who is authorized to exercise control over this material surface and what it supposedly involves. From the Nation-state, the Church, the family, couple relationships, private enterprises, civil society and its multiple forms of social organization, they remind us women that the meaning of our existence transcends our bodily boundaries; we are in this world for more than ourselves as individuals or as a community. Critically analyzing the geographic formation of this body that we are is of fundamental importance in understanding the phenomena that are trapped within it, and that turn out to be phenomena that constitute this geographic space. I locate sexual violence, and the geopolitics in which it is framed, as one of these constitutive phenomena. Sexual violence, as violence based on the sexualized body on which it is exercised, whose meaning, however, is porous with respect to the geopolitical defining line that is the skin, is a phenomenon both systemic and transhistoric, both intimate and personal as well as political and structural.

Feminisms have tried to understand sexual or sexualized violence from a non-victimizing to women, paternalistic or criminalizing point of view towards the subjects and bodies involved, denouncing the (self-)invisibilization and naturalization imposed to perpetuate it. It is in this feminist perspective, from the anti-racist and anti-speciesist Latin America in which I am formed and transformed, that I place myself as a woman raised and disciplined through experiences of violence and, nevertheless, here and now, living in a racist environment as a systematically privileged woman: white, young, with a European passport, university graduate, migrant. A system that becomes environment, surroundings, that has tried to silence my voice, my free walk and my experience, and guide them towards spatialities more appropriate to my conditions of gender, race and class. Sexism, racism and classism operate together to reassign us to appropriate legal territories. Whether we are urban or rural women, white or racialized, of different class, age, and geographic location, our identitarian conditions assembled in our bodies seek to be continuously oriented, corrected, straightened, and universalized by the most different maps. Our maps as urban women are, to cite one example, the immense advertising posters we see on the roads. They are uses and customs of our towns, neighborhoods, families: the legal system, more or less legislated, that founds or tries to found our territories. They are maps that pretend to orient us, although the only thing they do is spatialize the body, make it space, proposing the general rule, the desirable dimensions, both internally and externally, in this supposed Western polarization between body and spirit.

In committed academic research, accompanied by social mobilizations, feminisms have practically declined due to epistemologies and methodologies that have turned back to radical social change. Placing myself in this context, in the present work I will refer to an approach that considers the contributions of anthropology and geography based on feminist epistemology, which I will define as *feminist political geography of the body* (or *embodiment of geography*). It is necessary to underline here the political character of the (self-)knowledge intended to be generated through the proposed methodologies, whose objectives are to "visibilize, denaturalize and historicize" (Castañeda Salgado, 2012) sexual violence in women's experience, the experience made flesh in our bodies. Despite political efforts, both academic and "practical", the phenomenon continues to affect the lives and bodies of most of us women in the contemporary world.

I believe that conducting feminist research on sexual violence has to involve a deep analysis of our personal experience, from which we can re-acquaint ourselves with it. To affirm that the phenomenon is so generalized and rooted that it affects the majority of women's or feminized bodies means involving ourselves in recognizing ourselves as part of the subjects of the investigation. Indeed, recognizing female researchers as the first subjects and actors of the research: the body of the researcher as the first territory to be (counter-)mapped. This implies not only re-acquainting ourselves with the women with whom we are committed to working, but also transforming ourselves from the depths that we are, from our own bodies.

From this *re-cognition*, it seems to me immediate to think of academic research in the terms of a *co-labor* (Leyva Solano and Speed, 2015) of intimate, collective, social transformation. Committing to politicizing the phenomenon of sexual violence, to making it visible in terms of the political violence of the assemblages of power at the territorial level, implies two actions:

- to analyze the power relationships present in different contexts, in different dimensions and at different geographic scales: the analysis of the power relationships that are present in the "observed" and the power relationships between the "observer" and the "observed", in addition to the relationships that each person establishes with her/his own personal experience.
- to highlight the need for a critique of geography and ethnography as an analysis of a specifically public dimension of culture. Feminist political geography aims to

be a methodology that "repoliticizes" and "deprivatizes" the experience of women, which, in addition, questions the categories of modern spatial fragmentation, such as "public space" and "private space".

The spatialization of feminine experience: women's bodies

In this effort I intend to incorporate a critical geographical knowledge in a feminist perspective to understand and free us from sexual and sexualized violence, which also means understanding how our bodies were spatialized.

This materiality that we call body, the materiality that we are, has been approached in different ways from geography, in particular from feminist geography. The body has been defined as a place (Massey, 1994), the first geographical scale of analysis (Smith, 1993), a surface intervened by different actors and/or powers (McDowell, 2000), a territory for conquest (Segato, 2014).

In this article, the aim is to show how each conceptualization about the body is strategic for the political objective that we set for ourselves: in this case, it is about building participatory methodologies for the work of (de)construction of free and liberating body experiences for women.

Consequently, I am interested in approaching the body as a *territorial assemblage*, as a political territory composed of many other political territories that produce it, in which there are power relations from which it is necessary to free ourselves.

Women's bodies are historically configured as a *political territory* (Gómez Grijalba, 2012). The Maya-Xinka community feminist Lorena Cabnal states in this regard:

> interpretive categories such as "body territory" are shaped, which implies the first body territory of Indigenous women[1] in an action of recovery and

---

[1] In her words, the author refers to Indigenous women, although I personally consider that the categories she proposes

defense, that territory expropriated by the patriarchies and twice agreed upon to sustain them, a territory with bodily memory and historical memory, therefore the first place of enunciation, the place to be healed, emancipated, liberated, the place to recover and claim joy. *The body that embraces the "land territory"*,[2] which implies a meaningful and historical place where the long memory of the peoples lives, a territory of recovery by colonial expropriation, the usurpation of improper organizational models, the mercantilist imposition of private property, referred to be part of the colonial nation state but also in defense before the rise of neoliberalism through the extractive transnationals as another new form of dispossession, looting and threat to the life of the peoples" (Cabnal in Gargallo, 2012, p. 165).

It is the *territory that we inhabit, that we are* — territory-body and territory-land — that gives meaning to the methodology proposed here. In this sense, on the one hand, we consider the territory as the unit of measurement of the patriarchal and, consequently, capitalist extractive practices. In the acquisitive calculation of these hegemonic powers, women's bodies are read as a geostrategic territory for conquest (Segato, 2014), not only of the bodies themselves, but also of the entire community[3] and its territory-land. This assemblage between the territory-body and the territory-earth makes an analysis of the contexts of war in which massive phenomena of sexual violence are inserted become fundamental, particularly in the Central American region and in Mexico.

On the other hand, we recognize the body as the assemblage of our embodied subjectivity, our first territory, from which we push our processes of liberation.

The main characteristics of a cartography are the geographical scale, the system of representation and the symbolism, all of which are categories of spatial-temporal organization that are combined

---

can be extended to women's bodies, themselves traversed by different "hierarchizing" powers.

[2] My italics, to emphasize the way in which the author connects the body-territory and the land-territory through an embrace.

[3] The category of "community" is used here in a broad sense, not only referring to native communities but also to self-conformed communities of coexistence and communities in resistance.

for the (self-)appropriation of world representation. If our territories-body and our territories-land are indeed territories of power, it is time to de-functionalize them as territories of resistance, as political territories of insubordination, of spatial-temporal dislocation, reversing the geographic scales, the systems of representation and the symbologies of the territorial assemblages of power. Orthodox cartography, both corporal and municipal, state, national and global, constructs the territory by proposing systems of enclosure and definition (both sex-generic, like national borders) in order to functionalize us for extractive penetration: "each cartography is, above all, a project about the world. The project of each cartography is to transform, in anticipation, the face of the earth in its image and likeness" (Farinelli, 2009). Territorial knowledge and its representation are another way of exercising power, in addition to vehiculating its exercise; geography is a weapon for war, where, in cartographic production, the hegemonic subject occupies the central place, while the territories placed to the north and south are "functionalized" in relation to the north, each in its own way and according to the current perspective. The map is not the territory: "the map lies. Traditional geography steals the space, just as traditional economy steals the wealth, official history steals the memory, and formal culture steals the word," Eduardo Galeano says.

If we look at a map of what is intended to be a female body and a male body, a hegemonic representation of the two bodies, we see how the male body is drawn with straight lines that make it up, while the female body is characterized by curved lines. The straight line, in fact, is the shortest line to get from one point to another: it is the line of the modern map, the map of the conquerors, the map of the neocolonialist practices that seek to spatialize the earth, nature and, in turn, naturalize some corporalities as appropriable.

In the same way that the standardized and biologicist image of the female and male bodies is a violent and fallacious representation, so is the best known representation of the world, that of Mercator: Eurocentric, because it represents Europe at the center of the world, feeding a culturally vitiated vision that deforms the territory as it approaches the poles; it is rectangular. That said, there are no maps that are free of distortions, approximations and generalizations. Peters' planisphere, created to be more faithful to the real dimensions of the continents, respects the proportion of the surfaces, but not the distances.

Another issue to be discussed is: who establishes the boundaries of the bodies, of the Nation-states, and through which operations were the lines that defined them drawn? And, in the analysis of the planispheres, who decided that the north is up and the south is down? Evidently, people concerned with producing representations of the world that would functionalize a vision in which the north is "above" and the south is "below", perpetuating the master-slave, penetrator-penetrated dialectic. The planisphere commonly used in Australia shows us an "upside-down" world, although it does not question the centrality of Europe and the proportions proposed by Mercator. How to represent in a non-paralyzing, suggestive, freer, liberating, dysfunctional and open? How to reverse imaginaries in order to denounce, deconstruct and recreate better conditions of habitability in our world-territories?

Strategies of (self-)representation: "body-worlds" or embodying geography

Placing myself in this theoretical context, in this article I will put forth an approach that considers the contributions of anthropology and feminist geography, which I define as *feminist political geography of the body* (or *embodiment of geography*). I understand the *feminist political geography of the body* as a method of embodied research (the body as the first territory of analysis), which allows me to think about those geographic scales and territories analyzed in terms of *assemblages*.

Researching in the history of cartography we find forms of representation of reality that are the result of processes of (self-)awareness and represent alternatives to the hegemonic spatial form that characterizes the extractive approach of modern geopolitics. One of these examples is the artistic-literary production by Opicinus de Canistris, an Italian priest, mystic, writer and cartographer who lived in the 14th century. The images and

241

representations he produced were called "world-bodies" (Images, n.d.). They corresponded to the author's visions; they were representations of continents and oceans transformed into human figures, many of them self-representations used as a technique of self-analysis, to interpret his mystical visions in relation to his body and his life.

Opicinus de Canistris narrates: "My interior eyes were opened to the discernment of the earth and the sea and to integrate them into my conscience" (Whittington, 2010, p. 20). His maps appear as embodied maps. "On the one hand, creating the body-worlds allowed Opicinus to literalize and simplify micro/macrocosmic connections between bodies and worlds in a way that few had been able to do before him. But he also used this idea in order to create images unrivalled in their complexity and interpretive difficulty, multiplying maps and figures across the page in kaleidoscopic networks" (Images, n.d.).

What is most important in this context is making evident how most of his works depict the earth and the bodies as coextensive, made from the same material: bodies made out of the same matter as the earth (Whittington, 2010).

This co-extensiveness also leads us to overcome the ontological and epistemic distance placed between the "subject" and "object" of research, as well as the constant power relationship established between the two, the subjective and the objective.

Likewise, involving power relations in the analysis implies broadening the limited methodological horizon of the patriarchal and colonial social sciences, stuck in the universalism-relativism dialectic, macroscales-microplaces, structures and individual practices.

These research premises lead us to a constant rethinking of our position as female researchers and of our relationship with what we research, the object-subject of the research, to "place the researcher on the same critical plane as the explicit object of study" (Harding, 1998). It forces us to a continuous renegotiation of the position and the power relations that it implies at the moment in which mobility and reflexivity are considered as two characteristics of all the subjects involved in the research.

Figure 1. World Map of Opicinus of Canistris.

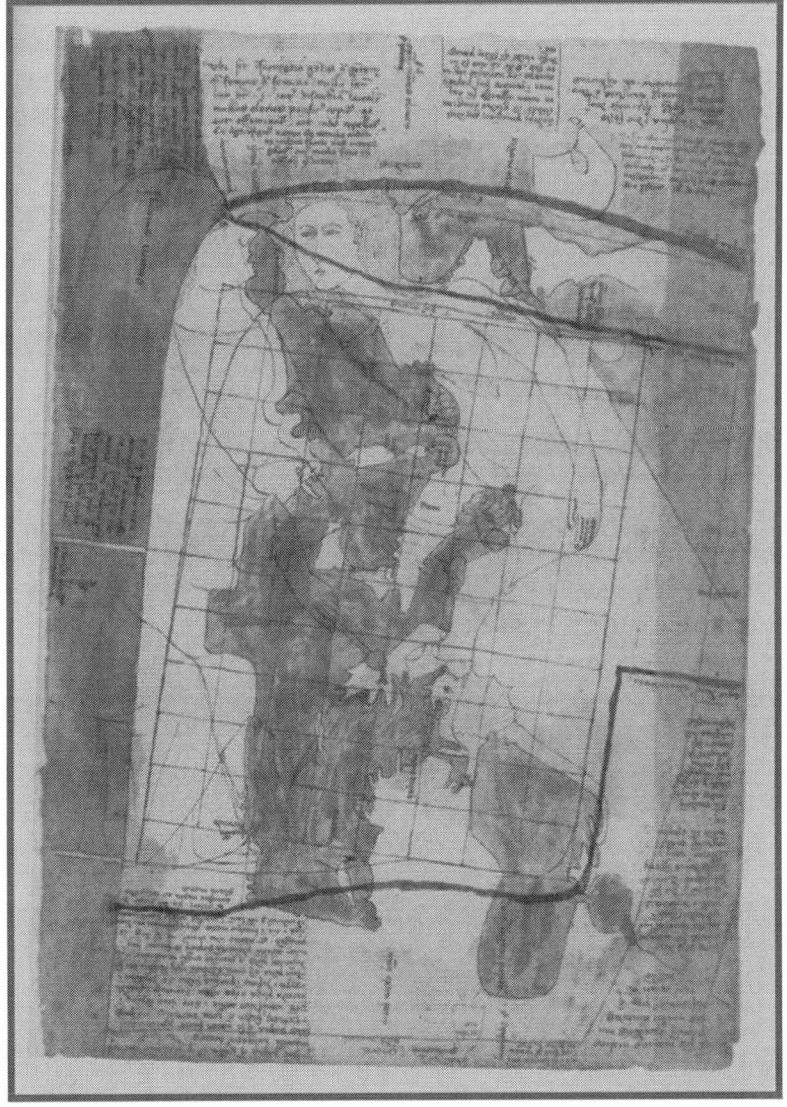

Source: https://www.alamy.es/457-opicinus-de-canistris-mapa-mundial-1296-1300-image187425963.html

Through this research method, we confirm that the political project neutrally defined as globalization masks multiform processes of domination of a neo-imperial and neo-colonizing style at different geographical scales. These processes constantly involve equally multiform spatial dynamics. From the geo-economy, the territory is partitioned into industrial and financial zones that shape territories as special economic zones, free trade zones, industrial parks, offshore enclaves, apparently identical anywhere in the world, while it becomes necessary to analyze the territorial assemblages that convey these zonings. Assemblages that articulate profoundly different, but equally functional, elements. The aim does not seem to be to eliminate differences, to exclude the different, but rather to work with these differences to construct corridors and routes in a world that is always more productively fragmented. Although this tendency can be regarded as apparently generalized, I consider that the spatial basis of the hegemonic political-economic system has always been heterotopic. Rather than in the direction of excluding "alternative" spaces and including "homogeneous" spaces, one should think in terms of the "hierarchical inclusion" of all spatial formations, addressing them and transforming them (doing violence to them) to make them systemically functional. What is different, rather than being excluded from the system, is absorbed by it and placed in spaces that are relatively peripheral, marginalized and precarized.

Figure 2. Mexico's open veins.

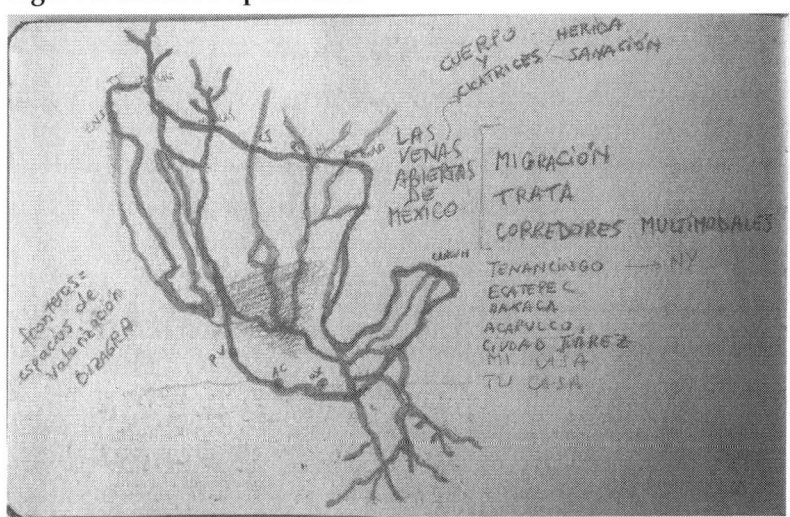

Source: Giulia Marchese.

It is necessary to change the *point of view* to understand how established hierarchies and exclusions are productive for the political-economic system.

I believe that this macro-micro polarization re-essentializes the geographic scales and the functionalist approach with which they were linked at the systemic level. In this discussion, it is necessary to bear in mind the defined "global connections", which allow for the articulation and territorialization of the abstract global space of flows.

There is a clear division and fragmentation of the geographical space into functionally specialized areas. Both our bodies and the Mexican space-nation itself can be read on the basis of a productive specialization that inserts them into a specific dynamic of the international division of labor and the global economy. Mexico is a country that offers at a regional and international level certain natural resources, among them, the resources of the subsoil, of nature and the bodies of people. Similarly, there are different zones that are formally recognized, such as financial zones and special economic zones, and others that are not formally recognized, such as zones for the extraction of natural resources and the harvesting of women's bodies for trafficking, that is, zones of territorial dispossession in broader terms. This represents a clear testimony to how contemporary geography is marked by the economy and its dynamics, such as the widespread warfare implanted in the territories to favor extractive practices.

While space marks limits and contents, geopolitics connects and functionally signifies spaces at a systemic level for their productivity. Revealing the assemblages that support essentializations and spatial and methodological fragmentations (geographical scales of analysis such as our views of the space under analysis) leads us to consider other methods and research techniques. The method of assemblages allows us to locate the articulation of oppression in terms that are neither hierarchical ("there is no hierarchy of oppressions", Audre Lorde) nor essentialist (categories or scales that configure established spaces of articulation), but rather interdisciplinary, multi-situated and multi-methodic. The assemblages denounce, on the one hand, the simultaneous localization of certain territories as "intervenable", moldable for the satisfaction of needs, spaces that historically can be identified as the earth (nature) and women's bodies, racialized, impoverished bodies; and on the other hand, a differentiation, a spatial zoning that confines the "intervenable" to a private sphere (massive privatization). Women and their specific body zones become the territory of the original accumulation on which capitalism is based (Federici, 2004). This necessary reconduction of sexual violence forms within the framework of bodies and lands as violated territorial assemblages allows us to explain how, historically, sexual violence is associated with practices of war and with contexts and systems of war, in charge of organizing destruction at a personal and community level through women's bodies and the annihilation of their subjectivities.

Work tools between situated anthropology, (self-) ethnography and feminist geography of the body

Feminist epistemology, as one of the social sciences that I believe it is necessary to involve in research, focuses, as I mentioned, on the reconstruction and resignification of women's experience in the contemporary patriarchal neoliberal capitalist system.

The subjects and female bodies can be historically located as subjects and bodies made others, placed in an unequal social position, hierarchized.

Co-labor is a practice consubstantial to the daily subjectivity of the "observer", a "built-in knowledge", a "know-how", in the literal sense of "knowledge with the body", that is, "a set of unconscious skills that pass through and are inscribed in the body" (Giglia, 2003, p. 90). The body is us, it is the territory through which, in feminist research, analysis and observation as well as self-analysis and self-observation have to pass. From the feminist epistemology as a creation of situated knowledge (Haraway, 1995), we want to give an account of the mobility of the "observed" and also of the mobility of the positions and the place of enunciation of the "observer".

We propose to critically discuss the concept of "multi-local ethnography" or "strategically situated ethnography [to] understand, in a broad way, the system in ethnographic terms and, at the same time, the local subjects" (Marcus, 2001, p. 121). From the methodological point of view, anthropology approaches geography in the search for a theoretical-practical link between the already mentioned macro-structures and micro-places. Marcus' proposal puts forth specific contributions to think about the link between sexual violence forms and bodily memory and the context of the patriarchal neo-liberal capitalist system.

> The empirical multi-situated research has particular connotations for feminist anthropology. It refers both to the geographical location of the context, and to the study of the places of concentration of power or marginality, of social reproduction, of personal or collective creativity, insisting on the *marks of gender in the construction of space* (Castañeda Salgado, 2012, p. 229).

The objective of the proposed methodology is to collectively construct a "partial and contingent" knowledge (Leyva Solano and Speed, 2015, p. 456) with ten women from the Mexican municipality of Ecatepec de Morelos, together identifying strategies for a life free of violence.

Giulia Marchese / Universidad Nacional Autónoma de México. GeoBrujas-Comunidad de Geógrafas

It is necessary to (re)cognize ourselves and have a strategic point of view to focus on the re-construction of our experience as women and the re-appropriation of our territories, starting with our bodies. The intention is to activate processes that allow us to exercise a policy of self-representation, to generate a re-signification of the territorial assemblage that we inhabit, that we are: our body.

Based on the objective and the proposed theoretical-methodological framework (assemblages and territories), we believe it is important to collect research techniques that I will define here as ethnogeographic. They help us to reveal the territorialization of categories in which power is put into play: the aforementioned categories of race, class, sex and sexuality and the territories (bodies and lands) that embody them. One of these techniques is the *(counter-)mapping of the body*, a graphic and discursive tool that allows us to reveal the assemblages of power that configure our bodies, the bodies of women, in our personal experiences of systemic sexual violence forms. In addition, the technique allows us to articulate the body through the different categories, establish new cartographic semiotics and abolish the orthodox visual hierarchies that are based on the essentialization of geographical scales, to make a self-history, as proposed by Gloria Anzaldúa, a life history made from self-reflection.

Figure 3. Body counter-mapping carried out in a group during a workshop of GeoBrujas.

Source: Comunidad de Geógrafas.

Finally, the (counter-)mapping of the body offers the possibility of re-constructing a place of enunciation of our own, drawn and realized from our personal experience. We seek to locate the mapping in the horizon of the playful, the artistic, the creative, the hysterical, to represent the time and the fractioned and simultaneous —assembled— space of women. We continue to search for technical-practical tools that show how "women move in liminal, border, transit and intermediary places" (Castañeda Salgado, 2012, p. 229), in general characterized by a context of militarization, conflict, war. How the border is shaped in the body, how the different structural geopolitical dynamics shape us and our lands: this is what we want to try to reveal and discuss.

Figure 4. Mexico-serrated vagina.

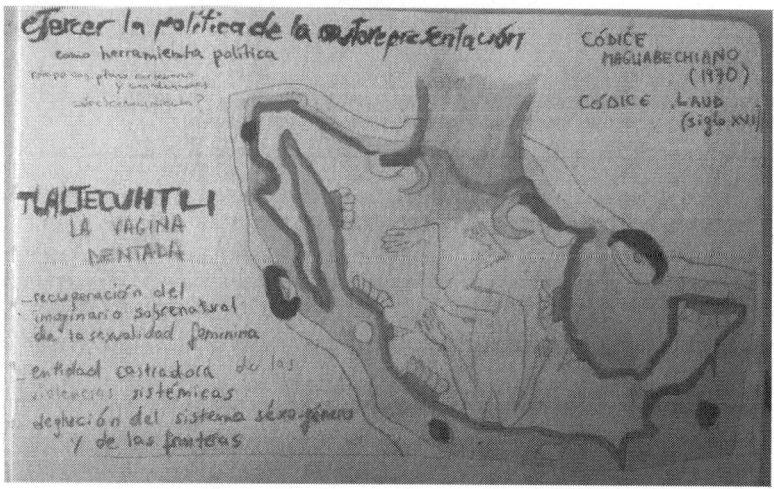

Source: Giulia Marchese.

Conclusions. Towards a (counter-)mapping of the body as a territorial assemblage

Feminist political geography invites us to recognize our bodies as territories that synthesize our articulations with power, which here I will call "assemblages of power", which appear embodied in our hierarchical conditions of gender, race, class, and sexuality. As far as the reorganization of the territory-earth is concerned, the result is a zoning of the territory. The territory of the extractable and penetrable geographies is a *stained* territory, in which violence occurs differently depending on the interaction and intersection between "territorial assemblages of power", "territories-land" and "territories-body" (Marchese, 2015). Far from thinking of the territory-earth as a uniform canvas undergoing violence and penetrated by absences or "power vacuums", I consider it fundamental, on the contrary, to make the saturation of powers that intersect in these operations visible. It will be fundamental to deconstruct "power" represented in monolithic terms, to enumerate and name the powers and their violences from the body, from the bodily fabric of the experiential, and to identify them at the intersection with the dimension of their territorialization. Through the technique of (counter-)mapping the body, we realize how our first territory was the first Cartesian space, even before the invention of the cartographic gaze of the world. The Cartesian space, as a medium that reiterates anthropocentrism and the fetishization of nature. That is why we believe it is necessary that there be a limit to "spatial" production as a liberating potential. Spatial materialization entails forms of "enclosure", which makes it impossible to keep spatial production infinitely open, as Lefebvre suggests. Unlike Foucault, who refers in his reflections to a universal and asexual subject/body and, therefore, to the female body as something given, through the methodology of assemblages we intend to reveal the assembly of power that specifically configures female bodies. In this sense, it is crucial to consider the body as a territorial assemblage of self-enunciation and re-signification of our experiences and not as a Cartesian space-container. Thus, we seek the re-signification of our bodies as territorial assemblages from which to think collectively and intimately about the processes of liberation.

Bibliography

Castañeda Salgado, M. P. (2012). Etnografía feminista. In N. Blazquez Graf, F. Flores Palacios and M. Ríos Everardo, *Investigación feminista. Epistemología, metodología y representaciones sociales* (pp. 217-238). Mexico: UNAM.

Crenshaw, K. (1989). Demarginalizing the Intersection of Race and Sex: A Black Feminist Critique of Antidiscrimination Doctrine, Feminist Theory and Antiracist Politics. Chicago: University of Chicago Legal Forum.

Farinelli, F. (2009). *I segni del mondo*. Academia Universa Press.

Federici, S. (2004). Caliban y la Bruja. Mujeres, cuerpo y acumulación originaria. Madrid: Traficantes de Sueños.

Gargallo, F. (2012). Feminismos desde Abya Yala. Ideas y proposiciones de las mujeres de 607 pueblos en nuestra América. Bogotá: Ediciones desde abajo.

Giglia, A. (2003). Cómo hacerse antropólogo en la Ciudad de México. Autoanálisis de un proyecto de trabajo de campo. *Alteridades, 13*(26), pp. 87-102.

GIULIA MARCHESE / UNIVERSIDAD NACIONAL AUTÓNOMA DE MÉXICO. GEOBRUJAS-COMUNIDAD DE GEÓGRAFAS

Giglia, A. (2010). Producir y habitar la ciudad informal. Reflexiones desde la antropología. In M. Alfie, I. Azuara, C. Bueno, M. Perez Negrete and S. Tamayo, *Sistema mundial y nuevas geografías* (pp. 337-368). Mexico: UAM/UIA/Porrúa.

Gómez Grijalba, D. (2012). *Mi cuerpo es un territorio político*. Brecha Lésbica.

Haraway, D. (1995). Ciencia, cyborgs y mujeres. La reinvención de la naturaleza. Madrid: Cátedra.

Harding, S. (1998). ¿Existe un método feminista? In E. Bartra, *Debates en torno a una metodología feminista* (pp. 9-34). Mexico: UAM-Xochimilco.

Harvey, D. (2004). The "New" Imperialism: Accumulation by Dispossession. *Socialist Register 40*.

Images, C. (s. d.). *Canistris Maps*. Tratto da Cartographic Images. Available at http://www.cartographic-images.net/Cartographic_Images/230_Canistris.html

Lagarde, M. (2005). El feminicidio, delito contra la humanidad. In C. E. Vinculada (A cura di), *Feminicidio, justicia y derecho* (pp. 151-164). Mexico: Cámara de Diputados, LIX Legislatura.

Lefebvre, H. (1976). *La produzione dello spazio*. Milano: Il Saggiatore.

Leyva Solano, X., and S. Speed, (2015). Hacia la investigación descolonizada: nuestra experiencia de co-labor. In VV. AA, *Prácticas otras de conocimiento(s). Entre crisis, entre guerras* (pp. 451-480). Guadalajara: Taller editorial La Casa del Mago.

Marchese, G. (2015). Lo sviluppo político del confine. Il femminicidio nello spazio pubblico di Ciudad Juárez. Bolonia: Tesi di laurea magistrale.

Marcus, G. E. (July-December 2001). Etnografía en/del sistema mundo. El surgimiento de la etnografía multilocal. *Alteridades, 11*(22), pp. 111-127.

Marx, K. (2005). Elementos fundamentales para la crítica de la economía política (Grundrisse). Mexico: Siglo XXI.

Massey, D. (1994). *Space, Place and Gender* (1st ed.). Minnesota: Minnesota University Press.

Mbembe, A. (2011). *Necropolitica*. Tenerife: Melusina.

McDowell, L. (2000). Género, identidad y lugar. Un estudio de las Geografías Feministas. Madrid: Cátedra.

Mezzadra, S., and B. Neilson (2013). *Border as methos*. Durham: Duke University Press.

Mies, M. (1986). Patriarchy and Accumulation on a World Scale. Women in the International Division of Labour. London and New York: Zed Books Ltd.

Monárrez, J. (2007). Bordeando la violencia contra las mujeres en la frontera norte de México. Ciudad Juárez: Colef.

Radford, H., and D. E. Russell (1992). *Femicide and the Politics of Woman Killing*. New York: Twayne.

Rubin, G. (1996). El tráfico de mujeres. Notas sobre la economía política del sexo. In M. Lamas (A cura di), *El género. La construcción cultural de la diferencia sexual*. Mexico: PUEG-UNAM.

Sassen, S. (2008). Territorio, autorità, diritti. Assemblaggi dal Medioevo all'età globale. Milano: Bruno Mondadori.

Segato, R. L. (2014). Las nuevas formas de la guerra y el cuerpo de las mujeres. Puebla: Pez en el árbol.

Smith, N. (1993). Homeless/global: scaling places. In J. Bird et al., *Mapping the futures: local cultures, global change*. London: Routledge.

Tzul Tzul, G. (2016). Lo indígena en clave comunal. In S. C. Tz'ikin, *Sistemas de gobierno comunal indígena. Mujeres y tramas de parentesco en Chuimeq'ena'* (pp. 37-62). Guatemala: Editorial Maya Wuj.

Whittington, K. P. (2010). *The Body-Worlds of Opicinus de Canistris, Artist and Visionary (1296-ca.1354)*. Available at https://escholarship.org/uc/item/2jc7h850

PART 3: DIALOGUES

15. On Genders and Territories. Does the land have a gender?

Gabriela Ruales and Sofia Zaragocin

This text is an invitation to revise our understanding of feminism and its relationship to territory and nature. It is a dialogue full of answered questions on bodies and territories that are undergoing permanent transformation.

Introduction

Our positionality

We both belong to the *Colectivo de Geografía Crítica del Ecuador* (Critical Geography Collective of Ecuador) and have similar but different trajectories on feminism and its relationship with the territory and land. Sofia Zaragocin analyzes space from the decolonial feminist geography and Gabriela Ruales from the body-territory relationship inspired by her work with *Colectivo de Miradas Críticas del Territorio desde el Feminismo*. We are interested in creating a dialogue between feminist geographies and Latin American feminist debates on territory, to provoke discussion around the central question: does the territory have a gender? The dialogue we propose in this paper is elaborated in relation to our action research experience and based on conversations on following authors and their work: Astrid Ulloa, Katy Jenkins, Lorena Cabnal and the Asambleas del Feminismo Comunitario (Assemblies of Community Feminism) in Bolivia. Following the desire to promote a discussion between different analysis of feminist spatialities, we have chosen two geographers who work on gender and feminist issues, an activist author and a collective that works on these issues from the perspective of communitarian feminism. All the authors analyzed rethink the linear and essentialized relationship between territory, gender and women that we develop below.

Does land have gender?

This question arises because there are those who claim that territory and land is inherently female, and furthermore, that *she* is a mother. But where does this affirmation come from? Why understand territory in terms of the feminine, woman and/or mother? If territory is given a gender, what happens to the other genders present in the diversity that land itself sustains and generates? What happens to the masculine, the father, the men, and those who are in transition? How do we understand land in gender terms and with regards to colonial heteronormative and homonormative frameworks? Why understand land in feminine terms when there is a diversity of gender posibilities?

We share a common discomfort, and it is the causal, homogenizing and essentialized relationship between women, land and territory. Specifically, the political use of Pachamama and Mother Earth, from which the land is given a gender, that of woman (Pachamama) and mother (Mother Earth). Woman, as a social reproducer of life, is related to the earth, which also gives life, acting as the mother that unites us and sustains us all. We have heard of this relationship for several years, in the everyday, academic, militant spaces, as in places that live or posit another worldview. The Pachamama, Mother Earth and many other feminine-maternal names at this moment in history draw our attention, and we question them because we believe that a patriarchal, utilitarian relationship has been established in these considerations that created a sexist culture deeply rooted in the practices and symbolism that is built on territories, including our bodies.

This discomfort comes from feeling that the land is being given an essentialized identity, which in other circumstances is already unsustainable. In the vast majority of political and academic spaces it is impossible to think of all women as cisgender, on the one hand, and, on the other, as an innate mother, following heteronormative, heteropatriarchal and heterosexist logics. This has been questioned by different feminisms for several decades. This is what creates discomfort. Why is the land given a fixed and stable identity that can no longer be given to people who are supposedly pigeonholed into a feminized identity? What makes us think that space can still be given a fixed gender, when in other spaces this is already highly questioned? Where does this thought come from and why?

Historical exploration of terminology: Pachamama, Madre-Tierra

As analyzed by communitarian feminism from the voice of Lorena Cabnal, of the Indigenous Maya-Xinca women of Guatemala, and the communitarian feminism of Bolivia, there is a type of original patriarchy, previous to colonization, that became one with the patriarchy stemming from colonization.

According to Cabnal, this patriarchal connection would have strengthened an *originary cosmogonic heteroreality* which

> is the norm that from ethnic essentialism establishes that all the relations among humanity and with the cosmos are based on principles and values such as complementarity and heterosexual duality for the harmonization of life. However, these constitute the most sublime ancestral imposition of the compulsory heterosexual norm in the lives of Indigenous women and men, which is legitimized through spiritual practices that are understood as sacred (Cabnal, 2010, p. 16).[1]

One of the main questions that Lorena Cabnal asks is directed to the male construction of original cosmogonic knowledge, since this epistemic construction of knowledge has generated and generates inequalities regarding those who are not part of the male collective.

Likewise, communitarian feminism in Bolivia states that "the understanding of Pachamama as synonymous with Mother Earth is reductionist and sexist, referring only to fertility in order to have women and Pachamama at their patriarchal discretion" (Cabnal, 2010, p. 18).

---

[1] Cabnal, Lorena (2010). Acercamiento a la construcción de la propuesta de pensamiento epistémico de las mujeres indígenas feministas comunitarias de Abya Yala. In: *Feminismos diversos: el feminismo comunitario*. Las Segovias: ACSUR.

It is interesting to find in this reflection a relationship between the exploitation of nature understood as Mother Earth and the exploitation of women, since the sexist interpretation of the Earth is related to fertility, that is, to a being who is sexed female in order to be fertilized and who, as a consequence, is a mother. Or, as Lorena Cabnal states,

> Pachamama is the mother earth whose cosmogonic role is situated within a female cosmogonic heterosexual order, as a reproducer and generator of life. Sired by Tata Inti: the sun father, the king star, the fertilizing male. This relationship establishes something that should draw our attention as communitarian feminist women, because of the position of power and superiority manifested by the one above as male and the one below, who is fertilized, as female (Cabnal, 2010, p. 19).

That is, the Earth in its complexity becomes declared exclusively as feminine, mother, and in a heteronormative relationship. Likewise, what is non-human is also humanized, heteronormed, and sustained on a patriarchal basis of creation of a world loaded with essentialisms.

On the other hand, understanding the land as a mother has served to establish a maternal imaginary. However, this same symbolic construction has deepened the abuse, use and usufruct of land.

How we respond to the question of whether territory has a gender

We respond from our situated knowledge, but also from the reflections that arise from collective work and with experience in anti-extractivist and feminist struggles.

For several years we have heard about the relationship between land, territory, women and mothers; we have questioned how we assume this vision of the world and we have begun to observe it by listening to other women and women's organizations who have taken issue with this essentialism made of territories and themselves. We wrote this text in conversation with one another.

Question 1: What are we really asking with regard to the central question of this paper: *Does land have a gender?*

SOFIA: When we ask this question we are also asking about who can give land a gender. What are the subjectivities involved in this process, and what do the processes that wish to give space, and especially territory a gender tell us? Feminist geographer Gillian Rose tells us that space reflects the heteronormative society in which we live. Taking that analysis to the ontological category of land reflects existing gender systems in a given context. This explains why spatial divisions are clearly reflected in gender divisions and vice versa. These dynamics show us the gender dynamics impregnated in society from other dimensions, such as space-time. When we ask if the earth has gender, we are also asking other questions; such as, who has the ethical authority to give land a gender? Could it be that land has gender dynamics impregnated in it?

At the same time, we recognize from an intercultural standpoint that there are other gender systems in which for example, stones have been given a gender, those that are feminine and others that are masculine, for example. We recognize that the danger of writing this paper is to fall into epistemic violence with respect to other ways of understanding gender relations where there is a variety of notions of complementarity and its relationship to different spatial identities. There is an already long discussion concerning complementarity within the context of Indigenous peoples and nationalities. Nevertheless, the spatial discussion of complementarity is limited.

GABRIELA: This question is a concern to recognize if this binarism, and in the eagerness to humanize the earth, is located as a woman, not as the feminine in its adjectival explanation, but as a woman, and not only as a woman, but as a mother, responds to a utilitarian practice of inferiorizing the earth in order to exploit it in the capitalist practices crossed by patriarchal logics.

By making woman responsible for gestation, and by equating land with women, the latter turns out to be the infinite reproducer; therefore, by being considered the infinite reproducer she will be considered the infinite mother. Even if we continue considering land a mother, where is the father, where is the male side of that land in that supposed duality?

And precisely in order not to fall into the epistemic violence mentioned by Sofia, I consider it indispensable to analyze in what way equating the land with a mother strengthens the logic of domination over it, contrary to the understanding of the land as an organism of reproduction of life from the ancestral Andean cosmovision, not traversed by capitalist patriarchy.

Question 2: What do we mean by territory?

GABRIELA: Territory, a planet, the conjunction of the different elements, water, air, earth, fire, minerals, their links cause the awakening of life in relation to the place where this conjunction occurs, because the state of being is not the same at sea level than in the mountains, just as it is not the same to be at latitude 0 than to be in one of the poles, and so on. Territory is diversified according to the geography it contains. It is the physical space that we inhabit, that we eat, that we smell, that we feel, that passes through us, therefore it is also our body. And at the same time it is the space that allows us to exist from the relationships that happen in it and that make up the territory, the society-nature relationships and social relationships in turn in the time and space relationship.

SOFIA: For me territory is a spatial identity, like others. However, I understand that the land as a spatial identity is prioritized from Latin America and for clear historical reasons. The land, in comparison with space or place, has a political sense of struggle and resistance. We see this now in relation to the struggles against extractivism, especially against mining.

However, from Latin American feminist geographies and Anglocentric feminist geographies, the body creates territoriality. There is a conceptual relationship between feminist geographies, and in particular feminist geopolitics with the proposals of body-territory in their feminist perspectives in Latin America. Sara Smith points out how the body through its reproductive possibility causes love and babies' bodies to be geopolitical entities, which create an intimate geopolitics as she calls it. This is a very particular way of understanding how the body generates territoriality.

Territory, then, is the spatial identity that will allow us to relate feminist geography to feminist debates about territory in Latin America. It is the spatial identity from which we will be able to build multi-spatial dialogues from different feminist perspectives.

Question 3: What is the existing gender-territory relationship that we are questioning?

SOFIA: We are criticizing the linear relationship, where territory is given an essentialized role of a mother as a reproducer of life. I do not question that the territory reproduces various forms of life, but I do question that it is given a gender. Who are we to give territory a gender? Why do we think we can humanize territory, and organize it into binary and heteronormative logics?

Instead of seeing territory as a feminized entity, I propose the possibility of looking at our gender relations to territory, in relation to the multiple territorial struggles that we have generated from feminist, decolonial and environmental spheres. Therein lies our learning. If we began to look at ourselves in terms of gender *in* territory, this woman-territory-mother relationship would not be possible. One way out of this debate, then, is to ask territory how we came to name it as a woman. Surely it will have a lot to tell us.

GABRIELA: From this, I ask myself, when is the earth humanized? And in this humanization, when is its only possibility of existence binary, male-female, feminine-masculine, seeing as even scientifically it is considered biodiverse? Why in this binary humanization is the feminine role maternal, and why are women equated with nature in their essentialized role?

Territory has been given a maternal reproductive role in different cultures and at different times; it would be necessary to investigate much further, in which moment the different cosmovisions — at least in the region— established and promoted a gender to the land in this way. We question the patriarchal link of this vision and use of territory in its maternal role, as the one that has to sustain, endure, deliver, sacrifice or reproduce to satiety everything that capital or any other predatory system needs.

I suggest understanding the land as an infinitely diverse being; non-human, but which also contains humanity, which in turn is land: that is, it is a diverse humanity, not only in forms and colors, but in sexual and gender representations. Understanding the land in its material, spatial, geographic, territorial, planetary, and non-generic sense allows us to broaden our perspective on the creative possibilities of humanity and non-human beings. Breaking with the patriarchal hegemonic duality of man-woman, reproducer-fertilizer, and so on, and understanding ourselves in our other facets, would generate, I think, a deeper relationship with the land and with the beings that inhabit it.

Question 4: So... does territory have a gender?

GABRIELA: The land does not have a gender, the land is a material being where the territory is constructed, which is a representation of the different relationships that occur in it. It contains an infinite number of forms and states to which a human quality cannot be granted. Territory has no gender, there are genders on the land, but these genders are assigned by people in a cultural attempt to understand the diverse forms contained in humanity, the geographical space and its territorial relations.

But, although this is the human intention, to grant gender to territory in order to decipher it, it is infinitely diverse and constitutes the space for generation of multiple combinations of vital processes and diverse beings. The historical process of feminization and maternalization of the territory can result in a dangerous containment of other forms of humanity, which are functional to the exploitation of the land and its elements for the benefit of capital. This also distances us from the embodied relationship with land, since it builds a culture of exploitation of the non-human when, on the contrary, those relationships should be sustained and strengthened for its care and respect.

As we mentioned earlier, this text is intended to encourage dialogue on the central question concerning whether territory has a gender. Therefore, to say that land does not have a gender is a position based on the context of the advance of extractive activities and land exploitation, where the struggles in its defense have also been strengthened.

SOFIA: No. Territory itself does not have a gender, it is a dimensionality of space-time and for that reason an identity cannot be imposed on it, be it gender or another axis of difference. Taking that analysis to the ontological category of territory, then the land reflects the existing gender systems in a given context. Land does reproduce life (beyond human life) and is central to the lives of humans and non-humans alike. There are dynamics in which women are leading political processes against mining, as Katy Jenkins shows us; processes in which there is a strategic essentialism about the usefulness of the woman-mother-Pachamama struggle.

However, outside of those moments where strategic essentialism can be understood, it seems to me that giving a gender to territory shows a tremendous lack of understanding of what territory is. There is no ontological understanding of what a multidimensional space is, where many systems of life and understandings of existence can co-exist. To give a gender to a planetary space such as territory is to simplify and dogmatize a space that leads to a profound disregard for how we live spatially. However, I do not rule out the possibility that territory may be a feminist entity. I believe that the woman-land relationship attributed to the planet allows and drives precisely a feminist response.

That is to say, it is possible to promote a feminist struggle for the defense of territory and at the same time advocate that the land not be given a gender. The more land has been feminized, the more necessary a feminist response is, and this implies a questioning of how it has been feminized.

This debate also makes it difficult, in my opinion, to discuss body-territory, where the (re)patriarchalization of territories and its effects on feminized bodies points out to us that even if the land is not gendered, it is still treated as if it were.

As a non-conclusion, we propose a necessary pause

We cannot draw a conclusion, because we are only proposing questions that should be widely discussed. We bring concerns with us, and propose an activist and conceptual pause.

We cannot draw a conclusion at this time about the process of land feminization. We have raised questions, concerns. We want to leave you with uncomfortable spaces and moments that, we hope, have been prompted by our questions. We do not want the debate on nature, decolonialism, feminism and extractivism to continue without generating a conceptual pause which in turn should be an activist, political, pause. We want to generate a pause because there is a need to rethink ourselves and live the land in a different way. Changing the woman-land-mother relationship is a first step.

We want to generate a pause so that environmental militancy can be rethought from its practices in defense of the territory. We think that the feminist, anti-extractivist and decolonial struggles are related in their practices, which have once again solidified binary processes from a gender perspective. To move forward, we need to see our gender relations from the land, from how we are creating gender on the land. There is a need to create feminisms for the land, from a relationship of political and conceptual complicity and reciprocity. We invite you to create a feminism for the land, not to give a gender to the land. That is the feminist ethic that we propose.

16. Women at the forefront of the fight. Conversation with Doña Felisa Muralles, from the Movimiento de Resistencia Pacífica La Puya, Guatemala

Jonatan Rodas

Presentation

Women's political protagonism has been evident in the face of neoliberal and neo-extractivist dispossession. They have been at the forefront of resistance struggles, breaking the silence, demanding their right to justice, holding back repressive forces, denouncing crimes against themselves and their communities, acting collectively for the defense of their bodies-territories.

This is the context for the experiences of Felisa Muralles, a member of the Movimiento de Resistencia Pacífica de La Puya (Peaceful Resistance Movement of La Puya) in Guatemala, who, like many other women on the continent, became a political subject that interrupts the inertia of capital and confronts the logic of domination, placing life at the center. With this conversation, we celebrate her organizational strength empowered in daily life, as well as her legacy of hope to radically transform the world.

Five years ago, in March 2012, a group of neighbors began a resistance struggle against the intended operations by a mining project near their villages, in the municipalities of San Pedro Ayampuc and San José del Golfo, Department of Guatemala. Known as the Movimiento de Resistencia Pacífica de La Puya, or simply La Puya, this neighborhood group has become a fundamental reference point for new forms of struggle in the country. As in many other experiences in Latin America, the role of women in this movement has been decisive. They are ordinary women, who have done extraordinary things, such as holding back the police forces, sustaining daily life in the camp and placing Christian faith at the center of their motivations. Women who, along the way, discovered others and discovered another world. Another possible world.

Even if it is part of her personal life, this conversation with Doña Felisa Muralles, known as Doña Licha, does not fail to express an experience shared by many of the women who to this day persistently continue to take care of their territory and avoid any onslaught from the police or the mining company. The task has not been easy, as Doña Licha's own account shows. In addition to the repressive force of the State and the mining company, there have been aggressions, defamations, political and personal differences, etc., which, as Doña Licha herself says, "would give anyone a stroke". Thus, the worth in these women is not that they are extraordinary beings, but precisely that they are women of their time, fighting against the history that has determined them and, as a result of their participation in the resistance, realizing that there is a world for women beyond reproducing and taking care of the house.

Conversation with Doña Felisa Muralles. Resistance sit-in, San Pedro Ayampuc, Guatemala

Doña Licha, tell us about your life: where were you born, what is your family like, what do you do?

I was born in 1967 in the village of El Carrizal, which is in the municipality of San Pedro Ayampuc, Guatemala. That is where I am from, that is where I live. I come from a close-knit family of eleven siblings, good parents. Unfortunately I no longer have one of my parents. I am the last of the family, the youngest. Of all the siblings, only nine are alive today, two have already died. We are always in touch, we all have good friendships, we have large families. Mine is a small family, with six children. I was widowed at the age of 35 and then remarried. My six children are from my first husband. I have a good family and a good husband. I have always had a good relationship with my family.

I have always liked the land, we would go and help my dad clean the land. It was not the same as now. There were other customs. We only used a hoe, but I liked it. Later, when my husband traveled to the United States, I always continued to do it with my younger children, to teach them to work the land; unfortunately the three boys I have did not like it. Whenever I asked them to do something, they always replied with "but": that it was bad for them, that they did not like it. In short, they did not like it. But I have always liked the land. We currently grow corn and beans, and we have always liked taking care of the land and planting it to obtain our food.

Does that link to the land have anything to do with why you joined the resistance? I understand that you were among the first to get organized?

Maybe I already had a love for the land, but also a love for organization. Because my father was a person who liked to organize. He fought for his community, he was president of a committee to build the road from Reyes to El Carrizal. So, in a way we have it in our blood, because my brother Chebo and I were very involved [in the organization]; in some way, we have it in our blood.

While I had my husband I lived a very closed life with my children, but when he passed away I left the circle, I felt independent, I started to get involved in the school organization, then I got involved in Church organizations. I enjoyed being in organizations, helping, supporting others. When this happened, I already had that organizational initiative, then when this began, I was chosen for Cocode[1]; I was vice-president of Cocode five years ago, in 2012.

---

[1] The Cocode or Consejo Comunitario de Desarrollo (Community Development Council) represents the most basic level of community organization in the institutional structure of the Sistema de Consejos de Desarrollo (System of Development Councils) through which the State of Guatemala,

From then on, the following period after the Cocode ended I was elected auxiliary mayor[2]; the auxiliary mayor office ended and this year I was re-elected again, but we are not registered because we have a clash with the mayor of San Pedro Ayampuc. But we are elected by the community. The mayor has always had issues with us because of mining: he does not want to admit this organization because he knows that we are going to be a thorn in his side. So he has not wanted to register us, but we are already working on legal issues, so it is definitely going to happen because we are not going to give up. We have already filed a complaint, and we have already summoned him to the Human Rights Attorney's Office and we are not going to give up now, now we have to get him to authorize us. We have lost six months without registration, so far, but we are organized. So they are not lost, because the community thinks of us as recognized; it is he who does not want to recognize us. We continue; when they do that to us, we work harder.

I feel that because of what my father did, we carry in our blood the initiative to organize ourselves, to support the community, to watch over it.

---

through the Secretaría General de Planificación (Segeplan, General Planning Secretariat) organizes and coordinates public administration for the formulation and execution of development policies.

[2] The position of "auxiliary mayor", although recognized by the municipal authorities, does not represent an institutional or remunerated position. Their activity is voluntary and they are elected for their legitimacy within their communities. Sometimes, the auxiliary mayor's office is intertwined with the figure of "community mayor" or "Indigenous mayor", in the cases of mostly Indigenous populations, but it should not always be taken as synonymous with these.

At what specific moment did you become part of La Puya?

At the beginning, in 2011, at school they would show videos about mining and my youngest son would tell me, "Today they showed us a video about mining", and he would talk to me and I would turn a deaf ear, as if I was not interested. Then my daughter was in a group of young people and she would tell me, "Mom, look, mining is here"; and we began to see that there were already wider roads there, we could see machines working there. So that's how that concern began, and they started to show us videos in El Carrizal. And that was when Tono gave us a warning and said, "Look, mining is already here, here in El Carrizal they are selling land, so it is time to push that away from us". I started to react and said, "Now where do we start?" And we watched videos about mining in San Marcos.[3] Seeing the destruction over there, we would say, "Where do we start?" And once we went to a meeting in El Guapinol, we were getting organized when the Marcha Campesina de Polochic (Polochic Peasant March)[4] was coming, so we had to commit El Carrizal to get organized and go cook for them in Llano Largo, when they passed through there. That is what we were doing when, in that organization that we went to Guapinol for, there was a man from El Carrizal, and I said to him, "Look, Don Victor, where do we start and what do we do?" And he said to me, "I thought that, to start with, we should send some banners and put them in El Carrizal, saying 'No to mining'"; so, that was like seeing that we were already organizing ourselves. We made a *coperacha*, a voluntary collection, we had two banners made, and we put them in El Carrizal, but that was where we were, at the "where to start" stage, when on March 2, 2012, around four in the afternoon they

---

[3] She refers to the case of the Marlín mine, the first mining megaproject installed in Guatemala after the signing of the Peace Accords. This mining project was installed between the municipalities of San Miguel Ixtahuacán and Sipakapa, in the department of San Marcos, in the western part of the country.

called us; a woman from El Carrizal was in San José del Golfo, and she told us that a machine was coming and it was coming here, and what should she do: should she stop it? And the brothers told her, "No, don't do it, because you will get into trouble", but she had her way, took the road shoulder, overtook them and blocked them with her truck. Then, just as she parked, the small bus from El Carrizal[5] passed by and she told them "get off and support me"; about five people got off and they began to call for El Carrizal. It was the first Friday of Lent and they were walking the Stations of the Cross[6]; I was not on the Stations of the Cross because we had just arrived home from bringing down some firewood. Then they called my daughter, who was involved in this the most, and they told her, "Come, because we need people". She told me, "Let's go to La Puya, because they are bringing in machines", and my son said, "You're crazy, why do you want us to go?" "Yes, Mom, let's go", she answered. "Well, let's go." And I said to my husband, "Are we going?" He did not refuse, he said, "Let's go", and we all got into the car without having eaten, even, because we had just arrived. There were already quite a lot of people. And we all saw that they had got the machine inside [the mine], because they threatened this woman by telling her, "If you don't remove the truck, we will turn it over". And as armed people came out of the mine, she began to argue and be rude to them because she was very foul-mouthed, so they began to speak rudely to each other, and she had to move the truck aside. But it was a machine that did not come complete, so it went in, but after a few days it went out because another part was missing; instead of being locked up there, it decided to leave.

---

[5] A bus that travels the route between the municipal capital of San José del Golfo and the village of El Carrizal at approximate intervals of between an hour and an hour and a half.

[6] It is also necessary to note that this information is relevant, since the population of El Carrizal is characterized by its constant religious activity. Other intense times when the mining company tried to bring in machinery were scheduled on days when there was religious activity in El Carrizal.

Well, we started to wait for more machinery to come, to discuss what to do. Then a man, Don Victor del Carrizal, said, "Well, then what we can do is to make a big ditch and divide the street, and when one of our cars passes, we put some boards on it and let it pass, and not the rest". Then someone said, "No, that is a crime, we cannot do that, it is an obstruction of locomotion and we cannot commit a crime", and so on, taking examples from other resistances where they quickly committed crimes, shooting, setting fire, beating up. We said that we did not want to go to jail, everything had to be done in a good way, and seeing all those news *por ay*[7], over there, that said that they had stolen explosives, that they were accused of it, then we said we should not do that, we must start to understand what we can do. We had that mentality of not hitting or being arrested.

That night was spent there, and they said, "Well, we are going to stay here and we are not going to let anything in." They went to bring a pot, they made coffee there on the road shoulder, and so on, out in the open. It was March, it was not raining yet. So we came day after day, day after day, to see what was going on; and the first few days, as workers were already coming in, there were *picopadas*[8], truckloads of workers who wanted to go in, and the people said, "No, you don't come in here, you don't come in." Then, on March 2 (2012) nothing was allowed to enter, there was a small gate there and they poured superglue[9] on the padlock, and then cars came and wanted to leave, and wanted to remove the key, but they could not because the padlock was sealed, so it remained closed.

There were several attempts. On May 8 of that same year, some trucks were coming at one in the morning, guarded by the mine police, and we were all on duty (because that is what I am talking about), a big group. And we said, "We won't last long like

---

[7] *Por ay* is a very common expression in Guatemala to refer to a place far away from one's own.

[8] A *picopada* refers to the load (of people or materials) that fits in the bed of a pick-up truck.

[9] Contact cement.

this, all of us here, all the time, so let's get organized; some of us today in a group, some others, tomorrow." That way, everyone could rest and go to do their jobs. "Well, let's make a group, who wants to get organized with me?" And we got about ten people in each group. I was the coordinator; since I made the list, they took me as the coordinator. But everyone made their own little group, and six groups were formed. And there was a chance to form seven, but we did not want to; because if you form seven groups, they all fall on the same day of the week, you do not rotate days. So it would be better to have six, to change the day each week.

Then, once we were organized, we could have a little more rest; but with the agreement that when necessary, even if it was not a shift, we would come. There were days when we stayed the whole day; or often we came as soon as the bell rang, because we adopted this strategy of ringing the bell. There were several eviction attempts, several provocations.

That was when we got organized. We came every six days, and we started to think that we should make a *champita*, a shelter. The group would come all the way to here (pointing to where our chairs are placed), some holes and caves were made, to put the pots in. And we would put a griddle in a barrel, and bake there. Here we had a good time: we made *coperacha*, we went to buy pork rinds, made coffee, bought bread. The same woman who put her truck there has a brother in the United States, and she sent him money to get portable toilets. Everything was going well, but this woman unfortunately retired (maybe she betrayed us, or just retired!), but she turned against us because she wanted to be given her place for what she did. But as Doña Yoli took the initiative, she went higher than she had been, and then started to get upset. She would come, and they didn't give her the importance she wanted. Sometimes organizations would come and say, "Who was the woman who put her car across?", and they would start interviewing her and she was all *chiviada*[10]. Then they didn't like it that they didn't get to where they had to get to her, and she went up very fast, so she started to

---

[10] Embarrassed.

be annoying. For example, for the first anniversary we made a walk from San José del Golfo to here, and she went ahead with her truck; she had it well decorated with little pieces of paper with pure insults. She wrote on the papers, "While I take little steps, others suck the little bones", insulting things, as if to say, "I did it and you're using it".

Doña Yoli told the police, "Look, this woman might provoke", because she was beginning to mistreat and insult us. She had it in for me, only in the last few months she no longer mistreats me. It was strange, because it was a good action, but she backed off because it did not reach the height she wanted. But we have survived. Doña Yoli retired because (maybe you have heard the story), she climbed a lot and from there she let herself fall, so it was a very ugly story because she was a great person. She encouraged us and everything as if she was the boss, we all gave her that credibility and she really believed. Then she started to make trouble because she would go to the meetings where she was taken, because she has a good way of expressing herself, very fluent, so all that helped her. But, when we saw that she went to any country and did not bring any information, people started to get upset and said, "No, this has to be stopped." They wanted to stop it, and everyone got so upset that it was a mess. There we thought, many people thought that without her we would not be able to continue, because they said, "We're in over our heads, and we won't know what to do." "No", we said, "we started from scratch and we have to learn along the way." So we have been developing. Maybe I went too far, away from what I wanted. Maybe it was not what I wanted to know, but I got way ahead of myself.

But notice how the story here helps other resistances: we tell them what problems we have had or how they should not get to that problem. We have given them some advice, what mistakes they should not make. Even though they may be small mistakes, but we have not been imprisoned; still there are little things that have hurt, and other things. So the biggest piece of advice we give is: do not fall into provocation.

If they mistreat you, do not turn back to look at them. Before, if they said "daughter of so and so", they would get a *pijazo*[11]; because no one gets to call your mother names[12], but now they can do it ten or twenty times and I do not care, it does not hurt me anymore or make me angry. The experience makes your skin thick like a toad's, and that helps you to tolerate things; because in between times I say, "Getting angry hasn't made any miracles happen for me". But I ask God for wisdom to tolerate it and to leave all anger aside, because anything can happen, to be criticized, to be looked at badly, but these are things that go with the wind.

I have something I took from Lolita Chávez[13]; I remember her often, as I like her way of being, and I have taken many things from her. On one occasion she came here and began to tell us everything that happened to her. "I've come this far because I've bathed in butter, now everything slips off me, they can say whatever they like." Because they call her a prostitute, that she has husbands everywhere, so she says that she bathed in butter; even if they tell her that she goes around with ten men, it does not make her angry, she knows it is not true and it does not bother her. And that is what you have to do, bathe in butter and everything slips off you. Because if you are very sensitive, with one bad look you leave here and do not come back. Many people have done it, very sensitive people, who maybe because of something small, because they were not offered a cup of coffee at the time, or because everyone was

---

[11] A beating.

[12] "Sacar la madre", a very common and offensive insult in the country.

[13] Lola Chavez is a recognized Indigenous leader from the Consejo de Pueblos de Occidente (Council of Western Peoples), an Indigenous grassroots organization in western Guatemala that fights, among other things, against excessive electricity charges in the region, a problem that contrasts with the lack of electrical power in homes and the installation of hydroelectric plants in the region.

eating and they did not think of offering them a *tortilla*, these are things that must be learned, because it is what helps people stay on.

You are one of the most recognized people in the Movement?

And you should know that I do not like it, do you know why? Because of the problem with Yoli. I would like more women to be here. I will not say I have received training, but I have learned in each workshop that I go, little things to go on developing or understanding. And I would like more women here, so that I am not the only one to be labeled. I would like a small group, I have even had the initiative to tell them, "Look, let's get together, so that you can develop a little more." Because as soon as there is a camera they hide, if they are interviewed their mouths are sewn shut. And that is why I am embarrassed to be mentioned a lot, as there are people who already think of me as the contact. And I tell them, "Don't say la Licha, say the resistance or a group that came, don't say my name", because they mention it a lot, and I do not like it because of that problem. Because she thought so much of herself, and I do not, she thought so much, so much that she went to the top and up there she did not want anyone to touch her.

Does this interest in not wanting to hog the spotlight help the movement stay horizontal?

I hope so and I hope that they do not look at me, so as not to create division or envy, because there has been some friction: here, what has been the rub is travelling. When there are chances to travel, there are certain frictions; and that is why I would like there to be more women who are open-minded, because more than anything else they pay attention to women, that a woman is going to represent La Puya, and I would like there to be more women who are beginning to grow more self-assured. I am not going to say self-confident, because I am not that confident either, but I would like some others, so that at times someone else can go. All these little meetings can orient, train and develop you, and they help a lot, but unfortunately there is no one who wants to do it.

From your experience here, why do you think it is that women are at the forefront of the struggle?

It is because the men are very violent. Or they were, because they were trained here. We said, well, so that they do not touch the men, we are going to put ourselves at the front. A man will not punch us women so easily, he will think twice, but will punch another man and get hit back and so on. That is what brought us to the front. And we were not so afraid, because we already know our rights, and we know that it is not so easy, they have to think twice before they hit us. And besides, there have always been cameras and that has helped us to catch anything that happens and there is evidence. That is why we started to take the lead.

But the miners use it to discredit us: they say that we hide men under our skirts so that they do not fight, that they are fearful, and that they run to hide under our skirts, and it is not true. They have courage, what we do not want is for them to fight. Look at my brother Chebo, he had *riata*[14] with a lot of men when he was young and used to drink, but here, oh God!, here he has become another person, not even half of what he was, because his character is better now. Here he is polite when he speaks; before, he only spoke vulgarities, but that has helped many men to work their courage. Because at the beginning they said, "Well, if this is not solved in the first few days we will buy gasoline and we will go to spray the machines and we will burn them all and we will see if we can't stop it." But that was not the solution, burning a machine is not enough money for them, they buy another one and we go to jail. That was what made us understand that we were not going to fix things with blows, it had to be done in the best way. That is why we women always go to the front, to protect them: we do not want them to be arrested, or to be beaten, or for them to beat others.

---

[14] To have fights.

Have you discussed this with other women, with other organizations?

Well, they see it as a good thing because we are preventing worse things. Nobody would like to know that a companion is in prison, because we have the blessing that we do not have any prisoners. Because that would be a downer, so we have not had the experience of having someone in prison.

But there were companions who were sentenced?

But we are happy that they are not in jail and that we managed to raise the money for bail and then we say, with God's help we have managed to laugh at them [the miners], because they are not going to take our companions away. We have the money, and the day they say, "Bring it here"[15], it will be delivered; and it does not hurt us, because we say, "God will reward us". We have doubts that they may not ask for it, because they know that this money will come unjustly to them; because it is not true, it is not fair. Maybe they will not ask for it, because we have had it for a long time and they do not ask for it.

The mine is closed, and although this represents a success for the population, the process is not yet won. In view of this, what are your hopes for the future? What will happen next?

What we think is that, God willing, we are going to win it, and that possibly we will recover the land in some way, so that it is no longer used for mining, so that they get rid of what is there and it can be used for something, a protected area, something that we can keep an eye on so it is used well. That is what we think and, God willing, we will not fade away and if this ends, if it is formalized and

---

[15] The judgment has already been made but the final resolution is still pending. If it is confirmed, the sentenced parties would have to pay a financial guarantee, which Doña Licha mentions.

finished, we can support other struggles. To go and give the advice that has worked for us, so that it can work for other resistances, too. We have visited several resistances, and they see the example of La Puya as something great. Notice that, for example, you can to a workshop where there are people from other countries, and the history of La Puya moves them, they like to listen to it. And seeing a La Puya t-shirt is like a trophy, they buy it as if it were something very valuable.

Here they thought that if we held out for a week it would be enough, that we were not going to make it to Holy Week, and that if we did it in that week we would leave because who would want to spend Holy Week here. Neither Easter, nor Christmas Eve, nor birthdays, nothing has taken us away from being here. For me, there is no date that takes me away from being here, whether it is my birthday, or anyone else's. We have spent two Christmases here, we are not worried about what date it is, whether it is Sunday, rain or shine. Thank God I have also been healthy and not even an illness has prevented me from coming here. I mean, there is nothing that prevents me from coming.

How do you reconcile this commitment to La Puya with your family life?

You see, my sons sometimes tell me that it bothers them a little that I talk to them so much about La Puya: that I am there at a meeting. My eldest daughter says, "Mom, we have to make an appointment to come and see you, when will you have a day off for me?" They say it with resentment.

And I tell her, "I am doing it for you. You don't go. It's fine, because you have small children, but you should go sometimes. But it is for you, for those little *patojitos*[16], that I am doing this". I tell people, "Look, I know that we can all do this because very old people have come here to take a shift, there is no age or pretext for not coming here". It is hard for me to come with her *[Heidi, her*

---

[16] Small children.

youngest daughter, who suffers from a neurological disease]. These last shifts I leave at half past four in the morning, I walk about 25 minutes all the way up to go out to the bus and not even that stops me, walking with her, stumbling all the way; then I say, "Why don't this people come? Healthy, strong people, with all comforts?" Then there is no reason for them not to come, because there have been pregnant people who have gone from here to get well, people with newborns have been here, so we all can, but there is some will lacking.

How has the resistance changed your life?

It has changed a lot, because it opened my mind, as if I had had a blurred, darkened mind, and it opened my mind to the reality of taking care of the water, taking care of the trees, taking care of the land, not throwing garbage wherever, that is, bad habits that one had as if it was normal, eat something and throw it on the ground. I have learned many things and it makes me angry when I see someone on a bus finish their water bottle and *poing!* *[making the noise of throwing something out]*, out the window. I wish I had more courage than I already have, because it took a lot of courage, a lot of courage, to tell them, "Don't be *shuco*, so messy, pick that up."

One day a woman said to me (and it hit me hard!), "But you wouldn't be like that if Tomás *[her first husband]* were still alive." I said, "Yes." Yes, because honestly I would not be like that, but things happen for a reason, because if he were alive things would be very different, I would be in a circle going around in the same place. So things happen for a reason, I have learned a lot from this, from that time until now. It has been about 16 years since he passed away, but yes, God knows why he does things, he does not do them for pleasure, he knows why he has a toad under a rock, he has everything well planned, then, everything happens for a reason. Yes, that woman told me, "If he were here, you would not be like that." Maybe she was right, because they knew him, but things are not like that anymore and sincerely it changed my life. I have learned more, I have been able to live with more people from different places. When I go to a one-week workshop, believe it or not, you adapt in five or four days to the people; by the last day everyone is sad to leave those people from another country. You adapt to their way of being, because those people are living the same struggles as you, maybe a little different but fighting for a common good, so it has changed me a lot.

Today, how do you think of yourself as a woman? Were you aware of being a woman?

I have discovered it. Unfortunately, I was brought up in such a small world that women were lesser, that women were below the power of men, that what men said went, the husband was the king, the woman was the employee. A very ugly little circle, which I began to see when I was young. I tried with my family, although it did not give many results, but I tried. Now I have solved it, but these are things that you discover, because when you are a child you think that you were only born to have children, to reproduce and to take care of the house, but that is not your function, your function is so much more than being locked up in a house.

The day I talked to you for the first time, you told me that you were writing your story. Where did it come from? Why write your story?

The idea came from my sister who is a nun. She is in a convent, and she told me, "Look, I would like you to write down what you are going through, and write a book". "Well," I said, "good idea". And I started to write from the first day, with all the details; I have written what I have lived. Not what I have been told, because when I have not been there I have missed some events. Because at the beginning I came and nothing happened; I left and when I left things happened. So I have not written that down, but what I have experienced, I've written: at what moment, at what time they have come, what they have done to me, how they have threatened me, how I have seen the danger, all that, so I have written it down.

The first writing was about the first two years. It was my sister's idea, she began to make poems of the first year about what she heard or what I told her, that is how she composed them. And that is how she made the first and the second for me. The third year, I said, "Well, I have to try it because I live it, I know it". Then, when I put together my poem, she told me, "You do it better because you are there; but me, I do it based on what they tell me, or what I hear." Now I write a poem for each anniversary. I have already written five poems in these five years. My book is simply dates: what happened, what we did, how we did it, but about my life. Maybe in general, but it is my story. I have been told that they will help me publish it, but I say no. Once a woman from an organization told me that she would take it from me, even if it was in my sleep, but I told her no. Because my purpose is to keep my story for my grandchildren; if they read it or not, that is up to them, but it is so they can learn a little something about me. My husband tells me that it is selfish not to publish it, or not to show it to other people. Maybe later on, because it would have to be improved; they are written my way. Someday.

Defendiendo la casa común. Poema para el V aniversario de La Puya*

Buenos días, buenas tardes

---

* "Defending the common home. Poem for the 5th anniversary of La Puya" Good morning, good afternoon. / Today we are celebrating / For we are five years old / And no one can deny it. / In the time we've had / Many things have happened / We feel very glad / Because they are not exploiting. / We are also one year old / Since we didn't let them in. / It's a gain for the planet / And we will celebrate it. / Company and ministry are the same corruption. / They only think about money / And they don't see the pollution. / Companions, women and men, / Who are here today, / Let's defend our land tooth and nail. / The government is silent, / They don't want to speak out. / Their silence has been bought, / But with us it will not hold. / The resistance of La Puya / Has given you a good example. / Organize your town / And let's not waste time. / Here I say my

Jonatan Rodas

Hoy vamos a celebrar
Pues cumplimos cinco años
Y nadie lo puede negar
En el tiempo que llevamos
muchas cosas van pasando
Nos sentimos muy contentos
Porque no están explotando
También cumplimos un año
De no dejarlos entrar
Es ganancia para el planeta
Y lo vamos a festejar
La empresa y el ministerio son la misma corrupción
sólo piensan en el dinero
Y no ven la contaminación
Compañeras y compañeros
Que hoy están aquí presentes
Defendamos a nuestra tierra con uñas y con dientes
El gobierno está callado
Y no le conviene hablar
Le compraron su silencio
Y con nosotros no va a aguantar
La resistencia de La Puya
Les ha dado un buen ejemplo
Organízate en tu pueblo
Y no perdamos el tiempo
Aquí me voy despidiendo
Con gozo y con alegría
Porque siempre nos acompaña
Dios padre y la Virgen María.

---

goodbyes / With joy and happiness / Because God the Father and the Virgin Mary / Always walk with us.

17. Violence affects the entire community, not just women

Dialogue between Cristina Cucurí[1] and Miriam Lang[2]

CRISTINA: I am Cristina Cucurí, from the Indigenous community Nitiluisa, Calpi parish, Riobamba canton, in the province of Chimborazo, Ecuador. It is one of the most populated, largest, and oldest communities in the parish of Calpi. I believe that about 2000 people live there. I am the first daughter in six brothers and sisters: four women and two men. My mother carries out activities traditionally considered for women: she is a housewife, she devotes herself to agricultural work, community *minga* (unpaid community labor, often to maintain certain infrastructures) and sessions or assemblies. My father was a worker at the Chimborazo Cement Company, a cement factory near the parish; now he is retired. About eight years ago, when my father retired, they began to live together again, because before that my mother assumed all the responsibilities of the home, community, agriculture and child-rearing, and my father only worked in the company and came home to rest, to continue his routine the next day.

---

[1] Leader of lands and territories of Ecuarunari between 2016 and 2019, native of the Puruhá people of the province of Chimborazo in Ecuador.

[2] Professor of the Environment and Sustainability Area in the Universidad Andina Simón Bolívar. She edited the book *Mujeres indígenas y justicia ancestral* (Indigenous Women and Ancestral Justice, http://repositorio.dpe.gob.ec/bitstream/39000/1172/1/ONU-024.pdf) in 2009 and was a screenwriter for the documentary film *Justicia nuestra. Mujeres indígenas latinoamericanas y el acceso a la justicia* (*Our justice. Latin American Indigenous women and access to justice.* https://www.youtube.com/watch?v=kGyoiG-HF1I).

My dad was very supportive of my education. When I finished school, my mom told me, "So far, we have supported you", but my dad said, "No, she is my daughter and if she wants to study I will support her"... He has seven siblings. At that time my three uncles were single and lived in the city, and since I was the first niece and first granddaughter, they said that they had to make me study, that I should have the best education. I studied up to fourth grade in the community school, and from there I went to the city to study, to Riobamba, in a religious school, Our Lady of Fatima. And my father intended to leave me in boarding school there.

So, when I went to the city they cut my hair, I had to wear pants, dress, use the school uniform.

MIRIAM: Did the nuns cut your hair?

CRISTINA: No, my uncles changed me.

MIRIAM: To get you to adapt?

CRISTINA: Exactly. When I finished college, I empowered myself again to take possession of what was mine, my traditional clothing, my customs, my language. Until this moment it was like I was in a world that was not mine, I was dressing in the clothes that were not mine, usurping. When I finished my higher education at the Chimborazo Polytechnic School, I got a degree in education and health promotion, which is equivalent to public health, so I stopped wearing my mestizo dress. Two or three years later, there was a call to become a doctor in health promotion at the undergraduate level, at the same university, and there I returned to study, but already with my own clothes. All my fellow students stared at me: "We'd always known you as a mestiza, but now..." I was already more outgoing, more expressive, more communicative. Because I remember that from school to university I was quieter, more self-conscious, I had to study and nothing else, and I did have a few friends, but not many. So I think that recovering my clothes, my language, was like recovering myself and expressing myself, what I am and where I come from. I think it was a strong resignification and vindication for me.

MIRIAM: And in your childhood, in the community, did people speak Kichwa?

CRISTINA: Yes, they did. When I went back to my community on weekends, I would put on my traditional clothes and speak Kichwa.

MIRIAM: So in a way, it was like dressing up to get out of there.

CRISTINA: Exactly, when I left the community, I would put on my pants. Not now, sometimes on the weekends I put on a tracksuit, but all that time I have been in my traditional clothes and I feel very good. I have recovered what is mine, because usurping an identity that is not yours made me feel very ashamed, so maybe I was shy, feeling self-conscious, not wanting to talk, all those things.

MIRIAM: And does your family have land, do they have animals there in the community?

CRISTINA: Yes, they have animals, they have a farm, they have land...

MIRIAM: And in your parents' house, do you eat what you sow?

CRISTINA: Yes, most of the things, because my mom always made, for example, quinoa leaf salad, made alfalfa juice, she toasted barley, corn and a lot of dry grain products, she would have them ground, she still does. So I think that good nutrition had a great influence on our progress in education.

And how was your trajectory in the Indigenous organizations, in the women's and mixed organizations?

CRISTINA: I live with my partner in the city, but I always go to my parents' place at weekends. Today, because of the leadership role I assumed, I also go to other communities and other provinces. I have been involved with community organizations since I was very young. In the community, you have to support your parents, to engage in the community *mingas*, in the sessions; my father is the head of the household. Since I was 15, 16 years old, I had to start building relationships with others. You don't represent yourself in the community, you rather represent your father.

So that's when I began to relate to others, and I also saw the problem of violence against women. In my house there was no physical violence, there were disagreements, anger, as far as insults. In the neighbors' house I did see physical violence, the drunk husband dragged her, hit her, kicked her, left bruises on her face. So that really shocked me.

One of the things I'm not good at is cooking, for example. Washing, yes, tidying up and cleaning the house, "moving things around" as my husband says, because I change things from one place to another, but cooking? I do it because I have to *[laughter]*. So my mom would tell me, "It's just that if you get married...", because supposedly it's a woman's obligation, and "If you have to cook and your husband doesn't agree with how you've cooked, if he hits you and you come to my house..." She used to tell me that if I went to her house, she would immediately take me back to my husband's house, that's what she said. And I said, "No, I have to study because at some point I'm going to get someone who can do the things in the house and I'll pay for it." So I think that from that point of view I began to question why women have to wash, iron and cook. And if he hits me, why isn't there someone to help, not even my mother? They tell you, "Then, you had to think very well if you got married or not, that is, if you suffer, it is your problem because you decided to make a new life as a couple." Maybe your parents would agree or disagree, but you decided, you are already apart, if you have problems they do not support you.

MIRIAM: That's tough, isn't it? Coming from a mother...

CRISTINA: I think that in some places it is still like that. So far my mom tells me that she has helped defend women who were physically attacked by their husbands many times. Then I start to reflect on what she told me and what she does. Did my mom want me not to get married, or not to get a partner who would abuse me, not to suffer? How do you explain this contradiction then?

MIRIAM: Obviously, in many places this is how things are, but I find it hard. Let's see, later on, when we met, you were a leader of women, you worked a lot on the subject of women there in Chimborazo. How did you come to that?

CRISTINA: From an early age I got involved in the community, because I am from the community, I represented my parents in the *minga*, in assemblies... I was also a leader of the local mixed organization. From there, I went to the women's organizations. Together with other companions we grouped the seventeen communities of the Calpi parish to found the Organización de Segundo Grado Mixta (Second Grade Mixed Organization). Then I was one of the founders, the articulators of this organization. I was also the first secretary of this organization that is called the Corporación de Organizaciones Indígenas de Calpi (Corporation of Indigenous Organizations of Calpi), I spent three years as a leader, then I stepped aside for a while so that other people could lead and I said, "Other people must work here," I don't have to be there always. And that's when I started working with women, because that's the issue that I started to question since I was a child: why do they say that we have to get married? Why do they say that we have to cook? Why do they say...? Why don't they value the work of women in the community? If I don't like to cook, what's the problem? And why do they beat us all the time? Not me, but the neighbor we've seen. So that's where I start to get involved with the Proyecto de Desarrollo de la Mujer Rural y su Familia (Project for the Development of Rural Women and their Families) financed by the European Community and the Ministry of Agriculture and Livestock. I go in strengthening my kichwa, asserting myself as a woman, as an Indigenous person, and learning and re-learning with the women about many rights and laws in favor of women. And that these laws are seen from the urban and mestizo points of view, and they do not fully protect us Indigenous and rural women, but it is useful to know them. I have been militating for twenty years, and I am an activist for the rights of women and of Indigenous peoples; I still support and work with rural and Indigenous women, in articulation. We have begun to articulate the organizations of Indigenous, rural, and peasant women at the provincial level, in order to build *Sumak Kawsay* and the plurinational state from our point of view. What do we need to do to achieve that?

For example, it was important at that time that we learned about Law 103[3], the Women's Police Stations and the role of the

---

[3] The Law 103 against violence to women and the family, of a civil and criminal nature, enacted in 1995 as an achievement of the feminist and women's movement, and largely repealed by the Código Integral Penal (Comprehensive Criminal Code) of

police, a lot of mechanisms that they gave you if you denounced violence against women, they gave you a little piece of paper so that the aggressor would no longer approach you. But in the community, how are you going to say "I have the paper here"? He takes the paper away from you and hits you because there is no police, because there is no Women's Police Station, because it is kilometers away, because at the Women's Police Station the officials also speak only Spanish and many of the older women don't speak Spanish very well. So Indigenous women have been subjected to mockery, they are called "Marías", or "cousins", or they are told "to speak Christian"; those terms denigrate us, so what do we do? There was another very strong trigger when an Indigenous Member of Parliament (MP) from the province of Chimborazo, who was president of the Human Rights Commission during those years, beat his wife and took refuge in the Indigenous justice system: in other words, "I embrace the Indigenous justice system, I am Indigenous". The woman denounced him at the Women's Police Station. So the community had to solve this problem.

MIRIAM: So he thought that the community was going to protect him in his right to beat his wife?

CRISTINA: And the community did. In fact, the community protected him because he was a provincial MP. Because otherwise, they wouldn't get his support for any public work, for any community requirement. They resolved that the woman was transgressing the function of a housewife, abandoning her husband and children, because she worked outside the home and the community, that she should assume her responsibility.

MIRIAM: So what happened? What reaction did this generate in you?

CRISTINA: We held a very large Indigenous women's march in the city of Riobamba against violence to women. We thought that women's access to Indigenous justice was the way to go: but that it should not be like that, unjust, inequitable toward women. So we

---

2014, introduced by Rafael Correa's Revolución Ciudadana (Citizen Revolution).

marched in support of Indigenous justice and against this decision, we began to work together for the Asamblea Constituyente (Constituent Assembly), saying, "We know that there are failures in Indigenous justice, but this is the path that will give us solutions to the problems of violence against us. Ordinary justice is a different arena, with different referees, it is played in another language, with other codes, it requires money, time, and it has not solved the problems of violence against women for us. In the Indigenous justice system, we have no guarantee either, but we know who is in the community, who the leaders are, we can have some influence and we want it to be resolved in the community, but not biased in favor of our companions. That was and is the struggle...

MIRIAM: What you are saying shows that the colonial state, of the hacienda system, are still in force in today's subjectivities. They sided with him because the man was powerful; that is not justice.

CRISTINA: That's not justice, that was another reason for the march. So we began to reflect and build proposals to reclaim our customs and traditions without discrimination or violence. In this work we were inspired by the Indigenous Zapatista women with their Ley Revolucionaria de Mujeres (Revolutionary Law of Women). Then we articulated with some Indigenous women, companions from Cotacachi and from Sucumbíos, to work on a proposal towards the Asamblea Constituyente.

MIRIAM: And what proposal did you bring to the Constituent Assembly in 2008?

CRISTINA: Basically they were two fundamental proposals from Chimborazo, I don't know if the other companions had other proposals. First, that they recognize the rights of Indigenous women in the chapter on the Collective Rights of Peoples. That was important, it was a significant contribution for the Indigenous peoples of Latin America, that the vindication of women's rights be included in the collective rights with the aim of living well, having welfare, harmony, and balance among peoples. For example, Article 57, paragraph 10, states that Indigenous peoples and nationalities can "create, develop, apply, and practice their own or customary laws, which shall not violate constitutional rights, particularly those of women, children, and adolescents. That was important, although of course, that was not exactly the text we had worked on, but it was the meaning of what we were saying: why, when they talk about collective rights, only men are visible while women are left aside, invisible, and the problem of violence is left out?

The other issue is Indigenous justice; without women's participation and decision, Indigenous justice can be invalidated in the cases resolved. But the only instance that can invalidate the decisions made, to which we can appeal, is the Corte Constitucional (Constitutional Court). Article 171 of the Constitution states that "the authorities of Indigenous communities, peoples and nationalities shall exercise jurisdictional functions, based on their ancestral traditions and their own rights, within their territorial sphere, with a guarantee of women's participation and decision making." We seek to ensure that the problems affecting women are also resolved in the Indigenous justice system.

MIRIAM: A decision that was made without the participation of women can be invalidated.

CRISTINA: Exactly. Not only on the issue of violence against women. All cases resolved by the Indigenous justice system must be resolved with the women's participation and decision. When we talk about participation, we're not just talking about numbers. Because we have always been quite a number in the assemblies, even in some cases almost the entire assembly has been women. We are talking about us deciding, us proposing, us putting forward proposals in the resolution of conflicts of any kind, and if it is the case of violence against women, women's presence, their decision, their proposal should be a priority, and not only their physical presence.

MIRIAM: So, you went as a delegation to Montecristi, in 2008, during the session of the Asamblea Constituyente. Do you remember which organizations went? Or how many?

CRISTINA: Well, let's see. The Red Provincial de Organizaciones de Mujeres Kichwas y Rurales de Chimborazo (Provincial Network of Kichwa and Rural Women's Organizations of Chimborazo), the

Central Committee of UNORCAC[4] of Cotacachi, and the women of AMNKISE[5] of Sucumbíos are the ones that were involved in this process. We didn't go there only once at the time, but several times: going back and forth to Montecristi to talk with the authorities, with the female assembly members, the Commission...

MIRIAM: And were you well received there?

CRISTINA: I think that in the end we were, but at the beginning... I remember that when the feminist and women's movement of Ecuador called for a meeting in Riobamba to draw up the women's agenda for the Asamblea Constituyente, they said that the women should send in proposals to draw up a document for the Constitution. We did send in our work, our proposal as Indigenous women, but it did not appear in the document. And when we participated in the events, we were told that Indigenous women cannot be apart because we were all women. So it didn't appear...

MIRIAM: And what did you think right then?

CRISTINA: We said, "We have to do something about this", that is, go there ourselves and tell what we are living through and how we want to live, how we want to build our future. Because it's not that we want to live in the communities with men apart and women apart, we are men and women, we live in community. But when we are living badly, the community is also not well, it does not advance, it does not develop. So how do we get our problems into the Asamblea Constituyente and into the Ecuadorian Constitution? We reflected and began to build the road, and walk along it. When we went to Montecristi to deliver the proposal of the Ecuadorian women, they delivered it and we also delivered our proposal to the president of the Asamblea, Alberto Acosta. Other women gave us bad looks: "That is a division, we are all women, and I do not know what else they want". But we had submitted our proposal.

---

[4] Unión de Organizaciones Campesinas de Cotacachi (Union of Peasant Organizations of Cotacachi).

[5] Asociación de Mujeres de la Nacionalidad Kichwa de Sucumbíos (Association of Women of the Kichwa Nationality of Sucumbíos), Ecuador.

Dialogue between Cristina Cucurí and Miriam Lang

MIRIAM: The alternative was to remain invisible.
CRISTINA: Exactly. We didn't want to remain invisibilized. I think that was the trigger for them to say, "All right, let's include them into the discussion." There were also female assembly members who had been activists at some stage in their lives, women's rights activists, who were very supportive of us. They gave us the opportunity to enter the Assembly and tell what we came for and what ideas we brought.
MIRIAM: And what reactions did you get from the Indigenous movement, from the male leaders of the Indigenous movement?
CRISTINA: They never knew. While you work so hard in the province, national leaders don't notice. They never found out about our proposals; from what I have been told, they never imagined that a group of women from three provinces could go and tell the Asamblea Constituyente what we are going through, what is happening in the communities, and how we want to rebuild our lives for ourselves and our peoples. They told me that, by the time they found out, it was too late, the topic was out there already. I remember that when we went to the Justice Commission led by Father Fernando Vega, and he had just been talking about the issue of Indigenous justice, when we went and said why we wanted women to be present, the other assembly members heard about the problems of access to ordinary and Indigenous justice that we women have: "Ah, you see, Indigenous women have also lived in violence." Father Fernando was a fundamental support, he helped us a lot. We were told that he said, "Either you include the women's proposal or the Indigenous justice won't be passed", so they said, "All right, let's include it, let's include it." I remember that when I returned from Montecristi, I saw the news on TV, and there a respected female Indigenous leader said: "On the issue of Indigenous justice, women have always been present; I do not know who has positioned the participation of women, but it must be a feminist who does not know the life of the peoples or understand the sense of community" and I do not know what else... But it was too late when she said that.
MIRIAM: And what do you think about that? I mean, because there's a whole debate, isn't there? The Constitution itself is an

instrument of the Western liberal state. In retrospect, do you think that appealing to this resource as Indigenous women's organizations from different provinces has helped you?
CRISTINA: I think it is a mechanism, but it is not everything. In order to be able to say "we are living very well with this", we still have a lot of work to do. One of the things I see is that as a result of this whole process, today, at least within the Indigenous movement, it has been possible for the expanded Conaie[6] assembly to resolve, in July 2016, that cases of violence against women and feminicide should be dealt with, resolved, and sanctioned in the Indigenous justice system. I believe this is an important step, but we still have a long way to go. Because it is in the Constitution, it forces you to deal with it. And also in the Sixth Congress of the Conaie in Saraguro, in September 2017, the women's round table positioned that the Conaie declare and mandate that the territories of Indigenous peoples be free of violence against women. Thus, it is generating discussions, positions, and proposals from women. The women began the work from a small place and are positioning these issues of violence against women and feminicide in Indigenous communities in larger spaces: that is important. I believe that the 2008 Constitution was a trigger, when we made it clear that we have problems, we have sexual abuse, violence against women, irresponsibility in assuming paternity, teenage pregnancies, feminicide within Indigenous peoples and nationalities. In the Sixth Congress of the Conaie, women raised their voices, saying that they must declare territories free of violence against women, which seemed to me another important step. Although as I say, it is only a mechanism, and it is not the end. We still have a lot of *chakiñan*, of path, to build; we must continue with a proud voice, with proposals, ideas.
MIRIAM: Of course, it's a step. And tell me, there are all those Indigenous people, men and women, who say that this might happen, but that anyway the good that prevails is harmony in the

---

[6] Confederación de Nacionalidades Indígenas del Ecuador (Confederation of Indigenous Nationalities of Ecuador).

community and that the women who are protesting —perhaps in the sense of what your mother said, when you get married— are dividing the community and breaking the harmony, and they can't complain, they have to endure. In other words, putting the collective right of the community as a whole before the individual right of a woman who supposedly wants to live free of violence.

CRISTINA: I remember that when in Chimborazo we had held several community workshops with women's organizations, especially at the cantonal and provincial levels, we already had a proposal. I personally was trying to look up something that would give an account of Indigenous women in the Bolivian Constitution, because they were very advanced in the constituent process, and there was a considerable group of assembly members from Indigenous peoples and nationalities in Bolivia's Asamblea Constituyente, but no, there was nothing. I also looked in the Mexican Constitution. An organization that supported women's organizations in Chimborazo helped us by hiring a jurist who specialized in Indigenous peoples. The lawyer also worked on the issue of Indigenous justice with another nationally-recognized lawyer who was close to the Indigenous movement. We spoke with the lawyer and explained the proposal that the companions were putting forward, so that she could help us transform it into articles for the Constitution. I sent her the document. She told me that the collective rights cannot be enforced by the State, nor is it possible to include a gender perspective... they belong to the Indigenous peoples. In these debates, she told me, "Rights are invented". I nodded and said, "If they are invented, we, the women from Indigenous peoples, want to reinvent rights in order to live better, with dignity; that's what we want." So that's what we've done.

MIRIAM: I recently read a research paper by an Aymara student from Bolivia who interviewed Mama T'allas[7] Aymaras on the *altiplano*, the highlands of La Paz. Her interest was to know in what way they exercise authority, in a system of authorities that always act in pairs, according to Chacha Warmi, the male / female

---

[7] Highest Indigenous female authority of a community.

complementary... And there are several women who express that they do suffer discrimination, but in their own words, they never state that "this hurts *me*", but rather they say, "Yes, I suffer discrimination, they make fun of me, they say that I can't", and I don't know what else, but "that hurts the community". I was amazed that these women never express a notion of violation towards their person, but that the violence they suffer directly violates the collective. Here in Ecuador, how would this be? The Kichwa women in the communities of Chimborazo that you have spoken to, that you know, that you have accompanied, how do they feel about that? Do they feel that the violence violates them as a person? Their personality? Or is it simply something that should not happen in general, or is it something that causes harm to the community, or to the family... what do you remember?

CRISTINA: Because of this situation I was telling you about, I was wondering, why do individual rights stand in opposition to collective rights? They should be on a par, not overlapping; they should be coordinating and cooperating for the good life and well-being of peoples and especially Indigenous women. What does this mean? That if my individual rights have been violated, this affects the entire community, not just me. For example, if a husband kills his wife, it affects the community, the children, the *ayllu*, it alters the communal and individual harmony and balance... It does not only affect the family, it affects the entire community because they also have relatives, they also have families. Where and with whom will the child be left? At some point he will be a leader, and under what circumstances will he be a leader? The situation that happened will have marked his life. How will he lead the community? Because at some point in your life you have to serve the community, you are not just appointed because you are more recognized, or because you have some property, or because you have a better last name. In the community, we all, female and male, have to serve at some point in our lives. So this child, in what circumstances is he going to be a leader, and what experiences will this child have had without his mother? Not only does it affect the child's life, but the life of the community.

MIRIAM: And what example will he set?

CRISTINA: What example will he set? So that's what we were saying: it does affect us women, it affects all of us, but it also affects the community. On the other hand, I believe that in Chimborazo the individual has been given precedence over the collective; since the time of the Colony, since the time of the *haciendas*, we have been divided, individualized. Then the State itself began to say, "You have no need to get organized", "You are a citizen who can directly be represented on behalf of yourself before the State." The ten years of Correa in office have been very strong in this process of individualizing us. In addition to this, the patriarchal, capitalist, neoliberal system...

From women's point of view, it is important to recover the territorial space, the communal space. This implies saying, "This does not only affect me as a person, but also the community". We live in that space and time. I believe that in some community maybe what you say about Bolivia can happen, the feeling that "it does not affect me, but the collective". But the liberal, individual influence has been strong in the life of women, in the life of the peoples, very strong; they do feel violence as a personal affectation. That is why they say that "the problem of violence is a personal problem", and that is why the communities have not attended to it, because they do not see that it affects everyone, female and male. We are in this process of recovering, reinventing, resignifying, reconceptualizing the organization, space, and time of women and Indigenous peoples.

I remember that in 2012, I participated in a research project on legal pluralism and Indigenous women in Latin America with CIESAS in Mexico. We did interviews with men in the south of Chimborazo, in Tixán. We wrote the question guide and a male colleague did the interviews. As a result, the men said that they feel bad when they exert violence, they do not feel good when they attack women. But it is the only way they have lived, the only way they know since the Colony and since the *hacienda*. If they had known another way of living, of living better, they would have been able to learn and would not have used violence, but their parents lived on the *hacienda* and they were abused a lot, first by the landowner, and then they replicated this at home. So that's the way they have known and lived together. It was interesting to see the perspective of the male companions with respect to this problem. We can talk a lot from the perspective of the women, but to know that they do not feel well either when practicing violence or living in it, that they feel very bad, is a way to rebuild harmony and balance in the community. Because Indigenous men have also suffered discrimination, exclusion and violence from men or women, white or mestizo.

MIRIAM: You have just named a series of influences, from the *hacienda* to the most modern form of State under Correa, that have impacted on the Indigenous territories of Chimborazo. There is this whole debate about where the patriarchy comes from? Guatemalan community feminist Lorena Cabnal claims, for example, that there was an ancestral patriarchy; while others, some Bolivian women for example, say: "No, the patriarchy came with the Colony and then came with peasant unionism, which imposed the male leader only: it is more recent." What do you think about this?

CRISTINA: I agree with Lorena Cabnal. There are various feminist currents —radical, autonomous, and others—, they are worth knowing, but I do not fit into any of these currents. I am part of a community, I belong to an Indigenous people, I have my own language, traditions, customs, worldviews, cosmoexperience, territory. The companions are our life partners, our community partners, our partners in struggle. So where do I position myself in order to work from a feminist standpoint? By understanding feminism as the struggle and the political life project of any woman anywhere in the world, from any culture, tradition, or people, at any stage of history, who wants to rebel or who has rebelled against the patriarchy that oppresses her or wants to oppress her. The struggle is not against male companions and men of any culture, it is against the patriarchy that oppresses people and Indigenous peoples, which affects everyone....

Many men in urban areas, but also in the Indigenous communities and different spaces, misunderstand feminism as the equivalent of machismo... Feminists are considered anti-men, against men, haters of men, more or less.

MIRIAM: But how do you feel?

CRISTINA: Again, I personally agree with Lorena, the sister from Guatemala. At some point I heard some female Indigenous leaders say that there was no violence in Abya Yala, that violence against women and patriarchy came with the Spaniards. I don't think that's true. There was patriarchy in Abya Yala, but in a different way, to a different extent because it was another context. I do believe that the Spaniards reinforced it very much, they strengthened the patriarchy and the violence with the Colony, from the State, through religion... I understand that this is what they mean when they say that "Indigenous women are three times discriminated against". But the issue is not so much discussing where it came from and how, but now, that it already exists, to ask how we have to work against this problem and what we should do, how we should confront it. I agree with Lorena Cabnal that there was patriarchy before, we can't say that there wasn't, it was reinforced with the arrival of the Spaniards to the territories of our great-great-grandparents. Now, what is valued is if you are a woman or a man, if you have money or not, if you profess some religion or not, if you know how to speak Spanish well or not, if you have a degree or not, that's why you are excluded, discriminated against, done violence to. In 1830, in the first Ecuadorian Constitution, only people who professed the Catholic religion, who were married, who had a certain amount of money and property, who could read and write, were considered citizens. If you did not meet these conditions, you were not considered a citizen. So Indigenous peoples, the Indigenous women and women in general were not citizens... But in the time of the Incas, they sent maiden women to be sacrificed, in the wars between communities they traded them in marriage to forge alliances. They also had to stay at home when the men went to war. So this is evidence that there was indeed an ancestral patriarchy, but it was not the same patriarchy brought by the Spaniards. On the other hand, they had the right to land, communal protection, among others. I totally agree that there was ancestral patriarchy.

MIRIAM: Well, you also say, more pragmatically, "What is important is that we see that patriarchy exists today, that it makes us live badly and that we have to do something", right? Since 2016, you have held the position of female leader of lands and territories in the Confederación Kichwa del Ecuador (Ecuarunari, Kichwa Confederation of Ecuador), which is one of the most important organizations of Conaie. What does this position imply? What are your tasks? And how do you see the relationship between violence and territory?

CRISTINA: For me it has been a space of learning and contribution, because Ecuarunari is a regional organization. I had been in mixed community, second degree, provincial, and doing activist work, supporting problems of Indigenous women, feminicide, sexual abuse, harassment, violence, working from the collective. When I became a leader of territories at the regional level, it was a much broader dimension. Territory does not only mean land, water, fire, air, but also means people, flora, fauna, rivers, those of us who live on top of the land and what is inside, such as minerals, among other elements. So it means working from the vision of the peoples, from the collective vision, from self-determination and control of the territory. For example, the defense of territory against mining, community management of water, territory and community. It is no longer just the defense of the territory-body, as Lorena says. It is the defense of the territory-land. From this leadership I am going to work and combine the defense of the territory-body and the territory-land: because our territory-body with our territory-land form elements that are conjugated, shared, configured and coexist in space; if some element is altered there is a loss of balance, there is disharmony, and the effects impact on the individual and community life of the peoples. Working on these issues from the perspective of being a woman is a challenge. The issue of the territory being free of violence against women fits into the defense of the territory-land and the territory-body. Another important aspect to deepen this work is to reconstruct, recover, and practice self-determination, autonomy, and self-government of the peoples, based on the international treaties of Indigenous peoples of the ILO, the UN, and the OAS, and of course also the Ecuadorian Constitution. The way forward is the reconstruction of Indigenous communities. The Ecuadorian state issued the Ley de Comunas (Law of Communes), which has been in force since 1937, and which contradicts the rights of Indigenous peoples. From my point of view, it destroyed, fragmented, divided and weakened community organization. It says that the community has a *Cabildo*, a local administration, formed by a president, vice-president, secretary, treasurer and trustee, for example.

MIRIAM: And with this, it imposes a specific form of organization.

CRISTINA: Exactly, it imposes a unique form of organization; this has caused the interior of the communes to create smaller organizations, in many cases motivated by the State, making them lose the collective sense of the community. And the *cabildos* limit themselves to small management, as if begging from the State authorities. For example, candies for Christmas, fences for the cemetery, road repairs. So control and self-government of the territory should not be exercised in this form of government that the State imposed with the Ley de Comunas. I am walking this path right now: to recover, reconfigure, resignify, reconceptualize the communal territory as a territory of struggle, of resistance and of proposal, regarding both the rights of women and the rights of Indigenous peoples.

MIRIAM: And free of violence, in what dimensions?

CRISTINA: In order to live in dignity, harmony, and balance in the community, we should not experience violence in the home or in the community, nor through mining exploitation in the territory. Being taken out of your habitat, having Nature stripped and exploited as a "resource", this is also violence against the territory-body of women and against the territory-land. The dimension of violence on the body and the life of women through mining is a new topic, an important topic, that should not be separated from the right of women to a worthy, balanced and harmonious life in the community. Because when minerals are extracted the land is polluted, as well as the water, the environment, and also the products that you will eat. So, if a woman eats these products she can get sick, she is violated in her diet, and she has the right to adequate, dignified and healthy food. This is related to food sovereignty. When there is water pollution, you don't have clean water, you can get many diseases; this is also a form of violence against women's bodies and community life.

Another significant issue is education in the communities. Formal education, as the State says, because the education that our parents give us from the time we are born until we die is another form of collective education. In the community we acquire a lot of knowledge and know-how about our peoples and nationalities. But from the State we should get a little piece of paper that says that you are a specialist in something or that you have a high school diploma. This is also an issue that concerns us women and Indigenous peoples. In the past ten years, the Correa government has closed thousands of Indigenous peoples' community schools. I have been involved in research on this issue. There are hundreds of community schools that were closed in the province of Chimborazo and especially in Indigenous communities. This has meant the rupture of community social cohesion. Before, the little school was the center of articulation of the communities; there were parties, the meeting of the *ayllus*, the sessions, the *mingas*, and a lot of activities around the school and the community. Some programs had the mothers cook for the children of the school, it was also a space of articulation for women. Closing the schools has meant the loss of that space. They have concentrated the children of other communities in one school, and with this, colonial problems have re-emerged. For example, in Chunchi, where it used to be a *hacienda*, one community was formed by the former *huasipungueros* of the *hacienda*, and another community by the former majordomos of the *hacienda*. As it happened, the little school of the *huasipungueros* was closed, and the school where the descendants of the majordomos lived was kept open. In this situation, for the descendants of *huasipungueros*, the pain of the discrimination suffered by the grandparents resurfaces. So they didn't want to send their children to that little school, they had to send them to the educational unit of the canton. That was a resurgence of colonial conflicts that we thought were over after the end of the *hacienda*.

MIRIAM: Unbelievable. Yes, under Correa there was a strong will to modernize and centralize education. According to the president, the bilingual community schools were "schools of poverty," unworthy. Then thousands were closed all over the country, and the millennium schools were made, modern, made of cement, for hundreds of children.

CRISTINA: Exactly, the only argument for closing the schools was that "there are not enough children to keep a little school open." The State had not invested anything in many of the community schools. The State should not have closed the little schools, because those belonged to the communities. What it should have done was to improve the quality of education from a collective approach, from two perspectives of knowledge, ancestral and worldly. Hiring the best teachers, with good remuneration. Often the State sent recently graduated teachers to the countryside for them to gain experience, while it should be the other way around.

MIRIAM: You say that the Ley de Comunas weakened community organization. Do you, as an organization, have any vision of what self-management of the territory should look like?

CRISTINA: I am proposing some strategies. Last year, the leadership of Ecuarunari produced a document in which we said that the first step was to empower ourselves with the international conventions and treaties on Indigenous peoples. It is also a matter of building community self-governments, so that we have control over our territory. Within territorial self-government, we must strengthen women's groups so that they can have proposals and a voice. The other fundamental issue is the Ley de Comunas. We want to file a lawsuit of unconstitutionality against that law before the Constitutional Court, because this law is in opposition to international treaties on Indigenous peoples and the Ecuadorian Constitution. International treaties state that Indigenous peoples have their own form of organization. The State has the obligation to guarantee this, adopting effective measures so that we Indigenous peoples can fully exercise our collective rights. In this way, we want to advance the construction of an intercultural and plurinational State.

It seems to me that another important issue is to have control of the territory: what is happening within the community? In the case of children and adolescents, many cases of sexual abuse and harassment in schools have recently come to light. The media has visibilized cases of children from urban sectors, from mestizo sectors, but there must be cases of violence, sexual harassment and abuse of children in Indigenous sectors. So what does the Cabildo or the community government do about these problems? There are the issues of violence against women, food sovereignty, mining, the *páramo*, water. We must know what we have and how much control we have over our territory, because now the mining companies are taking away our territories, they are easily taking over. The path is that of autonomy and community self-government: to reconstruct and exercise control over the territory. In order to reconstruct the territory, we are basically proposing that some elements must be recovered: a community has a territory, it is not only where the houses are, where the community lives, but the territory includes a few hectares, the *páramo*, the river, the streams. We have our own language, our organizational, political and civil system, which includes the Indigenous justice system. These elements have to be strong to build autonomy, well-being, and good living in harmony and balance.

And when we women say "good living in harmony and balance", this does not refer only to food: it refers to organization, to recognition, to the defense of our existence as Indigenous peoples, our experience. It also refers to a territory free of violence against women, against physical, psychological, territorial, and patrimonial violence, free of teenage pregnancy, among other issues. This also affects communal life and not only individual or couple life: it affects the *ayllu*.

18. What we talk about when we talk about reproduction. An ecofeminist dialogue between Ivonne Yánez and Cristina Vega

Cristina Vega comes from feminist militancy in Spain. She arrived in Ecuador more than seven years ago in the context of the Ecuadorian crisis. She is part of the feminist magazine *Flor del Guanto* and works as a professor in the Department of Sociology and Gender Studies at Flacso-Ecuador.

Ivonne Yánez, from the Instituto de Estudios Ecologistas (Institute of Ecologist Studies), is a co-founder and has been a member of Acción Ecológica for more than 30 years. She has worked on different issues such as forests, energy, climate change, environmental services, mining, programs for the REDD commodification of nature, as well as generating knowledge and reflection from the perspective of political ecology.

In this conversation, we discuss the idea of reproduction. What do we mean by reproduction, what do we mean when we talk about struggles for reproduction? And in what ways can spaces and experiences of reproduction (of care for life, the environment, people) be emancipatory?

Cristina and Ivonne meet to exchange views on the idea of reproduction.

From this dialogue emerges the text we share here.

What do we understand by reproduction, and from which viewpoint?

IVONNE YÁNEZ (IVONNE): A few months ago, you invited me to comment on a text of yours, "Rutas de la reproducción y el cuidado por América Latina" (Routes of Reproduction and Care in Latin America). The truth is that it wasn't easy, because as ecologists we have rather conceived the topic of reproduction in, for example, the protection of forests, rivers, and seeds against the expansion of mining, oil, and agro-industries. Campaigns in which our main argument is the defense of the right of nature to guarantee the reproduction of life. For us, the reproduction of life takes place in these spaces, understood as part of territories where peoples and communities live. Reading your article, and thanks to theoretical and historical bases on reproduction, from Marxism and feminism, learned with Silvia Federici, I was left with some doubts about what we can have in common in terms of the vision of what reproduction is, and if there are perhaps differences between our perspectives. Do we mean the same when we talk about reproduction? This makes our dialogue very interesting, and above all important, because what it is all about is building alliances and walking together.

CRISTINA VEGA (CRISTINA): I can offer some elements about how feminism understands reproduction. The central idea is that life, in some way human life, but also life in general, is given and has to be sustained. In our societies, the way in which life has been sustained is based on an unjust social order, which attributes the burden and responsibility to women in the private sphere. This is a very clear starting point in feminism to think about reproduction. In many places, and I think this is what is being revised now, feminists have thought about reproduction from the model of wage labor. They have thought that reproduction, as well as production, was everything that was visible in our society, and that the capitalist system ordered wage in a certain way and anchored it even if it was its opposite side. This, for example, is explained by Silvia Federici: the existence of a whole series of tasks, activities, etc., that were outside the world of production, but which ended up being anchored and modulated by it. Silvia explains what that anchorage cost.

By the way, this is not the case in all societies, but in many societies the productive and the reproductive are interwoven, they have not been separated nor absolutely mediated by wages. So, the concept of reproduction seems to acquire more weight in those societies that break it down, generating specialization and asymmetries of value. These are societies that divide tasks very clearly, assigning a social value and a wage to some and leaving others in the dark. It is when feminists begin to look at the injustice of this division of tasks that they begin to nourish the concept of the reproductive. And the reproductive, which is associated with this undervaluation, results in a set of activities that, when looked at, become more and more immense; instead of being marginal, they become more and more varied and rich. All or much of what we do is reproductive, and it is confused with social reproduction. Some components have to do with sustaining the materiality of the body: I mean hygiene, food, health, etc. Food alone involves many microactivities that feminism has yet to think about. What does it mean, for example, to feed oneself, to provide food, to transform it? The same applies to hygiene, health, rest and many other things. The tasks that have to do with the material support of the bodies cannot be separated from the affective, from the emotional well-being; we do not feed the children as if we were robots, but we feed them knowing what they like best, what they like least, what they need, what is good for them, what they ate yesterday... This involves moral, pedagogical, ethical and political judgments, a whole system of practices and values. Reproduction is a world that, from feminism, makes sense when it appears dissociated, linked not only to women but to racialized people, poor people, migrants, all those who are below and whose activities are less valued and more invisible. When this order does not happen, reproduction, as a concept, becomes blurred.

So, as I was saying, for feminists, it has to do first with the materiality of the body and then with the affective. It also has to do with the sexual division of labor and the absence of wages. Many feminists, who came from Marxism and saw its limits, associate reproduction with work, with the absence of a salary, and with the family. These are the two axes that articulated the first feminist approaches: work and family. If we look at societies where these divisions are not so strict or are posed in a different way, even if we think of societies of exploitation, for example a plantation, a reference point for black feminism, reproductive work takes on other meanings. It is rather a site of humanization, and not so much the place of subjugation, of lack of wages, of the house, of family exploitation.

For certain sectors of feminism, rethinking reproduction has to do not only with the misery of the family or with oppression, but with positively valuing those spheres and activities that are part of the cycle of life, and that the first feminism, for example Simone de Beauvoir, considered as a repetition in which nothing transcendent occurred, where there was no emancipation, but something that had to be shaken off in order to be free. Feminism, at this time, is looking at the complexity of reproduction beyond the regeneration of workers for the market for free. It revalues reproduction in order to understand how to rescue it politically, how in it there are processes that also potentially contravene the logic of capitalism based on the capital-life tension, something that some feminist economists talk about. It is a tension that emerges again and again and reminds us that economics is the science of concealment and instrumentalization. We understand, then, that what is sought is to reproduce subjects, but not just any kind, but subjects that fit the market by assuming little socialized responsibility and transferring labor to those at the bottom, both within countries and among countries. So, in a way, what feminism does is say: we can build political leverage from the wealth of reproduction and the possibilities of challenging the social order as a whole. Can we make politics by thinking from there? And that is what has been called the "(political) perspective of reproduction". Others refer to this as "placing reproduction at the center". *Placing* reproduction because it is a place where potentially, not automatically but potentially, you can challenge the capitalist social and gender order. I believe that this thought has been nourished by ecologism and other experiences. But before I go on I would like to know what you think about reproduction.

IVONNE: We —when I say we, I mean an equatorial ecologism, that of the women of Acción Ecológica, because ecologism, like feminism, is obviously very diverse—, we have been in this struggle for thirty years, accompanying local organizations and communities threatened by extractivism, by agrarian policies, by the advance of capital. In many cases, we have seen that women are the ones who fight the most, because they are most affected by the impact or because it is from their experience that the so-called alternatives to the predatory model are forged. Thus, ours is not only a reflection from an intellectual-academic, institutional, or urban activist position, but from practice, from contact with local people. We have been inspired by the struggle for life given by women in rural Ecuador. Yes, they are struggles for reproduction, of course they are. The reproduction of their cultures, of their communities, which is reproduction of life itself.

This has made us see and understand the issue of reproduction in a conflict scenario, where what you call the sexual division of labor and roles are seen and lived in a way that I think is a little different. For example, clearly in Indigenous or peasant communities that are threatened, not everything is harmonious between men and women: there is machismo, community patriarchy. But there are tasks that are proper to men and others to women. Hunting is a male task, the farm is a female task. There is even knowledge that can belong either to men or to women. This is called the division of tasks, or of care and reproduction labor in the communities. When the mining or oil company arrives, everything gets more upset. For example, in some Shuar communities more closely linked to the forest, men were in charge of hunting and providing bush meat, while the women stayed in the communities to take care of the farm, the animals, the children and the elderly, collectively. And this is very important, the collective. Because the families are extended, and the care tasks, including the preparation of food, are collective. So I think this is a difference in the way we look at the issue of tasks and roles. It is not men who confine women to the home, it is a gender division, but in communality. In the community itself is the key.

But what happens when mining or oil activities come into communities? What we saw in a Shuar community in the very south of Ecuador is that the men can no longer hunt because the forests are disappearing, so they stay in the community. And the women have two or three times as much workload. The men spend more time in the community, the women get pregnant more often and have more children; they have to deal with the presence of idle, childish men, who drink more; and violence against women increases, and women have become slaves. Of course, the division of reproduction tasks that had been agreed on is no longer possible: everything was disrupted with the arrival of mining capital. The mining, oil and logging activities completely changed the relations between men and women in the communities.

So, it is clear that for us, as ecologists, the issue of reproduction is to look at how the tasks of reproduction and care are carried out in the communities, in social relations, but also including the reproduction of the life of trees, birds, dolphins, insects, or spirits, and their relations with humans. It is the reproduction of life in its widest concept; this is not merely social or biological/ecological, it is Nature as subjects.

Thus, when we started this path of approaching the idea of bodies, territories and feminisms a few years ago, it seemed that there were pitfalls that had to be overcome. Because it seemed that reproduction as seen by feminists was more linked to a conception of women's work. This approach has made us see that this conception is very useful for understanding what happens in areas of socio-environmental conflict, but it must be complemented. When we see the situation of women in these contexts of conflict, the issue of care and reproduction is related to the situation of women's bodies, biologically speaking, which are more affected because we have more fat in our bodies and more toxins are deposited there, with polluted rivers, with deteriorated soils, with deforested forests, with animals that disappear; there are more sick people, more violence, the relationships among people and between people and "ecosystems" are broken.

Finally, we must say that not only does the workload increase for women, but also for nature: it has to work harder to clean itself up, to carry out its carbon and water cycles, to do photosynthesis, to provide shelter for animals, to keep soils' capacity to provide food, etc. All of nature's tasks —turned labor through environmental services— are part of the reproduction of life as well. Therefore, the work of reproduction transcends the human.

CRISTINA: I find what you say very enlightening; and this helps reformulate the conceptions of reproduction that urban feminism had, of the North, of societies where production and reproduction are so separated that they need to name two different spheres —

production/reproduction— to describe themselves. In those increasingly fewer societies that do not separate both and do not devalue the latter, to speak of reproduction has another meaning, even if there is a sexual division of activities. The concept of domestic work itself is absolutely alien to a community that, for example, does not live the relationships of child rearing as part of a closed, urban home, etc., but in an open natural environment. I believe that in this sense some feminisms start from experiences that have conditioned and limited their way of thinking. And I think that feminisms from other locations help to situate and historicize what now appears as something absolutely normalized. There are places where reproduction as a support for social and natural life can respond to a more comprehensive, evaluative logic, which makes different processes revolve around it. Reproduction then takes on a different meaning.

IVONNE: When you say "it takes on a different meaning", what do you mean?

CRISTINA: It takes on a different meaning because it is organized and connected in a different way. For example, if you talk about a society that is organized in a communal way, even if there is a sexual division of labor, food, care, celebration... everything is done together and this causes support to be lived as a continuum and not as something isolated or broken, subject to a special dynamic. The production-reproduction division is not so marked, so we speak of *life support* at best, or we speak of something more general. In my view, the concept of reproduction has to do with these four things: separation, hyper-specialization, devaluation, and the subordination of everything that concerns the regeneration of people and their daily well-being.

There is a whole discussion in feminism about whether the concept of gender is relevant to all societies, or we could think of societies where there is a division, but where what women (or others who live different genders) do is not devalued. Their activities are complementary, which is what you described when you spoke of the Shuar community before the oil companies. Perhaps the tasks are divided, but perhaps it is not that some are more valuable than others. It seems difficult to think about it in the contemporary world, to me it is difficult, but in any case we could reflect on societies or experiences where the relational, the interpersonal, goes through not only the reproduction but also the production. One produces *in relation* to the community. The Andean communities could be a good example of this in some cases. One does not produce to accumulate in individual terms, but produces in community terms, in which case production is as relational, as much a regard for others' welfare, as reproduction. There are no individuals in one and relational subjects in another; everything is thought and done for the common support, from interdependence. In my opinion, the very conceptual separation between production and reproduction already reflects a certain social order, the capitalist order; it reflects Western modernity, which classifies, divides, isolates and hierarchizes. This creates subjects who think of themselves as individuals, except when they arrive at their urbanized homes and somehow discover that they exist in relation to others. Then they go out again and so on.

What I find very interesting is how feminism in its diversity has been expanding and making the concept of reproduction more complex, and that has a lot to do with feminisms that came from non-Western societies. It has also had to do with the dialogues with ecologists, because many feminists thought about the contributions of Marx and he considered reproduction within the market. Thinking, what do we need to reproduce? Is it what the market produces? Feminists say no, there is something else that is the work of women, and I think that ecologists say no, there are many other things, there is our relationship with natural cycles, with the environment, with activities that are not in the market. In the end, what we have lost is the idea that we are living organisms, and that life also has its limits, which is something that Marxism, with its anthropocentric and androcentric outlook, has not considered in detail.

IVONNE: This is not exclusively mediated by human labor.
CRISTINA: It is mediated by human labor and by the social order, but it has its own limits, its own cycles and its own potency, which is something that we humans find difficult to understand. And we

feminists, as good heirs to Marxism, find it hard, very hard to think that.

Production and reproduction, from different perspectives

IVONNE: I find the need not only to redefine or reconceptualize what can be understood by reproduction from different points of view, but also what production is, interesting. I think it is very important to talk about this duality of reproduction and production from different perspectives. Let's see. Most people live in urban areas, and there are also many communities that still live in non-capitalist forms, or let's say, immersed in capitalism but living in a more communal way. Here there are forms of production with another meaning; for an Indigenous or peasant community, what is production? In other words, why does growing food —even if they sell part of the products— fall within the sphere of "production" and not reproduction, the reproduction of life? The same is true in the space of cities, where there are also those production-reproduction relations that are different from those of the capitalist model. Preparing your food, caring for your children, your mother, or reproducing the family spaces that are so important, are they not necessary for life? Furthermore, a society like ours, the Ecuadorian society, in a capitalist context, would not have been able to continue functioning if the family did not exist, not the family of Tradition, Family and Property or the family of Engels, but the family in the case of Ecuador, culturally speaking, which is an extended family in every sense. All of this falls within the scope of reproduction or even more, of cultural survival. So how can we recognize and claim these spheres of reproduction of life in order to make them emancipatory? Of course, by eliminating the assignment of roles, because indeed they are assigned; unfortunately it is we women who call our mother, our sister, who organize family meetings, who take care of the children, or go to the market. But if these pre-assignments, so beneficial to capital, are broken and become collective tasks... they are tasks in the realm of the reproduction of life that must be strengthened, because they must exist and must be reclaimed in order to become liberating.

CRISTINA: I think it's a challenge to think of reproduction not as a set of activities, but as a cycle that connects activities, that is, not to think of it as a list, but as an articulated continuum. Thinking in terms of articulation is more interesting in that sense than thinking about the set of tasks, the productive and the reproductive ones. If we think about how they are linked to each other, we will also discover the idea of cycles, of ages and courses of life, and then we can understand how wage labor is linked to what we do at home, to transport, to water, to supply, to market, to territory. The challenge is to rethink the connections. In the cities everything is ordered, systematized; children at school, women at work, the house in another place... an absolutely classified, hierarchical and ordered universe. When I leave the house, reproduction ends, when I arrive here, production begins. But the challenge is to break through those classifications that order us and arrange us into hierarchies, to break through them in a synchronic and diachronic sense. That is, when we live, we get sick, we get old, and this happens in all the spaces we inhabit. We have a very present-bound thought, that's why thinking about care is something that sometimes becomes strange to us until we have children, until we get sick and until we get old. Breaking apart with the thought of individuality, of maximization, of rationality, also happens by putting that in the center of existence and seeing it in what sustains it, as you say, if the Ecuadorian family was not what it is this would fall.

IVONNE: But beyond that, not only the Ecuadorian family as a way of confronting the capitalist situation that finally imposes this type of life and relations. Advantageously, what we maintain now is also an ancestry, but which acquires another dimension, almost of survival.

CRISTINA: That's where feminism comes in, to think about the costs for women of resolving these conflicts and crises that are more and more frequent, because capitalist society imposes more "work" on nature and more work on women. So women have to be constantly compensating for the conflict imposed by a hierarchical, divided society, etcetera, and it is plenty. Feminism questions the idealization of the family. These family networks, as ancestral as they are, must be thought of critically, because the family is a space of violence, and this has to do with what has occupied a good part of feminism. Division and devaluation have to do with the dispossession of women as collective subjects. They are dispossessed of their own bodies, their knowledge, their work. All this is expropriated and instrumentalized by men specifically, and by capitalism in general. For me, that reflection is very important.

IVONNE: Ecologism does not criticize the family; on the contrary, it is defended, because in Latin America, and probably in other countries of the South, the family is different from the European or "modern" family and we must fight so that in situations of conflict the family has a healthy life, more dignified, without such a burden for women, for children, for everyone.

CRISTINA: I feel much more skeptical about the family because I believe that the family is a space of support, but it is also a rather violent place; and the data on Ecuador reveals this, that violence against women and girls happens mostly within the family. So we need to problematize the family. Families are a very important support system, as are communities, but what constitutes that very important support is women within those families and communities.

IVONNE: In our countries, finding a way to end these evils is a challenge. One way to do this is to fight to prevent relationships in the community, and within the families that make up the community, from being affected by factors that generate violence such as disease, loss of food sovereignty, pollution, displacement, impoverishment; violence is perhaps not intrinsic to the family in its broadest sense, but it is the result of social and environmental problems that exist and have an impact.

CRISTINA: The family has been changing along with the system and it has not remained a stronghold. I don't have any nostalgia for any lost family. What interests me about the family, but also about other social formations, is the establishment of relationship and support bonds, and I believe that is something we can observe in and beyond the family. When we speak of communities we usually refer to Indigenous communities: we find it very difficult to imagine ourselves as communities in the first person, people who cooperate to move their daily lives forward.

Reproduction of the human and the non-human. How do we understand affectation?

IVONNE: I would like to return to the theme of the reproduction of life besides the human aspect. That is, the reproduction of life beyond what we have been discussing: the production that humans do, the production of culture, in the family, etcetera. Nature, which has its own cycles of reproduction.
CRISTINA: Yes, I remember that we talked about "second nature". Actually, I have my doubts and I wanted to ask you about this, about the dynamics of nature besides the human.
IVONNE: We are not talking about nature as an entelechy. Nature here and humans there; nature is everything, humans within, and nature has cycles of reproduction apart from those that exist in human societies themselves.
CRISTINA: I think it would be good to give an example.
IVONNE: For example, the depths of the oceans, or the snow-capped mountains. Even if these places are in some way influenced by human activities, such as climate change, which is the result of human activity affecting glaciers, the glaciers, in fact, have their own reproduction cycles that are not necessarily linked to human nature.
CRISTINA: This, for me, makes a difference. If a child is born and we leave it there in the middle of the cold, of the inclemency, it dies. Our body has limits, and it has its own relational conditions of survival. On the other hand, as with glaciers, if our body is filled with toxins, it also dies. We can recover that idea of a natural, corporeal materiality that interacts as an organism. If we think about our own corporeal materiality I think it reveals exactly that: we are being affected by a series of conditions that affect our own limits. What are those limits? They are very connected to social organization, to how we are going to relate. What is organic

mutates, but maybe it will mutate into situations that we cannot or do not want to sustain.

IVONNE: Sometimes it seems to me that when you talk about reproduction, people end up referring to the human, the family, the children, etcetera, but I think there is another sphere of reproduction that is neither human nor social.

CRISTINA: Could you explain that?

IVONNE: Life is not just what is "alive". What is life? Human beings, animals, spirits, stones? For many Indigenous peoples stones have life, oil has life. We cannot say that rocks are not alive. Which leads me to think, then: what do we mean by "reproduction of life"?

It is useful for us to think about it in terms of action because there I see a possibility of anchoring and uniting struggles that defend reproduction in territorial spaces of humans and non-humans. To act so that people can continue to live in good conditions. And because it also allows us to understand that there are affectations to other spaces that are not necessarily human spaces and that this must hurt us. When you are affected by the lives of other human beings and by the lives of non-humans, it hurts, and this drives you to act. For isolated villages, for pink dolphins, for fishermen, or for the bottom of the oceans where they want to mine. It is not just a political tool, but it allows you to connect with that other life that is not necessarily linked to yours and to the social.

CRISTINA: I think I understand your point a little better. There is an element in this discussion that has to do with interdependence and affectation, what we were saying about pollution, but there is another element you bring up now, that has to do with the autonomy of the non-human and how we engage with its mere existence. Areas where the human is not even relevant, where life flows on its own terms. That autonomy involves us in some way, sometimes from interdependencies and affectation, sometimes from the feeling of knowing oneself in this world, from ethics. This makes me think of this animist idea that everything, in the end, is connected to everyone at all times. In Galicia there is a reflection on this: "San Andrés de Teixido: vai de *morto* o que non foi de *vivo*".

Your particles will somehow reach San Andrés de Teixido in one way or another during your life, and if not by then, they will once you have died. That is, your matter circulates, and everything ends up interfering with it. Everything is interconnected, and that invites us to conceive the human from another place, in its relations (between humans) and also with other existences, animate and inanimate. We are no longer going to talk about life in a restrictive sense, but about material existence.

IVONNE: About existence, that's all: it can be material, spiritual, whatever.

CRISTINA: I am interested in what you say about a life that transcends the human, and about the human committed to that existence. The Yasuní, in its remoteness, matters (to us). And that is the thought that I think we have to bring up, to question anthropocentrism and androcentrism as well. This idea that women are still marginal, that men think of themselves in relation to the control of other things; that which they cannot control scares them, so they defend themselves (even before being attacked). So, it is this idea of a thought that is rational, that is based on control, and for which everything that cannot be known is immediately a threat. I believe that we have to explore out there, the areas of existence, as you say, where we do not touch each other, where autonomy can exist, but where there is affectation. And then, I wonder, why are we affected? In other words, why does it affect you and not thousands of other people? Where does affectation come from? Because if you are polluted and you can see it, there is a clear link of affectation. But, where would an affectation be born that is not directly related to your existence, where does the affectation that ecologists feel for territories that they have not seen, nor will ever see, come from?

Do you remember what the government said about the ecologists, regarding the defense of Yasuní? They said, these people live in the city, and it is very easy for them to talk about these territories, when in fact they have a car and they do the same as any urban person. So why are ecologists affected by these places? It seems to me that this is related to criticism of anthropocentrism,

androcentrism and control of territory. I think that women feel a little more marginalized by that thought.
IVONNE: I don't understand what you mean.
CRISTINA: I think that the affectation has to do with thinking the world in a relational way, with thinking of oneself together or close to others who are different, in a relationship of interdependence with others, and not in vain is the environmental movement a very female movement.
IVONNE: I think what you say is interesting, because it is thought that women are more sensitive, but it is not a question of sensitivity...
CRISTINA: I think that women are less individualistic.

Women and reproduction in the territories

IVONNE: It seems that we women, who are really immersed in these spaces of reproduction of life, also in political discussions, feel more involved with the reproduction of life in completely alien or distant spaces, or with environmental issues. I believe that this happens not only because we are less individualistic, but also because deep down we perceive that it is the same struggle, that fighting the issue of reproduction on a social level as a feminist movement is the same as fighting for the reproduction of life in spaces where there is not necessarily an associated societal condition.

They are the same struggles because it is the same life, because it is the same condition of oppression that concerns nature and that women suffer. If you understand nature as a subject, as a space for the reproduction of human and non-human life, and you understand that women are not subjects because of capital... then you see the connection. That's why I think the ecofeminist movement, or this union between ecologism and feminism can be so powerful, because it's really like bringing together a lot of people who are fighting for the same thing. The same thing happens with the Indigenous peoples who fight for the defense of the territories; it's the same fight as that of the ecologists, with their particularities.

CRISTINA: For me, there is something that Indigenous feminists say that is very relevant here, and that is the body-territory. You have worked on it and it is this idea that is spreading throughout Latin America of how women are problematizing the struggle for territory through the body. The struggles against sexist violence are becoming more and more spatial. It is understood then that the struggle for reproduction has to do with the struggle for the integrity and support of the body, especially bodies that are violated, threatened by environmental conditions but also by male dominance which, as we saw, is interwoven with control of the territory and everything that populates it. This triangle between territory, nature and body is something that Indigenous feminisms teach to the rest of the movements and to other feminisms. So when they talk and we talk about reproduction, we are talking about reproduction and the viability of bodies, of everyone, including women's bodies. One element of threat and violence, of the destruction of bodies, is sexist violence, which also increases when territories are deprived of their own forms of reproduction. For me this nourishes the struggle and gives it a very powerful meaning. What Indigenous feminists say is that we can talk about the support of the community, of the territory, but that women are also being done violence to at the same time. Seen from that perspective, the struggle for reproduction has to be a struggle for the support of women's and children's bodies. In other feminisms, these connections between the body and the territory have not been there.
IVONNE: There is still a certain reluctance in the ecologist movement to incorporate the issue of the body. There was a graffiti placed next to the Acción Ecológica house that said: "Without body sovereignty, there is no food sovereignty". We are still discussing what the person who wrote it meant. And I think we need to keep talking about this. It will do us good.
CRISTINA: Talking about reproduction is talking about the body: for me, that is just it.
IVONNE: Okay, but we do incorporate other non-human bodies as well. For example, the body of the pink river dolphin, which is affected by oil activities, same as the bodies of women.

CRISTINA: Yes, I was talking about the human bodies of women. I think that the discussion about reproduction and care has to do with all this, with a way of connecting, from feminism, the relations of reproduction in the territory. We cannot defend life in the territory and ignore that this life is absolutely threatened. Transcending the human-centric does not mean not talking about the human. When we began to dialogue, with Silvia coming in, we discussed how extractive projects generate a series of social relations that change men and women, and the relations between them, for the worse. Men stop hunting, and a series of problems begin. The contribution of Rita Segato, who will soon be visiting us, is also along those lines. There is a connection between the destruction of territory and the destruction of women's bodies; it is a contribution to thinking about the forms of violence that take place today.
IVONNE: Yes, it is a contribution and a strategy to fight for women's rights. If I defend the pink river dolphin's body, I defend the living conditions, sustenance, and reproduction of women, which are also being violated by oil companies; just as when you defend women's bodies from violence by oil or mining companies, you also defend the pink river dolphin. We are on the same wavelength, and from now on, when we talk about bodies, we can do so in this broader sense, with greater power.
CRISTINA: We have mutual challenges, feminism has the challenge of developing non-anthropocentric thinking, and ecologism has the challenge of thinking about reproduction by connecting it with the support of women, of women's bodies, and thinking about that very seriously. Because there is resistance, and you say so yourself; there is a tenacious resistance to connecting body to territory, to territory struggles.

There is another challenge that we have in common, and it is thinking about the urban issue, the urban as a territory, too. Territories are not just there, but here. And we have to think and imagine our territory, our care, our reproduction, our families in a different way, which I would like to think about and beyond the family, above all because I do not have my family here but I have a dear extended family, which is very important to me in my daily life. Since the concept of family is so overloaded with couples, with heterosexuality, with this and that, then we have to think beyond it. That's an important challenge, like weaving communities in care and in the urban.

IVONNE: Of course, the urban gardens on the terrace of your house, the collective care of children, but also the defense of green spaces, which are like our forests in the cities. Turning them into spaces where life is reproduced through fun and pleasure. Along those lines we must continue our conversation.

19. Mirrors of each other: consciousness-raising in Minervas

Gabriela Veras Iglesias and Lorena Rodríguez Lezica[1]

Introduction

In this space we would like to share some of our reflections on the consciousness-raising experiences that we have been feeling-thinking in the Minervas collective in Uruguay. Minervas is a collective of feminist women, diverse in age, color and experience; we have organized ourselves since 2012 to seek new ways to channel our feelings and political concerns together and with others. We got organized because we want to change everything (Furtado, 2017):

> To say *no more*, so that we are not forced to do the things that we are expected to do as women, both at home and in wage labor. We have stopped doing the things we are expected to do, including keeping quiet. We say *no more* to a life plagued by precariousness; of housing, health, work and education. We say *no more* and we do not ask for permission. (Dissemination flyers for Colectivo Minervas.)

Since then, we have recovered a powerful tool of the feminist movement: consciousness-raising, which we understand as spaces and moments that we give ourselves to stop, look and listen to each other, to tell one another our sadness, our worries and our joys, to ask each other questions and to try out answers, to reflect on one another's stories, stories that are sometimes different, and most of the time are very similar. Consciousness-raising has allowed us to become closer sisters, to understand each other, to help manage our differences, to strengthen that fabric between women that is so urgent and necessary to face daily violence.

---

[1] Activist members of the Colectivo Minervas, part of the Consciousness-raising Group.

To write this text we begin by situating this tool of struggle at its origins in the practice of radical feminists in the United States, and then we gather feelings-thoughts from the voices of four members of Minervas, with whom we shared a number of questions in order to establish a dialogue between the lines about our practice of consciousness-raising. In order to define which companions would be interviewed, we thought of women who in some way reflected the diversity within the collective: companions in their twenties, thirties and over forty, members of the Consciousness-raising Group (that is, those who have participated in the planning of these instances) and who have frequently participated in the activities promoted by the Group.

Recovering a tool for struggle

Consciousness-raising practices as struggle action were first raised in the late sixties by the group Radical Women of New York, which belonged to the Women's Liberation Movement. These women proposed consciousness-raising meetings as a way of addressing personal problems from a political perspective; that is, they reflected on how private life was framed by patriarchal mandates. In the text "The Personal is Political"[2], Carol Hanisch makes a defense of consciousness-raising as a necessary practice for women's liberation. She vindicates this experience as a political therapy, differentiating it from individual therapy, thus responding to criticism put forth by some leftist groups:

> The very word "therapy" is obviously a misnomer if carried to its logical conclusion. Therapy assumes that someone is sick and that there is a cure, e.g., a personal solution. I am greatly offended that I or any other woman is thought to need therapy in the first place. Women are messed over, not messed up! We need to change the objective conditions, not adjust to them. Therapy is adjusting to your bad personal alternative. [...] these analytical sessions are a form of political action. (Hanisch 1969, in Franulic, Jeka, 2016, p. n/a).

---

[2] The title for the text was chosen by Shulamith Firestone and Ana Koedt, its editors.

By focusing on the objective problems that women face in the private sphere, they acquire a political dimension in the exercise of looking at them from a critical perspective in search of collective solutions. This process of politicizing the private becomes one of the best known slogans of the feminist movement: "The personal is political", and it goes on to represent a political project and a reconstruction of the female subject.

The slogan raises a new fighting banner for the feminist movement, extending its demands to the everyday dimension of women's lives in all its spheres, placing sexuality, motherhood, child rearing, work, marriage on the table; spheres of life where they come to identify the various forms of oppression experienced, and which help support the institutions of the patriarchal system.

To visualize the dynamics of consciousness-raising, let us take Campagnoli's consideration:

> They were characterized by work in small cells with sessions of denunciation. These were guided by informal organizational criteria: they were composed exclusively of women, based on collective work, numerically reduced, and they denounced certain practices of power associated up to that point with individual morality and marginalized from public discussion (Campagnoli in Andujar, 2005, p. 156).

Women's "ought to be" is now being questioned from their personal experience. By sharing personal narratives in the practices of consciousness-raising, oppressions experienced individually take on a collective dimension, which opens up the possibility for the construction of new subjectivities.

It is interesting to note the relationship that Campagnoli proposes between consciousness-raising and Foucaultian categories. The process of making aspects of private life public "allowed the neutrality of the public to be uncovered and the socio-historical character of intimate relationships and the construction of subjectivities to be made evident" (Campagnoli, in Andujar, 2005, p. 160).

The author takes up the category of biopolitics in order to contextualize the forms of power devices centered on bodies through sexuality, for example. In *The History of Sexuality*, Foucault describes how institutions and their discursive practices (medical, legal and religious) acted as powerful devices over bodies, generating subjectivities linked to certain socially expected behaviors. Campagnoli discusses the power that the concept of governmentality makes possible in the process of resistance:

> Governmentality highlights the dimension of "subjective constitution" of the subject, of self-production in the intersubjectivity. This dimension is constructed by the feminist collectives of the 1960s and 1970s which, based on a practice of intersubjectivity, produced a "we" and opened up a new possibility in the personal view of women [...] we can consider awareness as a technology of the female self (Campagnoli, in Andujar, 2005, p. 163).

Where power is exercised, there is resistance. In this sense, the author situates the power of consciousness-raising within the "technologies of the self"; through the act of speaking about oneself, the power games that sustain expected behaviors are revealed, which allows for the process of breaking and the creation of the new. Thus, it becomes a tool for struggle to promote the constant reconstruction of the female subject.

An inward look: consciousness-raising in Minervas

We share an exercise of reflection on our practice of consciousness-raising, in the form of a dialogue. For this exercise, we asked some of our companions for a definition of consciousness-raising, to know how they felt about it. We also asked about the emergence of this political tool in our collective, about the importance that each one gives to this space, and invited reflection on consciousness-raising as a tool for struggle.

There were instances of consciousness-raising in which we worked on certain issues, or worked on them at certain moments that marked the collective, and also individually. From these experiences, they share their memories. We asked the companions about their "personal" transformations based on consciousness-raising. All of them asked how this personal transformation affected the collective, whether it was Minervas or other inhabited spaces.

Based on the transformations that consciousness-raising has generated within the collective, we are interested in questioning what its effects are on the outside; asking ourselves how these practices are important for strengthening the links between women's collectives and for the feminist movement as a whole.

We understand that the body is key in the process of consciousness-raising, since the narrative is about expressing what the body feels and what it has experienced. This is how we conceive of it as the territory of this experience that mobilizes us to build another "us" in this interweaving of women. In this sense, we asked the companions: how is the body put into play in the practices of consciousness-raising?

How did they start?

> [...] It wasn't something that was brought up, that is, we didn't sit down to think about how to implement consciousness-raising, but rather it was something that happened almost spontaneously. Later we realized that this was also unknowingly anchored in the history of feminism in the seventies and in consciousness-raising groups. But we knew that later, they emerged more spontaneously at the beginning. I remember a meeting in which a colleague was particularly moved by personal and work issues and from the most structured logic of organization we had an agenda to discuss, and well, it was impossible because affection, anguish, discomfort broke out. And it was good, because unlike many other collectives —I compare it to other collectives and activist spaces that I am in—, we had the capacity to say: "Well, let's take a moment, what's happening here, what's happening to this companion, what's happening to the rest of us with what we're listening to?" Well, this is how this need to include listening to each other began to emerge, and to make room for feelings, emotions, affections. And then it began to take a little more shape in the organization chart, in the proposals of Minervas' political practice. The Minervas consciousness-raising group was formed. We began to think in terms of working on these issues as an agenda. That's when the idea of working on consciousness-raising began to be more structured. I think it was also a finding, not by chance, that we started to work in a different way, by putting our bodies into it, our affection; not dissociating them, because there is always the body and the affection, but not dissociating them as we were used to doing (Alicia).

Consciousness-raising for us

> For me, consciousness-raising is a process in which we all start from ourselves, to be able to collectivize it and have a collective political vision, common to this group of women [...] We all tell something about a pain, a

joy, a way of thinking about a certain reality, or a particular moment, at any stage of our lives, we put it in common, and that is what makes us mirror one another and feel that our problems are not only ours, or that our powers are not only ours, and that by talking it out with others it is possible to find solutions or improve them (Andrea).

It is a space that we find among women in which we empathize with each other. We empathize in our oppressions and resistances, pains and joys, and we politicize them, and we transform them. We take them out, we expose ourselves, we see ourselves, and we transform ourselves. And we see the forms of resistance that we also generate among ourselves, that we have been generating, the transformations and the things that we can do together. That is, without a firm proposal, perhaps not as much as an objective, but it generates a confidence in the companions once you share your pain, or your oppression, or your experience, or your life, as a much more solid bond (Dava).

I believe that it is a practice that allows us to see issues of our own, of our experiences, of our lives, of our bonds, in an atmosphere of great trust. I believe that an atmosphere is created in the consciousness-raising sessions that relates to a question of trust [...] after each session a deeper understanding is generated, let's say, of the other companions, of oneself. And in a way it allows you to feel that the things that have happened to you have not only happened to you. Sometimes you also see the differences in lives and experiences. And then this kind of relocates you. You have lived through such issues in your life in a certain way, and this resignifies it. You kind of find another meaning to it. I mean, on a more personal level. I think it also does a lot to make the bonds between us closer, and to make political trust take on a deeper sense. And I think it's about putting "the personal is political" into practice. To be able to talk and share what is going on in your daily life in political terms (Rossana).

On the importance of consciousness-raising for our collective

[...] we are learning a little bit more about ourselves individually, and about ourselves collectively as companions. And it seems to me that this is important for any process of women's emancipation, any movement that understands itself as feminist. Because we live oppression in our bodies in this way, on a daily basis, so what makes us a political movement is to be able to share it collectively (Andrea).

I think it's important for Minervas and for women in general. But for Minervas, because we generate meaning, we are building meaning in the consciousness-raising sessions, and also in the plenary, and in the formation sessions. But in the consciousness-raising sessions all the things we have been learning, all the things we have been thinking, are also shaped. Or the fights that we are giving are also shaped in the issues of consciousness-raising, how you are processing it through the body, how you are processing it through your mind. Your body lives that, it is not only something that you have read, but you are already living it. So, your body is transforming, and that kind of empowers others, empowers the changes in others. At least I feel like I am super empowered by the changes in my companions. They offer a mirror back to me. They mirror me, and I see myself and I can change and be better. And it works for us because we must transform ourselves. We can't avoid transforming ourselves, in this sexist, patriarchal system. Impossible. We can't avoid transforming ourselves, avoid seeing ourselves. Otherwise, we'll continue with a structure of activism... (Dava).

For me it's very important, it makes for bonds of greater trust with the companions. That does not imply, and I say it as a psychologist, it does not imply that this a space where one talks and the other listens and helps to give meaning to the other — that would be a psychological practice, rather — ; instead, it is a place of greater horizontality. Where I listen, but I am also listened to. So I think that creates an enrichment and a strengthening of the political ties between us (Rossana).

I think that they are fundamental because they have to do with the type of feminism that we have tried to build in these years. I believe that consciousness-raising was a discovery and a re-invention in any case. It was like making ourselves part of the long history of feminism again, of embodying the slogan "the personal is political", and in that sense being able to make politics pass through our bodies, through our histories, through our affections, disarming them collectively, talking about them, sharing, not only always from the word, but also appealing to other languages, to other ways of sharing. I think that when we began to think about some of the hard core issues of the feminist agenda — abortion and violence are the two that come to mind, but obviously there were many more— we found those resistances in ourselves, which also had to do with the need to be able to see how those issues related to our personal, family, and collective histories, and find in all that what we could heal, reinvent, restore to remake that pain into strength (Alicia).

Consciousness-raising as a political tool

At a time like the present, when people are alone, when bonds tend to melt, when everyone lives a constant race against the clock, and sometimes you have no time to dedicate anything or very little to the beings that matter most to you in life, I think this says: well, we get together, we take this issue, we share it, we give ourselves the time to do it, that is in itself a political power and a political tool, because I think it will counteract not only the patriarchy, but everything. Yes, we do it because we want to, we get together because we want to. [...] It seems to me that there is something of a desire to come together, to speak, to meet, and that is a political tool (Rossana).

Maybe consciousness-raising is often something you can do collectively with your friends, right? But what it implies to do it from a political collective is that you look for a solution for all women, to be transmissible not only to those who are present then, but also that you'll want to transmit everything you find positive. And it is like that exercise: it is a back and forth between what we are, what we feel and what we do, and what we want. We project our desire from there. And, for me, consciousness-raising has that. I am, I feel, I think, but I think together with others. I don't think alone (Andrea).

Moments that marked us

A moment that marked me individually, which was very strong, was abortion, because I had not been able to see it so clearly. I hadn't been able to talk about it that way. The times I had an abortion, I couldn't speak about it, and I did it alone. I talked about it with very few people, and then to talk about it in such a big space, and loaded with a lot of pain, because we were all crying. And for me it was liberating, it was totally liberating. Because after that I never felt bad again. It's not that I go around yelling out "I had an abortion", but I don't feel guilty about that. I don't feel guilty about it anymore, I understood, I didn't want to go through that. [...] Another [moment] that seemed to me important for the collective was that one of the burdens, the kepis. [...] I feel that when you can see the essence of the other person, when you can see that the person breaks down and shows herself like that, I don't know, you sort of love her more. I feel that I love her more, because she shows you that she's all broken. So, she is a person who is trying to do what she can, with all her burdens. So you kind of love her more, you understand her more. More tolerant. We talk to each other with more love. I feel closer, much more trusting (Dava).

I remember the first one I went to [...] What I felt there was that I was talking to women I barely knew. I had just started a couple of months ago, I barely knew them, and yet I was able to talk and share things, and I felt surprised at how other colleagues had thought and lived things that I would never have questioned. I remember the discussion about pills. As for me, I took pills for a long year in my life, and I always understood them as a liberating thing; to me, they solved a problem! And there, seeing it from another side: you got a lot of stuff into your body, for a lot of years! That was very nice, very long, we left very late. That was an experience where I thought, "I've met a group of women!" And maybe another one that was very recent was that of the kepis, where most of us went to the figure of the mother. That was very healing for me. Because there were things that I, for example, had done from a therapeutic framework. So in a way that reconciled me with the deep ambivalence of exercising motherhood and being the "daughter of" [...] after that I felt more at peace with myself (Rossana).

Before and after consciousness-raising: personal and collective transformations

Before, it was much more like I couldn't see the other companions [...] and I feel that since I started at Minervas and started participating in consciousness-raising, I appreciate the essence of the companion much more, which is what she is trying to say [...] why she feels this way. I didn't use to be like that. Before, it was like closing the door and judging the other, that very sexist logic of relating to women. [...] And then, my body. I began to love my body very much. Like, I love myself! *(laughs)*. Before, I didn't like myself, I didn't like my body at all. At all. And now I like my belly, I like the way I am. I didn't use to like my hair, I love my hair now [...] it's like gaining confidence: you are you, and that's it. Little by little. And I think that's thanks to consciousness-raising (Dava).

What it gave me was enormous confidence, a new trust in the encounter between women, the power of the encounter between women. And I think that has meant that now I have much more practice in seeking agreement, uniting with women in the different spaces where I move, being a better companion, so to speak [...], registering this [...], looking for ways to take care of yourself, to defend yourself with another, from this (Rossana).

The place of the body in consciousness-raising

It seems to me that the body is very important because if you don't connect with what is happening to the body, all the pains of the body that you are going through, it is very difficult to see what is the root of the burden, of the pain, of the weight, of what you are carrying, of what is happening to you. If you cannot go back to your body, think about your body, about the different parts, it will be more difficult. It will be more difficult to understand how your life affects you. [...] And in capitalism there is more and more disconnection, so for me it's totally necessary to go back to the body. Where does it affect you? Where does it hurt? What illnesses do you have? Now I think a lot about diseases and the body, and why we get sick, why we take so many pills and stuff. In a way, if you look at yourself, the parts that hurt every day, or what hurts the most, it always has to do with a burden or a way you live your life. I don't know, it seems to me that if you don't, it's more difficult for you to understand the root, or get rid of it (Dava). It's hard for me to become aware of my body [...] It's like a process that I need because my body hurts, my shoulders hurt, my spine hurts, my head hurts, my arms hurt, now my throat hurts. And I think that relaxes me. And that beyond the fact that it's hard for me to process it in my body, and that's why I'm so stiff, I'm open to doing it. Yes, I need it, I need this to affect my body, this other companion, or this other sensation or this emotion, and to relieve me in some way. I'm willing to put my whole body into it (Andrea).

I believe that different meanings of the body are in play. Sometimes the work is from the body in the most concrete sense [...] there is a dynamic, touching, looking. And it's planned, it's very concrete, it's part of that consciousness-raising. But I believe that the body is also put into play in another sense, precisely the lived body, the felt body, what happened to me, how I perceived it, how I lived it, and there I am, speaking from the body. I think it's like that, I don't know if I can explain it. It is not only because there is a dynamic, but simply because it is spoken, and when you are part of a consciousness-raising session you cannot put much into it. In another scenario you can say "I do this political reading", rather more 'frontal lobe'. But not in a consciousness-raising session, in a session you speak from yourself, and suddenly you bring up things like, there are things that hurt you, and things that hurt you about yourself, and things that you don't like about yourself: you bare yourself a little. Then it seems to me that this is not in vain. After that, you know more about who you are with (Rossana).

To continue to mirror each other: the challenges of building new subjectivities

We want to change everything, we shouted out to the world once and we keep on trying, encouraging the construction of new subjectivities from, among other tools, our practice of consciousness-raising. And this has been a challenge, not without tension, as one of our companions put it.

> I believe that a first challenge arises when consciousness-raising is structured, so to speak. That tension between being able to define topics and having them enter the agenda and the organization chart of Minervas' tasks, without them becoming bureaucratic. I think that has always been in tension; how to handle the "we want to work on certain issues" and "when do we want to work on them, when is the best time?" I think that this is one more tension that arises from relating issues or life, the evolution of the organization, of times and spaces. Later, I think there was another issue that also began to be a challenge, especially when the collective began to grow more, and especially in the last few years when it began to diversify. [...] We started out with a very intimate consciousness-raising format, very much an awareness-raising group, a small group. And I think, and we've talked about it sometime, that there are some limits to that. It's not the same to talk when there are fifteen of us, as it is to talk when there are fifty of us, in a way. Because of the number of people, but also because of the bonds that are created. And I think that another issue is the generational question, and the different age experiences. There are times of the year when we are eaten up by madness, by the vertigo of all the tasks that need to be done, and it is very difficult to give ourselves time for consciousness-raising. [...] Another tension has to do with the difficulty of systematizing, and well, what you are doing is an effort to systematize. At some point we had proposed to keep a record of the techniques used, and that became a little difficult, but I think it is more than necessary (Alicia).

As a collective, we share the importance of making an effort to systematize our political-affective-collective practices based on consciousness-raising. We recognize that these are practices that, unknowingly at the beginning, we inherited from the feminists of the seventies, and just like them, we tried with this tool another form of activism, where the body and emotions take on a fundamental role. As we share these dialogues, it has been central to our consciousness-raising to create an atmosphere of trust, in which we can reflect on ourselves, and make our personal ailments and resistances into collective ailments and resistances. Consciousness-raising has been very powerful to recognize in our bodies the violence experienced and the forms of resistance generated. From the point of view of shared experiences we politicize the personal-individual, and we make it collective. We continue to search for the construction of a feminism from below, which can serve as a tool to support our lives. Because we want to strengthen our bonds within the collective and also with other women's collectives and female companions, sororized against the daily oppressions imposed on us by a society sustained by its patriarchal institutions, we have found in consciousness-raising a tool for struggle, where our body, the first territory in resistance, is the protagonist of that transformation so desired.

Bibliographical references

Campagnoli, Mabel Alicia (2005). El feminismo es un humanismo: la década del 70 y "lo personal es político". In Andrea Andújar, Débora D'Antonio, Nora Domínguez, Karin Grammático, Fernanda Gil Lozano, Valeria Pita, María Inés Rodríguez and Alejandra Vassallo (Comps.), *Historia, género y política en los '70* (pp. 154-168). Buenos Aires: Feminaria Editora.

Hanisch, Carol ([1969] 2016). Lo Personal es Político. In Andrea Franulic and Insu Jeka, (Eds.). Santiago de Chile: Feministas Lúcidas Ediciones. Available at http://autonomiafeminista.cl/wp-content/uploads/2016/07/lo-personal-es-pol%C3%ADtico_lucidas.pdf

Furtado, Victoria (2017). Nosotras queremos cambiarlo todo. *Zur Pueblo de Voces*. Available at http://www.zur.org.uy/content/nosotras-queremos-cambiarlo-todo-entrevista-al-colectivo-minervas *ibidem*.eu